Writing the 9/11 Decade

Writing the 9/11 Decade

Reportage and the Evolution of the Novel

Charlie Lee-Potter

Bloomsbury Academic
An imprint of Bloomsbury Publishing Inc

B L O O M S B U R Y
NEW YORK · LONDON · OXFORD · NEW DELHI · SYDNEY

Bloomsbury Academic
An imprint of Bloomsbury Publishing Inc

1385 Broadway	50 Bedford Square
New York	London
NY 10018	WC1B 3DP
USA	UK

www.bloomsbury.com

BLOOMSBURY and the Diana logo are trademarks of Bloomsbury Publishing Plc

First published 2017

Library of Congress Cataloging-in-Publication Data
A catalog record for this book is available from the Library of Congress.

ISBN: HB: 978-1-5013-1319-6
PB: 978-1-5013-1320-2
ePub: 978-1-5013-1321-9
ePDF: 978-1-5013-1322-6

Cover design: Alice Marwick

Typeset by Integra Software Services Pvt. Ltd.
Printed and bound in the United States of America

To Kit and Mia

CONTENTS

ACKNOWLEDGEMENTS

Many people have made significant contributions to the writing of this book. I would like to thank Tim Armstrong for his invaluable advice as I worked on my research, and Jeremy Lee-Potter for his detailed analysis of the final manuscript. I interviewed many artists, writers and journalists for this work, all of whom were unfailingly generous with their time and insights. I owe a great debt to Rowan Williams, Richard Ford, Kamila Shamsie, Amy Waldman, Mohsin Hamid, Eric Fischl, Kevin Marsh, Fergus Walsh, Stephen Evans, Adrianne Ryder-Cook Joseph, Roger Mosey, Graham Kings and Sunetra Gupta. I would like to pay particular thanks to Haaris Naqvi and Mary Al-Sayed at Bloomsbury for their faith in this project and for their expert guidance. Thank you, too, to Balaji Kasirajan, Jothilakshmi Ganesh, Srinivasan Ramu and Alice Marwick, and to everyone involved with the book's layout and design. I am indebted to Sally Bayley for her wise and intelligent observations, and to Robert Eaglestone for sharing his knowledge and expertise. My family and friends have been stalwart in their support and made many helpful suggestions about the manuscript. Thank you to Emma Lee-Potter, Ali Huntrods, Liz Bauwens, Chrissie Probert-Jones, Alison Culverwell, Adam Kingdon, Non Morris, Jemima Hunt, and Andrew and Caroline Meynell. I am grateful to the Rothermere American Institute, University of Oxford, whose award of a research fellowship enabled me to finish my manuscript, and to all the staff in the Vere Harmsworth Library. Thank you to Lady Margaret Hall, University of Oxford, and to the English Department at Royal Holloway, University of London. Finally, my special thanks go to the late Lynda Lee-Potter, Norman Higginson, Sally Adams and Susie Berry whose advice I often recalled while completing this book, and to my children who have been unfailingly encouraging, even on days when my manuscript was at its most unruly. This book is dedicated to them – and to all the families of 9/11.

Introduction

The shock provoked by the 9/11 attacks was followed almost immediately by announcements that 'something must be done'. The mood was characterized aptly by the hand-wringing of a leading British politician who said that 'it seems almost inevitable that there will be some sort of military response at some point – although at the moment we do not know where, when, or against whom'.[1] George W. Bush injected more steel into that retaliatory paradigm with his binary proclamation that 'either you are with us, or you are with the terrorists'.[2] The resultant acquiescence of the news media was summed up vividly by TV news anchor Dan Rather when he said, 'one finds oneself saying, "I know the right question but you know what, this is not exactly the right time to ask it"'.[3] Self-censorship evolved into what US journalist and author Norman Solomon called a form of news coverage that 'is more akin to stenography for the movers and shakers in Washington'.[4] In a similar vein, once the military offensive was launched in Afghanistan, Howard Zinn reported that news values had shifted:

> The head of the television network CNN, Walter Isaacson, sent a memo to his staff saying that images of civilian casualties should

[1]Charles Kennedy, MP, speaking in the House of Commons, 14 September 2001, *Hansard*: 14 September 2001, http://www.publications.parliament.uk/pa/cm200102/cmhansrd/vo010914/debtext/10914-02.htm#10914-02_spnew1 [accessed 29 February 2016].

[2]George W. Bush, *Address to a Joint Session of Congress and the American People*, 20 September 2001, http://georgewbush-whitehouse.archives.gov/news/releases/2001/09/20010920-8.html [accessed 16 March 2013].

[3]Dan Rather, interviewed by Madeleine Holt, BBC *Newsnight*, 6 June 2002, http://news.bbc.co.uk/1/hi/programmes/newsnight/archive/2029634.stm [accessed 15 March 2013].

[4]Norman Solomon, 'Foreword', in *No Questions Asked: News Coverage since 9/11*, ed. Lisa Finnegan (Westport, CT: Praeger, 2007), p. xiii.

be accompanied with an explanation that this was retaliation for the harboring of terrorists. 'It seems perverse to focus too much on the casualties or hardships in Afghanistan,' he said.[5]

A key consequence of the political and journalistic solidarity was, against the odds, the re-election of George W. Bush in 2004. He was voted back in by a newly risk-averse nation that, since 9/11, had been seemingly desperate to forge a sense of continuity and stability in the face of catastrophe. Before Bush's re-election, the journalist and former Republican speechwriter Peggy Noonan wrote approvingly and bathetically that when she looked at him she could not help but think of 'earnest Clark Kent moving, at the moment of maximum danger, to shed his suit, tear open his shirt and reveal the big "S" on his chest'.[6] Susan Faludi, who also pointed to Noonan's invocation of Superman, reported that in the days after the attacks she was called numerous times by journalists seeking to take the narrative in a particular direction,

> among them a *New York Times* reporter researching an article on the "return of the manly man" and a *New York Observer* writer seeking comment on "the trend" of women "becoming more feminine after 9/11". By which, as she made clear, she meant *less feminist*. Women were going to regret their "independence", she said, and devote themselves to "baking cookies" and finding husbands to "take care of them."[7]

Thus the journalistic default was set, and not just in the United States. The former editor of BBC Radio 4's *Today* programme, Kevin Marsh, declared that daily journalism failed in Britain too. Marsh, who later became editor of the BBC College of Journalism, has consistently said that 9/11 and its political consequences reinforced journalists' dislike for intellectual depth and complexity:

> Journalism – even that from non-jingoistic, xenophobic quarters – was hugely influenced by the political consensus in the face of the

---

[5]Howard Zinn, *A People's History of the United States: 1492-present, Third Edition* (1980; Harlow: Pearson Education, 2003), pp. 679–680.
[6]Peggy Noonan, 'The Right Man', *Wall Street Journal*, 30 January 2003, http://online.wsj.com/article/SB1043895876926710064.html [accessed 18 March 2013].
[7]Susan Faludi, *The Terror Dream* (2007; London: Atlantic Books, 2008), p. 20.

9/11 attacks. Both that consensus and the speed at which events careered towards war. And those failings are the usual ones: daily journalism's aversion to complexity; its centripetal tendency, dragging the apparent plurality of multiple outlets towards common framings; its inevitable preference for the striking event over the telling trend; and its eternal excuse – we're just telling stories.[8]

In the early days after the attacks, many novelists rehearsed their later fictional responses by acting as journalists, writing commentaries, essays and fragments of prose for the newspapers and magazines that queued up to commission salving words. An analysis of much of that journalism and prose non-fiction demonstrates that it, too, suffered from the 'aversion to complexity', a 'centripetal tendency' and a craving for the 'common framings' that Marsh identified. For those who attempted to respond – Ian McEwan, Martin Amis, Richard Ford and Don DeLillo amongst them – their themes were as curiously symbiotic as the international community's had been on its more macro-scale. To paraphrase, perhaps a little harshly, each of them fumbled in one form or another for the nostrum that in the end, love will overcome. Unconvincing at the time and, for the most part, rejected by each of them in their novelistic responses some years later, the 'love' solution has persisted as the grand narrative for some writers of 9/11 fiction, such as Karen Kingsbury, for whom a restorative and fortifying exceptionalist doctrine, often underpinned by Christianity, has been the stirring rejoinder to terrorist assault.

At the circumspect end of the 'love-spectrum', there was a more literary response. While it avoided explicit exceptionalism, it still relied for its heft on the nourishing notion of consolation. It is the lyrical realism eschewed by Zadie Smith in the context of Joseph O'Neill's 9/11 novel *Netherland*:

[It] knows the fears and weaknesses of its readers. What is disappointing is how much it indulges them. Out of a familiar love, like a lapsed High Anglican, *Netherland* hangs on to the

---

[8]Kevin Marsh, 'Afghanistan, Truth and the Unexamined War', in *Afghanistan, War and the Media: Deadlines and Frontlines*, eds Richard Lance Keeble and John Mair (Bury St Edmunds: Arima Publishing, 2010), p. 81.

rituals and garments of transcendence, though it well knows they are empty. In its final saccharine image (Hans and his family, reunited on the mandala of the London Eye Ferris wheel), *Netherland* demonstrates its sly ability to have its metaphysical cake and eat it, too.[9]

Smith's remonstrations against the indulgences of O'Neill had at their heart the objection that to wreathe prose in metaphorical excess is to console, when no such consolation should be proffered. As she phrased it, '[t]here was the chance to let the towers be what they were: towers. But they were covered in literary language when they fell, and they continue to be here.' That tension between mimesis and metaphor is one of the dialogic tussles that I examine in this work, along with the broader contest set up by Smith between 'misguided ideologists', such as DeLillo whose rejection of realism has been a 'fascinating failure' that 'lacked heart', and lyrical realists, such as O'Neill whose work may be nothing more than the 'bedtime story that comforts us most'. Smith's assertion that *Netherland* is an 'anxious novel', because it is conscious of the literary struggle in which it is a combatant, has fragments of truth to it, as does her definition of *Netherland* as a 'post-catastrophe novel, but the catastrophe isn't terror, it's Realism'.

To use Smith's word, I will define much of fiction's response to 9/11 as 'anxious' to a degree, certainly in the early years. That is not to say that all novels fixate upon the means to be 'true' or 'real' or that they simply give up the struggle, but that they wrestle with Iris Murdoch's evocation in 'Against Dryness' of 'the consolations of form'.[10] Murdoch's distinction was between the 'crystalline' novel (in other words the 'small, quasi-allegorical object portraying the human condition') and the 'journalistic' novel which is to say the 'large shapeless quasi-documentary object, the degenerate descendant of the nineteenth-century novel, telling, with pale

---

[9]Zadie Smith, 'Two Paths for the Novel', *New York Review of Books*, 20 November 2008, http://www.nybooks.com/articles/archives/2008/nov/20/two-paths-for-the-novel/?pagination=false [accessed 18 March 2013].

[10]I am grateful to David James of Queen Mary, University of London, for thoughts about the 'false consolations of form' in the context of Murdoch and Smith, in addition to his journal article. David James, 'A Renaissance for the Crystalline Novel?', *Contemporary Literature*, vol. 53, no. 4 (Winter 2012), pp. 845–874.

conventional characters, some straightforward story enlivened with empirical facts'.[11] It is a helpful distinction in the context of this work, since Murdoch identified the false-friend that she saw for writers of both crystalline and journalistic novels, which still entraps the 9/11 novelist now: 'The temptation of art, a temptation to which every work of art yields except the greatest ones, is to console. The modern writer [...] attempts to console us by myths or by stories.'[12] That drive to 'console' was characteristic of the earliest non-fiction experiments of those novelists who were commissioned to respond immediately to 9/11 in newspapers and magazines, as this work will go on to demonstrate. Foremost amongst them was Richard Ford. A few days after 9/11, he was asked to contribute his reflections on the attacks to the *New York Times*. He began by describing his father's death more than forty years before and he is precise and graphic in his description of smelling the 'large, sweaty body' and 'flaccid self, loose-limbed and malleable...'. But Ford concluded in a way that seemed far removed from the crystalline, unsentimental prose that his readers had become used to:

> It is an axiom of the novelist's grasp on reality that a death's importance is measured by the significance of the life that has ended. Thus to die, as so many did on Sept.11 – their singular existences briefly obscured – may seem to cloud and invalidate life entirely. Yet their lives, though amazingly lost, remain indelible and will not by simple death be undone. They live still, and importantly in all but the most literal ways.[13]

Ford had, quite consciously it seems, succumbed to the temptation to make people feel better. The *Boston Globe* columnist and Pulitzer Prize-winning-journalist Don Murray put this craving for the consolation myth into words in his contribution to a book

[11]Iris Murdoch, 'Against Dryness: A Polemical Sketch', in *The Novel Today: Contemporary Writers on Modern Fiction*, ed. Malcolm Bradbury (London: Fontana, 1990), pp. 23–31.
[12]Ibid.
[13]Richard Ford, 'The Attack Took More Than the Victims' Lives. It Took Their Deaths', *New York Times*, 23 September 2001, http://www.nytimes.com/2001/09/23/magazine/23WWLN.html [accessed 30 March 2013].

published by the American Press Institute, the organization founded by newspaper publishers in 1946:

> I needed facts in the confusion following the attacks, but even more I needed stories, narratives that ordered experience and instructed me on how to behave in the face of tragedy. I found myself reading editorials and op-ed opinions, background and interpretive articles, poems and letters to the editor as much as hard news.[14]

Ford had been struggling with that conundrum: how to 'order experience', how to grant post-death meaning to the lives of those who perished, even though on the face of it there was no meaning, no sense at all. However, unlike Frank Bascombe, who Ford had finessed for thirty years, thereby giving him 'significance', the victims of 9/11 were largely unknown and unknowable in the immediate aftermath of the attack. Ford's reinvigoration of the victims, his salving drive to give them back their lives 'in all but the most literal ways', did not, in the end, convince. He was encumbered, too, by his sense that he did not have adequate language. In a later piece of non-fiction that combined responses to both 9/11 and Hurricane Katrina, he admitted that he 'lacked the words', conceding that 'we still do not have an exact human vocabulary for the loss of a city'.[15] As the first chapter will show, using an extended interview I conducted with Ford, his failure to find the words persisted when he attempted to write his 2006 novel *The Lay of the Land*. There is good reason to assume that Ford did not write a 9/11 novel: where, after all, is his text? However, using his testimony and an early draft of *The Lay of the Land*, I demonstrate that he has in fact produced a 9/11 work, but from an angle so oblique that it is at times hard to recognize. Ford told me that he found it impossible to address 9/11 directly, but that his effort to define it by other means has gone largely unobserved by his readers. He admits that he could only describe the collapse of the Twin Towers by re-envisaging them in his novel as a decaying hotel destroyed in a controlled explosion.

---

[14]Don Murray, 'Behaving in the Face of Tragedy', Forward, *Crisis Journalism: A Handbook for Media Response* (American Press Institute, 2001), p. ii.
[15]Richard Ford, 'Elegy for My City', *Observer*, 4 September 2005, http://www.guardian.co.uk/books/2005/sep/04/hurricanekatrina.features [accessed 13 March 2013].

Novelists, acting as journalists, who chose not to offer the consolation myth risked vilification and even threats of violence. Shortly after 9/11, novelist Barbara Kingsolver wrote an essay seeking to reclaim the American flag from what she called 'bully-patriots' who were using it to promote intolerant nationalism: 'the loudest mouths get the most airplay, and the loudmouths are saying that in times of crisis it's treasonous to question our leaders. Nonsense. [...] It is precisely in critical times that our leaders need *most* to be influenced by the moderating force of dissent.'[16] After publication, Kingsolver was subjected to what she later described as 'a monstrously angry response': 'Magazines and newspapers printed horrible things, they misquoted me, made me a figure of hatred. It was so frightening. Awful. I was scared that my family might be at risk. It was really one of the worst times of my life. A dark, dark winter.'[17] Susan Sontag's experience was similar. She asked in the *New Yorker*, where was 'the acknowledgment that this was not a "cowardly" attack on "civilization" or "liberty" or "humanity" or "the free world" but an attack on the world's self-proclaimed superpower, undertaken as a consequence of specific American alliances and actions?'[18] She was vilified for it. While politicians' rhetoric that 'we're going to fight back and win' was at odds with the traumatized fictional response of 'but how?', there was still a unifying logic to the two positions. Sontag and Kingsolver, meanwhile, found themselves flung out to the margins by the centrifugal force that appeared to be dictating which questions could even be asked. Musicians, too, were expected to say/write/sing the right thing. Bruce Springsteen has described the moment that he realized he was 'needed'. It was only a few days after 9/11 and Springsteen was leaving the beach:

A man drove by, rolled his window down and yelled, 'We need ya!' Then he rolled his window up and kept going. 'And I thought, "Well I've probably been a part of this guy's life for a while,"' Springsteen says. 'And people wanna see other people they know,

---

[16]Barbara Kingsolver, 'And Our Flag Was Still There', in *Small Wonder* (London: Faber & Faber, 2002), p. 238.

[17]Kira Cochrane, 'Barbara Kingsolver: From Witch Hunt to Winner', *Guardian*, 10 June 2010, http://www.theguardian.com/books/2010/jun/10/barbara-kingsolver-orange-prize [accessed 8 September 2014].

[18]Susan Sontag, 'Tuesday, and After', *The New Yorker*, 24 September 2001.

they wanna be around things they're familiar with. So he may need to see me right about now. That made sense, like, "Oh, I have a job to do." Our band, hopefully, we were built to be there when the chips are down. That was part of the idea of the band to provide support'.[19]

His album, *The Rising*, duly did that. Its title track takes the image of a man ascending a stairwell filled with smoke and skilfully reverses his trajectory, so that he is not rising to certain death, as so many firefighters did, but to redemption. It was a long way from the wealth-fantasy World Trade Center (WTC) of his 1984 song *Darlington County*, but it was another form of consolation myth nevertheless.

Novelists, who offered up that same consolation myth in their immediate journalism, still had to negotiate the longer-term ethical question for writers of fiction as to the 'ownership' of experience. Even if they *could* write about it, should they? For those people who escaped from the towers or from the surrounding streets, there can be a deeply ingrained reluctance to look again at the events of that day. The former Archbishop of Canterbury, Rowan Williams, was taking part in a series of theological debates on September 11, in a building owned by Trinity Church only yards from the WTC. He has rarely spoken publicly about his experiences since then, beyond publishing a short essay, 'Writing in the Dust', in 2002, and speaking briefly to the BBC on the tenth anniversary of 9/11. He tried to explain to me why he has found it hard to speak and why he has encountered such difficulties in trying to read any fictional accounts of 9/11. It is important to note that the former symbolic head of the Anglican Communion[20] has always been expected, like a major novelist, to find words adequate to any historical situation. This time he could not:

When you think of the visual images of 9/11, they are very, very hard to capture or to rework because they're so enormous and

[19]Mark Binelli, 'Bruce Springsteen's American Gospel', *Rolling Stone*, 22 August 2002, http://www.rollingstone.com/music/news/bruce-springsteens-american-gospel-20020822 [accessed 17 January 2016].
[20]Rowan Williams was appointed as Archbishop of Wales in December 1999 and as Archbishop of Canterbury in July 2002.

the actual sight of the plane going into the tower and bodies falling from the windows and dust clouds in the street ... who has managed that? I find it very difficult to read any of the novels. It's a difficult question because it's just that the visual images do still bring back a moment I haven't really got words for, and, having been close-ish to it, I think there's almost a resentment about people who're not so close to it finding words on my behalf.[21]

The 9/11 novel is, perhaps inevitably, ensnared by competing dialectics, and here Williams presents yet another one: the tensions between the direct and the indirect witness. He expresses the sentiment that there appear to be implicit gradations of entitlement to represent 9/11 artistically, because while everyone saw it, comparatively few witnessed it, in the sense of experiencing it first-hand. For the purposes of clarity, I attempt to untangle the interwoven dialectics that so obfuscate the artistic response to 9/11, but of course an inevitable part of 9/11's complexity is that oppositional forces which compete with each other – the direct witness versus the spectator, the immediate response versus the considered, the literary versus the non-literary, commemoration versus memorialization, fiction versus historical record – present in multiple ways and often simultaneously. For Williams there was yet another layer of complexity: his and his colleagues' belief that they were unlikely to survive revealed a fundamental truth about the immediate experience of such a traumatic event that seems relevant to any artistic representation of it. At the height of the crisis, Williams found that there seemed very little to say:

I think we were rather assuming that we would be fortunate to live through this. [...] We prayed a bit together, being mostly clergy. There wasn't a lot to say. I do remember somebody saying as we bundled ourselves down the stairs towards the basement, 'Well, if we've got to die, this is quite a good group of people to be in company with'.[22]

---

[21]Dr Rowan Williams, interviewed by Charlie Lee-Potter, 3 April 2013.
[22]RW, interviewed by CLP, 3 April 2013.

The simple realization that 'there wasn't a lot to say' is central to any discussion about the appropriate lexicon to represent trauma, or indeed whether that trauma can be represented at all. It is arguably a more astringent and economical definition of Zadie Smith's criticism that the towers 'were covered in literary language when they fell…'.[23] If a witness to the catastrophe such as Rowan Williams, and one for whom nuanced and apposite language has always been so easy to summon, found that words were redundant, what chance of success could there be for the spectator-novelist? Others voiced the same sense. BBC journalist Stephen Evans, who was in the North Tower on 9/11, told me about an interview he did some time after the attacks:

> I can imagine that there would be very little to say. I interviewed a woman who was very, very moving. It was in the home she and her husband had created – we sat at the wooden table which her husband had made. She lived in Connecticut and – amazingly and tragically – died herself in a plane crash five years ago. Her husband had got trapped because the impact was below the place where he was. They spent thirty minutes on the phone talking about getting him to the roof. She was watching it all on TV and trying to guide him to a place of safety. Telling him to try going up to the roof, that kind of thing. He would leave the phone and try a way out but then come back. Eventually they realized that there was no way out. After that they simply talked about the big things – the 'I love yous'.[24]

For Rowan Williams and his colleagues, trapped in the basement with very little to say, it was becoming increasingly difficult to breathe. One of them, Courtney Cowart, described what happened when they tried to escape. They emerged into a landscape where 'Sidewalks, streets, cars, windows, ledges are deep in lavender-grey ash. The crystalline blue sky of the early morning is bruised, purple-green. The smoke in the sky continues to partially obscure the sun. It strikes me how unnatural this painter's palette is. The colors are

---

[23]Smith, 'Two Paths for the Novel'.
[24]BBC journalist Stephen Evans, interviewed by Charlie Lee-Potter, 13 February 2016.

wrong; deeply unsettling. It feels like an alien planet.'[25] Just a few moments later, the North Tower collapsed behind them:

> Above the decibels are so high the air is crackling. Below the ground is roaring and writhing like some mythical savage beast. The sound is bewildering because it is two noises coming from two directions. It feels like it might swallow us. [...] I see it barreling toward me 1,368 feet high. My mind is almost paralyzed, but not quite. I think in milliseconds. I think, 'When it gets to me I'll die or live. I have time for one more thought'.[26]

It is little wonder, then, that Williams has contempt for those novels that attempt to soothe and to resolve: the consolation myths, the 'love-spectrum' texts and, in particular, the Christian novels that proselytize. Williams describes those texts with some passion as 'horrible, *really* horrible actually. Novels ought never to be propaganda. They do have their philosophies. They just do. There are very few innocent novels in that sense. But again the good novel is not one that leaves you with more conclusions, but with more room in your mind.'[27] What therefore should, could the novelist do to define such an event as 9/11, while eschewing propaganda, avoiding resolution and resisting rhetorical excess? Given Williams's remark about 'resentment' at the audacity of those who did not witness and yet who try to write, should the event somehow, impossibly, be reserved only for those who experienced it directly? Perhaps it is appropriate that his response avoids resolution:

> No, no. I just report a reaction that anyone involved in serious trauma must feel, even somebody let's say who has been recently bereaved, picking up a book on bereavement and saying 'How *dare* they? What has this book to do with me? This is my territory'. [...] With any traumatic experience, at some point you have to make it part of your own story and part of your own narrative. You've got to talk about it. I don't mean in a cheap,

---

[25]Courtney Cowart, *An American Awakening: From Ground Zero to Katrina: The People We Are Free to Be* (New York: Seabury Books), 2008, p. 11.
[26]Ibid., p. 13.
[27]RW, interviewed by CLP, 3 April 2013.

therapeutic, let-it-all-out way. [...] And as soon as you've done that you're admitting that it can be talked about, and if it can be talked about then other people will talk about it too. [...] It is quite risky. Because if you hold something to yourself, you know that it's safe and you're safe. It's locked up. But you also need it to be recognized, and you need acknowledgement. And if you go out looking for acknowledgement then you take a risk that something will be misrecognized, the risk that you yourself misrecognize what you've been talking about, that you've betrayed something. But that's the process you go through. I once met Elie Wiesel but I didn't quite have the nerve to ask him, 'How do you do it? How do you write about [the Holocaust] without somehow thinking that you've shrunk it?'[28]

While lacking resolution, his candid response goes some way towards explaining why he has chosen to speak publicly now and why, on a larger scale, novelists may find 9/11 more 'speakable' as time elapses. However, in the shorter term, his view that to write it runs the risk that 'you've shrunk it' is allied to the idea that if a traumatic event is described in its fullest detail and form, it will somehow attract the wrong kind of attention. In other words, there is yet another troublesome dialectic at play here which is of importance to novelists, particularly those who attempted to describe the terrorist attacks immediately after 9/11 – the tension Williams sees between the responsible and the irresponsible spectator:

I'm always wary of what you might call trauma pornography. You read it because of the sense of being in touch with an extreme experience. It does get the adrenalin flowing in some ways. I'm very wary of that. Even your own text can work that way sometimes. I don't want to get excited by it. Let's be very blunt about this. If something like that happens in the world that we're in, it makes you interesting. 'Ooh! You were *there*?' And I have to be very aware of that and I have to be very suspicious of it. [...] And there have been times when I have very deliberately backed off saying anything about it because I don't want to say 'Hey, look at me! I'm interesting. I was *there*!'[29]

[28]Ibid.
[29]Ibid.

As the book will go on to suggest, it is the particular difficulty posed by the scale of the event and the public nature of the catastrophe that makes it so perplexing for the novelist to contain. Implicitly invoking Jean Baudrillard's definition of the 'hyperreal', Williams defines the event of 9/11 as almost beyond the scope of the novel:

> With the massive, world-altering, boundary-challenging experiences, whether it be the life and death of Jesus or the Holocaust or a modern trauma like 9/11, it's almost like saying 'well how much bigger, how much deeper do you want things to be?' The event itself almost does the work of the great novel for you, because it pushes the boundaries. It deepens things. It creates places in you that weren't there before. So isn't the novel just going to domesticate that a bit? [...] I once supervised a thesis years ago on Holocaust fiction and one interesting point made by my very gifted student was that if you look at some Jewish writing, like that of Isaac Bashevis Singer, you have fictions about life in the *shtetl* before, and fictions about New York Jewry after, and in the middle you have this great silence which people will not really refer to and that in itself is a very powerful fictionalizer, [...] the empty space.[30]

The idea of 'the empty space' is, in some respects, a counsel of despair for the novelist seeking the vocabulary to write about 9/11: for the writer, conceding that the most powerful way to confront 9/11 is to leave a 'great silence' is, potentially, to admit defeat. However, as Richard Gray points out, 'even in denying or dismissing the tools of the trade, [the writer] is using them. [...] The solution is either to surrender – which is not really a viable option, practically or emotionally – or to go on writing, continue trying to find some way of saying the unsayable.'[31]

In what follows, I address a variety of responses to the challenge of 'saying the unsayable', all of them written from different political and aesthetic positions. The particular conundrum of the 'great silence' that Rowan Williams identifies would seem familiar to my

---

[30]Ibid.
[31]Richard Gray, *After the Fall: American Literature since 9/11* (Malden, MA: John Wiley & Sons, 2011), p. 54.

first example, Richard Ford. My second chapter provides an analysis of what I term 'narratives of retrogenesis' by Don DeLillo and Jonathan Safran Foer, in which their consolatory fictions attempt to subsume the trauma of 9/11 by regressing in time. Chapter 3 provides an examination of Paul Auster's immediate response in essay form on the day of the attacks themselves, and an analysis of his perplexed and at times perplexing counterfactual fictional response much later. It is an engagement that I term 'hyperparallel', using the hyperbolic geometrical term that combines both the notion of the parallel and yet the divergent. (It is a fortuitous coincidence that the hyperparallel invokes, once again, Baudrillard's notion of the hyperreal.)

The fourth chapter concerns the 'extraterritorial' novels of Mohsin Hamid, Kamila Shamsie and Nadeem Aslam, whose reactions to 9/11 have been to eschew the neurotic fixation on the day itself and to focus instead on 9/11's historical context. Aslam's contention is that 'history is the third parent'; in other words, 9/11 was one of the perhaps inevitable consequences of history's long twentieth-century shadow. All three novelists point to the failure of political and journalistic discourse to anticipate 9/11 and the woeful lack of understanding of 9/11's place in history. The approach they decry is perhaps an inevitable consequence of what novelist Will Self describes as journalism's neglect of history: 'where we exist in news is in a kind of continuous now. It's even begun to project out in front of the present to schlap up the immediate future as well and that is why news has started to take on a character of sameiness and banality.'[32] The current defining practice of the journalist to focus on the time-defeating, sense-defying mantra of the endless now has, as a consequence, the effect of avoiding a contextualization of the past or an anticipation of the future via historical analysis. In this book, I examine the efforts made by novelists, some more successfully than others, to escape from an endless present tense, in which the past has been incorrectly framed or even ignored. As Richard Crownshaw has suggested, the false framing of the past can produce not memorialization, but merely commemoration:

> Commemoration results from the divorce of history from memory, the disarticulation of their interdependence, the unmooring of

---

[32]Will Self, interviewed on *Making News: The Endless Cycle*, BBC Radio 4, 9 April 2013.

history from the particularities of witnessing and testimony. It is these particularities that obstruct commemoration's desire to conclude upon past events.[33]

Commemoration is expressly what Shamsie and Aslam have been striving to avoid in their work. Their rejection both of commemoration and the 'continuous now' is further illuminated by Paul Connerton's analysis of the commemorative[34] in the context of Paul de Man's idea that 'invites us to consider "the idea of modernity" as consisting in "a desire to wipe out whatever came earlier, in the hope of reaching at last a point that would be called a true present"'.[35] In an interview I conducted with Shamsie, she highlights both the consequences of approaching events as 'continuous now' or 'true present' and of refusing to place 9/11 in historical context, as well as the particular difficulties of writing fictionally about Guantanamo detainees, where the situation is still evolving and remains unclear.

The final chapter examines the work of journalist-turned-novelist Amy Waldman, whose work published almost ten years to the day since 9/11 seeks a new temporal drive by forcing the fictional response forwards rather than nostalgically or paranoically back, combining both context and progressive momentum. Again, in an interview, she explains to me the tensions she sees between the so-called arbiters of fact: journalists, artists, politicians and historians. Her novel is the most journalistic in its rhetoric of all the texts that I examine, while eschewing the 'love-spectrum', any form of retrogenesis or temporal avoidance tactics. The former *New York Times* reporter lays out her own definitions of the journalistic versus the fictional response to 9/11. Given that this book assesses the trajectory that novelists have tried to follow since their early journalistic experimentation, Waldman's status as journalist, then 9/11 novelist, brings new insights into the field, defined by her as 'bringing chaos to order'.

---

[33]Richard Crownshaw, 'Introduction', in *The Future of Memory*, eds Richard Crownshaw, Jane Kilby and Antony Rowland (New York: Berghahn Books, 2010), p. 4.
[34]Paul Connerton, *How Societies Remember* (Cambridge: Cambridge University Press, 1989), p. 61.
[35]Paul de Man, 'Literary History and Literary Modernity', *Daedalus*, vol. 99, no. 2, *Theory in Humanistic Studies* (Spring 1970), pp. 384–404, pp. 388–389.

Waldman's proleptic conclusion and her novel's title are mirrored in Michel Houellebecq's work *Soumission* (Submission). The French novelist imagines the year 2022 and draws a new political landscape in which the Socialist Party does a deal with an imagined Islamic party to defeat *Le Front National's* Marine Le Pen. Whether Houellebecq's or Waldman's approach guides the novel away from the consolation dialectic, as defined by Crownshaw, or the exceptionalist mode defined as so inadequate to the task by Michael Rothberg, or, in the case of Houellebecq, the proselytizing approach decried by Rowan Williams are questions that this book will consider. In the case of Houellebecq, there are further questions to consider about the mutability of the literary text, given the fact that his novel was published on the day of the *Charlie Hebdo* murders in Paris. Houellebecq, whose face was on the cover of the satirical magazine that day and whose friend was killed in the attack, has said that his novel would have been much more violent if he had finished it after January 2015 rather than before.

* * *

Notable attempts to fictionalize 9/11 without relying on words alone include the typographical games played by Foer, outlined in Chapter 2. Philip Metres, meanwhile, in his poetry collection *Abu Ghraib Arias*, published ten years after 9/11, used textual experimentation to find a bridge between historical record and artistic expression.[36] He drew on news reports and transmuted them into redacted fragments, with occasional words or even whole lines obscured by an imagined censor's black pen. The cover of the collection was made of 'combat paper', or recycled military uniforms, by Chris Arendt, an army veteran who served at Guantanamo Bay. There was a synchronicity to the effort: the Combat Paper project is a paper-making workshop that encourages veterans to use their own uniforms in the process. According to the project's founders, the uniforms are 'cut up, beaten into a pulp and formed into sheets of paper. Participants use the transformative process of papermaking to reclaim their uniforms as art and express their experiences with the military.'[37] There is a

---

[36]Philip Metres, *Abu Ghraib Arias* (Denver/Rosslyn: Flying Guillotine Press, 2011).
[37]The Combat Paper Project, http://www.combatpaper.org/index.html [accessed 15 March 2013].

defensive fixation here on objectifying the word, the page, the cover, while exploring the therapeutic value of the book-making process. The insistence that the uniforms should be 'beaten to a pulp' would suggest that creating paper for *Abu Ghraib Arias* was as much about concentrated retaliation against a perceived aggressor as it is about literature. The news reports, the redactions, the recycled uniforms, even the revelation that Arendt spent precisely fifteen months, 'the length of a modern Army deployment',[38] collecting stories as a homeless veteran, hint at a neurotic fixation on trying to say more than language can, or perhaps to bridge what Rowan Williams called the 'powerful fictionalizer' of the 'empty space'. It is an exhaustive, even exhausting, attempt that ultimately struggles to find itself adequate to the task.

Artists, too, found it challenging to find ways to express what they had seen. The German painter Gerhard Richter, who was on a flight from Cologne to New York on September 11 and was diverted to Canada, attempted to depict on canvas the moment that the second plane hit the WTC, calling his work simply *September*. The artist was born in Dresden in 1932 and so has always been preternaturally conscious of the realities and consequences of the 'loss of a city', to use Richard Ford's phrase. After 9/11, he took for his inspiration a photograph of the second plane's moment of impact, but like so many other artists, he found the images problematic:

> The picture I used for this painting was very beautiful, with flames in red and orange and yellow, and wonderful. And this was a problem. Of course I painted it first in full colour, and then I had to slowly destroy it. And I made it banal. It doesn't tell much. It shows more the impossibility to say something about this disaster.[39]

Richter's drive to remove paint, to erase specifics, appears to ally his work with Rowan Williams's idea of the powerful fictionalizer of

---

[38]Ibid.
[39]Gerhard Richter in conversation with Nicholas Serota. Extract taken from recording for the Tate Channel and reprinted in *Tate Guide*, December 2011–January 2012, p. 15.

the empty space. Robert Storr, in his essay about Richter's painting, reframed that idea subtly, arguing that the artist's 'blurring of the explosion in the South Tower places gratification of any desire to see and thereby seize death pictorially beyond the viewer's reach. It is painting's reply to a photographic myth; painting's discretion counteracting the camera's voyeurism.'[40] The uncanny effect of Richter's refusal to allow the 'beautiful' red, orange and yellow flames to remain on the canvas was to render it more specifically representative of the event since the effect of the grey, black and white smudges and scars produced by his scraping is evocative of the planes themselves (Figure I.1).

The ambient musician William Basinski, who witnessed 9/11 from his Manhattan-facing apartment in Brooklyn, experimented with the 'empty space' too, in his work *The Disintegration Loops*.

FIGURE I.1 September, *2005 © Gerhard Richter 2016.*

---

[40]Robert Storr, *September: A History Painting by Gerhard Richter* (London: Tate Publishing, 2010), p. 52.

Basinski had been working on the loops since August 2001. He had a collection of music on fragments of magnetic tape and wanted to preserve these short loops by lacing each one onto a reel-to-reel tape machine and recording it onto CD. One day that August, he says he left the room to make coffee while one of the loops was playing, and when he returned, he saw dust starting to collect around the tape head: the constant friction as the tape passed repeatedly over the head was causing the magnetic tape to disintegrate, taking its stored sounds with it. By making a recording of the endless, deteriorating replays of a French horn playing the same eight notes over and over again, he produced a mesmerizing soundtrack made uncanny by its gradual effacement to silence. The sounds' connectedness to a painted canvas is resonant: an analogue tape is constituted of minute magnetic oxide particles on a narrow strip of plastic film. It was the falling fragments of those particles that Basinski could see around the tape head. Like Richter, Basinski was orchestrating the removal of paint from a canvas.

There is a counter-intuitive and dissident quality to Basinski's experiment, certainly to someone who has worked with magnetic tape as I have done as a radio reporter. Editing tape is a curiously intense business: headphones on, razor blade in hand, yellow wax crayon behind the ear, rolls of narrow, white sticky tape gummed to the top of the editing machine. Each phrase or sentence sliced out with the blade must be hung round the neck in case it is needed later. The tiniest slivers of tape, no more than a quarter of a centimetre long and imprinted with just a single breath, are stuck to the back of the hand, ready if the rhythm of a sentence needs the insertion of an extra pause. I can think of no other journalistic process that entails being literally draped in the words that are its currency. To allow that precious tape, with words, breaths and sounds magnetically attached to it, to play to the point of erasure is a subversive act. But bizarrely, Basinski's soundtrack is still recognizable forty minutes into the recording, even when there are virtually no particles left, because it leaves a sound imprint on the mind. It is a post post-echo of what had once been there, eerily redolent of the post post-image left in the sky above lower Manhattan after 9/11. Basinski finished the recordings on 10 September and fell asleep. The following morning, he awoke to see a plane flying very low past his window, through the gap above his sagging curtains. He and his neighbours spent much of that day on their roof, compelled to watch the grotesque 'show'. Their view from that distance rendered the scene in macabre Cinemascope, and, once again, Basinski expressed what he saw as a form of erasure:

> We [...] saw the South Tower crack and fall off and we just ran to the roof. [...] And then we sat there and watched the other tower going down...cascading glass...slow motion...and it was just...God. We couldn't believe it. We were all in shock. [...] We went downstairs and put on the music. It was like, 'This is the greatest show on Earth. Armageddon, here we go'.[41]

Basinski left a video camera in a fixed position on the roof and set it to record the towers' negative space, in a bleak reversal of Andy Warhol's assertive film *Empire*.[42] The following day, he retrieved the footage of the black clouds of smoke coiling around the empty space where the towers had stood, and married it with his disintegrating looped sound track. The footage ends in darkness, pierced only by specks of distant light and punctuated by the slow funereal beat of the almost-exhausted tape. Rather than viewing the breakdown of the tape as representative of mortality and decay, Basinski found the strangely eerie erosion of sound restorative: 'The most profound thing to me immediately was the redemptive nature of what had just transpired; the fact that the life and death of each of these melodies was captured in another medium and remembered.'[43] However, Richter's and Basinski's assertive power to somehow turn the gradual removal of colour and sound from their artistic expressions of 9/11 into much-admired aesthetic strengths has not always been shared by their fellow artists. In Chapters 2 and 5, I examine the opprobrium directed at sculptor Eric Fischl and architect Maya Lin in their attempts to memorialize

---

[41]John Doran, 'Time Becomes a Loop: William Basinski Interviewed', *The Quietus*, 15 November 2012, http://thequietus.com/articles/10680-william-basinski-disintegration-loops-interview [accessed 4 January 2016].
[42]Andy Warhol's 1964 work *Empire* is an 8-hour 5-minute, fixed-camera film of the Empire State Building.
[43]Doran, *The Quietus*.

and bear witness to the traumas of 9/11 and the Vietnam War, respectively.

The representation of 9/11 has been a vexed and fractured story. In serious literary terms, it has tended to wrestle with temporal conundrums involving the turning back of time, stopping time dead, and attempting to envisage counter-historical narratives. All of these approaches carry risks of entrapment by the 'continuous now'. However, the greater risk is the decision by some novelists to maroon themselves in the dead territory of what could be called the 'missing person' scenario, in which 9/11 acts as a kind of lumbering deus ex machina, arranging for people to vanish or reappear. These works include Clare Messud's *The Emperor's Children*, which allows a character to disappear, and Jay McInerney's *The Good Life*, in which 9/11 becomes the means by which two unlikely characters meet and in which 'apocalypse and atrocity yielded to adultery and conversation'.[44] These awkward, syncretic attempts to bind public trauma with private missing persons have produced a kind of hybrid fiction that is part memorialization, part sleight of hand. Other novelists have tried what might be called the reflex angle of making glancing reference to 9/11 and swiftly diverting their attention elsewhere, such as Audrey Niffenegger in *The Time Traveler's Wife*, where the protagonist's 'chrono displacement disorder' allowed him to know 9/11 was imminent but nevertheless decline to intervene. Niffenegger admitted that 9/11 occurred as she was completing her novel and, although she did not want to include it, she felt that 'you have this gigantic thing and if you don't at least nod at it, it's going to seem glaring in its absence'.[45] (Niffenegger's hesitant 'nod' is in opposition to DeLillo's assertive rejection of the reflex angle: 'I didn't want to write a novel in which the attacks occur over the character's right shoulder'.[46]) Lorrie Moore's *A Gate at the Stairs*

---

[44]Adam Mars-Jones, 'As His World Came Tumbling Down', *Observer*, 13 May 2007, http://www.guardian.co.uk/books/2007/may/13/fiction.dondelillo [accessed 15 May 2013].

[45]Audrey Niffenegger, interviewed by Veronica Bond, December 2003, http://www.bookslut.com/features/2003_12_001158.php [accessed 14 March 2013].

[46]Don DeLillo, interviewed by Mark Binelli, 'Intensity of a Plot', *Guernica*, 17 July 2007, http://www.guernicamag.com/interviews/intensity_of_a_plot/ [accessed 15 May 2013].

suffers from the same compulsion to 'nod at' 9/11, while Nick McDonell relegates 9/11 to a curious subplot in *The Third Brother* in which someone does not die.

Richard Gray, citing Messud's, McInerney's and DeLillo's 9/11 texts, defined them as works in which the 'crisis is, in every sense of the word, domesticated. [...] all life here is personal; cataclysmic public events are measured purely and simply in terms of their impact on the emotional entanglements of their protagonists.'[47] Gray observed that novelists had emphasized the 'preliminary stages of trauma: the sense of those events as a kind of historical and experiential abyss, a yawning and possibly unbridgeable gap between before and after'.[48] (Once again, this definition resonates with the 'empty space' described by Rowan Williams.) However, Gray suggested possible strategies to bridge that 'gap'. In recommending that 'some kind of alteration of imaginative structures is required to register the contemporary crisis', he proffered a 'deterritorialized' approach, in which novelists can respond to the challenge of 'new forms of otherness that are at best virulently critical and at worst obscenely violent' by placing themselves at the heart of those conflicts and, through their writing, 'by means of a mixture of voices and a free play of languages and even genres, they can represent the reality of their culture as multiple, complex, and internally antagonistic'.[49]

It is important to note, here, one of the key critical debates about the future of the 9/11 novel. While Smith objected to the way in which, as she saw it, O'Neill attempted to indulge the reader, Michael Rothberg, responding to Gray's notion of deterritorialization, detected in *Netherland* not the empty 'garments of transcendence' or the false lure of 'domestic' fiction, but a 'vision of a deterritorialized America', in which lies 'the ethics of the immigrant encounter'.[50] While Gray recommended a fictional response to 9/11 that opened up the homeland to the immigrant, Rothberg suggested that we need 'a fiction of international relations and extraterritorial

---

[47]Gray, *After the Fall*, p. 30.
[48]Ibid., p. 24.
[49]Ibid., pp. 18–19.
[50]Michael Rothberg, 'A Failure of the Imagination: Diagnosing the Post-9/11 Novel: A Response to Richard Gray', *American Literary History*, vol. 21, no. 1 (Spring 2009), pp. 152–158, 157.

citizenship'.[51] Congratulating Gray for demonstrating that although 'American novelists have [...] announced the dawn of a new era following the attacks on New York and Washington D.C., the *form* of their works does not bear witness to fundamental change',[52] nevertheless Rothberg argued that Gray's remedy of deterritorialization was not 'entirely sufficient'. He suggested, instead, a move away from the homeland altogether, by seeking 'a centrifugal literature of extraterritoriality' in which the 9/11 novel should provide 'cognitive maps that imagine how US citizenship looks and feels beyond the boundaries of the nation-state, both for Americans and for others'.[53] This 'extraterritorial' approach is addressed in Chapter 4, where I consider 9/11 texts written by novelists from Pakistan.

Gray's concern about novelists' fixation on the 'preliminary stages of trauma' is important, in that he suggested that the writer is acting 'as both victim and witness'.[54] This is perhaps an inevitable consequence of writers' early attempts at direct reportage. Paul Auster produced a tentative fragment of prose on the day of the attacks, while Martin Amis wrote an essay soon afterwards in which he reached for the lexically and intellectually threadbare idea of the nightmare/dreamscape in which an event becomes the substance of film. He attempted to have it both ways, however, by saying that it is 'already trite but stringently necessary to emphasize that such a *mise en scene* would have embarrassed a studio executive's storyboard or thriller-writer's notebook'.[55] Amis conceded that an 'unusual number of novelists chose to write some journalism about September 11', while Jonathan Lethem said that 'most of the novelists in New York were asked by one magazine or another to write something, and to me it seems our voices, at that moment, blended into one vast impotent scream'.[56] Indeed, he confessed that his own attempt written on September 12 and 13 was 'a pale

[51]Ibid., p. 153.

[52]Gray, *After the Fall*, p. 51.

[53]Rothberg, 'A Failure of the Imagination', p. 158.

[54]Gray, *After the Fall*, p. 24.

[55]Martin Amis, 'The Second Plane', in *The Second Plane* (London: Jonathan Cape, 2008), pp. 3–4.

[56]Jonathan Lethem, 'To My Italian Friends', in *The Ecstasy of Influence* (2012; London: Jonathan Cape, 2013), p. 227.

scream of protest, nothing more'.[57] Amis, in a later essay, explained his and his fellow novelists' choice to go 'into newsprint'; they were 'obliged to snap out of their solipsistic daydreams: to attend, as best they could, to the facts of life':

> For politics – once defined as 'what's going on' – suddenly filled the sky. True, novelists don't normally write about what's going on; they write about what's not going on. Yet the worlds so created aspire to pattern and shape and moral point. A novel is a rational undertaking; it is reason at play, perhaps, but it is still reason.
> September 11 was a day of de-enlightenment.[58]

While novelists were temporarily writing about 'what's going on', some journalists were writing about what was not: they were turning news into stories. Some reports at the time were fabricated from rumour posing as fact, seasoned with heavy doses of psychic paranoia. Newspapers reported that the Al Qaeda leader Osama bin Laden was driven by rage at his sexual inadequacy[59] and that Nostradamus had predicted the collapse of the Twin Towers.[60] Stephen O'Leary noted that within twenty-four hours of the 9/11 attacks 'over one hundred of the 120 students in my class at the University of Southern California's Annenberg School had received emails containing the spurious Nostradamus prophecy'.[61] Journalism will always be diminished by its flirtation with fiction, but even for journalists and novelists who were doing their best to find accurate words to represent the deaths of so many in Manhattan, at the Pentagon and in a field near Shanksville, Pennsylvania, the task was formidable. Martin Amis confessed that after a 'couple of hours at their desks, on September 12, 2001, all the writers on earth were considering the

---

[57]Ibid.

[58]Martin Amis, 'The Voice of the Lonely Crowd', *The Second Plane* (London: Jonathan Cape, 2008), pp. 12–13.

[59]S. Elizabeth Bird, 'Taking It Personally: Supermarket Tabloids After September 11', in *Journalism After 9/11*, eds Barbie Zelizer and Stuart Allan (London: Routledge, 2002), p. 151.

[60]Stuart Allan, 'Reweaving the Internet', in *Journalism After 9/11* eds Barbie Zelizer and Stuart Allan (London: Routledge, 2002), pp. 133–134.

[61]Stephen O'Leary, 'Rumors of Grace and Terror', *Online Journalism Review*, University of Southern California, 2 April 2004, http://www.ojr.org/ojr/ethics/1017782038. php [accessed 4 May 2008].

course that Lenin menacingly urged on Maxim Gorky: a change of occupation'.[62] He explained their journalistic endeavours as 'playing for time',[63] apparently suggesting that responding to 9/11 as an essayist was somehow the means by which the 'real' and difficult task of the novelist could be temporarily avoided. Novelist Mohsin Hamid admitted that he too turned to non-fiction: 'my fiction floundered in the face of world events, so I turned to journalism and essays instead'. [64] Kevin Marsh, who as a BBC programme editor frequently commissioned writers of fiction to define or to comment on the news of the day, takes a different view on this, seeing it not as a means of 'playing for time' but of being entrapped by the *lack* of time:

> The right thing for McEwan to have said when asked to do that was no. Because when journalism crashes into fiction, or a journalist crashes into a novelist, one thing disappears from the equation which is time. Surely the one thing that any novelist or artist needs is time, because you need that reflection, to go outside the concepts that you're happy with, familiar with, comfortable with. You need to step outside those and when you invite McEwan to write a piece or Rushdie, you're almost saying 'we'd like you to be a novelist, but we're going to take away your most important tool which is time'.[65]

There can be no doubt about the particular demands that 9/11 placed on all writers, whether of fiction or non-fiction. Marsh, who presided over *PM*, one of the BBC's flagship radio news programmes, on 11 September 2001, recalls a journalistic crisis unlike any before or since in his twenty-seven years of editing. It is worth citing his comments at length because they set in context perfectly the resounding lacuna at the heart of all initial attempts to define 9/11 in words. What was the vocabulary supposed to be?:

> It was one of those rare things that almost broke the system. There wasn't a framework, wasn't a conceptual framework

---

[62]Amis, 'The Voice of the Lonely Crowd', p. 11.
[63]Ibid., p. 12.
[64]Mohsin Hamid, *Discontent and Its Civilizations* (London: Hamish Hamilton, 2014), p. 28.
[65]Kevin Marsh, interviewed by Charlie Lee-Potter, 8 March 2013.

to fit this into. People were moving very slowly, it was a very strange afternoon. You would expect everyone to be rushing about, but everyone was going very slowly. There was almost a feeling that 'if I walk too fast I might upset things': a very, very weird atmosphere. And trying to work towards the headlines at 5 and 6 o'clock when you do have to say something resounding it was almost impossible actually, almost impossible. At 6pm the format kicked in: 'there has been a terrorist attack on the World Trade Center in New York and on the Pentagon in Washington'. So there was a format for that, a framework for that. But then, what does that mean? It was almost as if anything you could say couldn't explain it. Because that doesn't explain it, does it?[66]

Marsh's description of how the day evolved runs counter to Andrew Hoskins and Ben O'Loughlin's suggestion that familiarization eventually comes via endless repetition. Their view is that 'the default mode of both continuous and extended [television news] and even the more punctual (bulletins) [...] is repetition. "Recognition" and even "familiarity" actually sit with novelty, immediacy and surprise as news values'.[67] However, this did not seem possible either in the first responses to 9/11 or even subsequently, because 9/11 could never be 'familiar' enough for Hoskins and O'Loughlin's paradigm to work. Repetition became intolerable too and orders were finally given to television news networks to avoid repeated use of footage of the planes flying into the towers. I suggested to Marsh that 9/11 was a unique historical event: both known but not familiar, unthinkable and yet actualized. It could even be described as the first 'perfect' news event, in that it occurred on live television throughout the world and in some ways did not need writers' interventions in order to be mediated; 9/11 signalled a reduction in the power of the writer as negotiator, in inverse proportion to the gathering strength of the mere observer. Marsh agreed that the spectator has become part of the news:

You're in the news story. You're watching it happen. The downside is that you've got no one bearing witness, telling you what you can't see, no expertise telling you what *isn't* happening.

---

[66]Ibid.
[67]Andrew Hoskins and Ben O'Loughlin, *War and Media: The Emergence of Diffused War* (Cambridge: Polity Press, 2010), p. 22.

No journalistic input. 9/11 as the first 'perfect' news event absolutely puts the finger on it. Because if you now look at the news priorities of the BBC it's to get news cameras there to *show* you. It's not to get a reporter there anymore. The reporter comes second. And that is now the expectation, that like 9/11, we will watch the thing for ourselves and take away from it whatever we take away from it.[68]

To interpret the idea of unmediated news less pessimistically, if everyone is a witness, it should be less easy for journalists to veil the event with their much-loved 'common framings'. However, in the case of 9/11, that did not appear to happen, in part because of the cravings I identified earlier for consolation and reassurance. James Curran, professor of communications at Goldsmiths, University of London, expressed it slightly differently. His view is that 9/11, the 'ultimate instant story', may have been universally witnessed but was universally misrepresented too, certainly in the West:

It's become almost a paradigm for how you should report the news. An urgent story that tells the unfolding of events, a story that narrates what is happening, an eyewitness report. All that is good but it can also produce misunderstanding. Looking back on it, the reporting of 9/11 encouraged a spasm of rage. It didn't produce a fully contextualized account of what could have given rise to 9/11 and what could be the consequences. The very focus on the tragedy and horror encouraged a visceral reaction, a reaction that in hindsight probably didn't serve the interests of the West.[69]

The misrepresentation of the event has had additional consequences for fiction writers because the 'continuous now', the 'common framings' and the drive to occlude alternative points of view have made it arguably ever harder for them to find the vocabulary, the form to redefine what has already been seen. This book uses the flaws and lacunae in fiction and non-fiction writers' immediate

---

[68]KM, interviewed by CLP, 8 March 2013.
[69]James Curran, interviewed on *Making News: The Endless Cycle*, BBC Radio 4, 9 April 2013.

responses to the 11 September catastrophe both as context and as starting point for a study of the post-9/11 novel, beginning with the work of Ian McEwan and Richard Ford. Ford was a writer who was somehow expected to write fictionally about 9/11, but who was unwilling to do so. The book begins with Ford's perceived failure for two reasons: firstly, because it sets the context for the struggles that all novelists have faced in the past decade; secondly, because, as this book will show, Ford did write fictionally about 9/11 in the end. Like all the writers that I assess, Ford finally found some words that wrenched the 9/11 experience out of the 'continuous now', while avoiding the 'missing person' narrative. His drive to console, however, remains as a legacy of his first journalistic experiments in September 2001. McEwan too, in his novel *Saturday*, seemed unable to shake himself free of his journalism.

In my choice of novels to address, I have sought out those that seem to confront the issues most cogently. My findings would suggest that there has been a gradual transition towards a more historical accommodation of the event, concluding with *The Submission*, a far more schematic work than its predecessors. All these novelists attempt to renew the tradition of the novel in responding to the history of their own times. I have consulted widely; however, my response has been at the level of the practice of the individual writer. Indeed, I have gone to novelists themselves to seek their explanations as to why they have found it so challenging to render 9/11 in fictional form and what literary approaches they have been able to devise to overcome their artistic anxieties. It is an approach that seems to me to be important in the context of the history of the novel as cultural discourse, and one that relies on close readings to extract a sense of what is at stake in individual texts. In assessing the novel's capacity to respond to and contain an unimagined traumatic event, *Writing the 9/11 Decade* stands as a contemporary history of the form. Rather than pursue the tradition – present in western thought since Kant – that philosophy is somehow adequate to the sublime object of catastrophe, I wanted to make the novel itself the object of enquiry.[70]

---

[70]This philosophical tradition is analysed by Hans Blumenberg in *Shipwreck with Spectator: Paradigm of a Metaphor for Existence* (Cambridge: MIT Press, 1997); arguably it is alive still in the work of Badiou and others.

1

Richard Ford and Ian McEwan: Transactors and Redeemers

Introduction

Richard Ford's literary creation Frank Bascombe has had an unexpectedly long life. Ford appeared to believe that Frank would not evolve beyond his first incarnation in *The Sportswriter*, published in 1986. 'I would write a book', explained the author, 'and then that book would be over and that would have exhausted all of my ammunition.'[1] Yet, Frank's nudging insistence on coming back to life, not once but three more times, makes his fictional evolution a rare, percipient and above all un-choreographed chronicle of American life over four decades. Each novel was published in the middle of the decade with which it concerned itself, each roughly ten years apart, constituting a three-book cycle that is perhaps uniquely placed to reflect America's experience in the closing years of the twentieth century and the opening years of the twenty-first century. In 2014, Frank appeared again, this time in a collection of four short stories.

The expectation may have been that Ford, leading literary transactor of America's pre- and post-millennial crises, would write a novel in which he attempted to decipher or at least chronicle the neuroses provoked by the 9/11 attacks. It had been the natural

---

[1] Richard Ford, interviewed by Ramona Koval, Sydney Writers' Festival, 4 June 2007, http://www.abc.net.au/rn/bookshow/stories/2007/1941373.htm [accessed 4 May 2008].

trajectory followed by novelist Ian McEwan, who wrote two journalistic essays about 9/11 before embarking on his novel *Saturday*. Don DeLillo did the same, as did Paul Auster. But while Ford, too, wrote journalistically about 9/11 with little apparent difficulty, he appeared to avoid engaging with it fictionally. Ford admits to loving journalism because 'it's so easy and swift',[2] perhaps a partial explanation as to why he felt able to contribute to newspapers on the subject but apparently not to his own fictional canon. However, using an extended interview I conducted with Ford, I demonstrate that, far from avoiding 9/11 in his fiction, he did write a novel about it, albeit one that his readers failed to recognize. In this chapter, I establish that Ford's 9/11 novel is *The Lay of the Land*, a work in which he also engages with the environmental trauma of Hurricane Katrina that devastated his former home city of New Orleans. By analysing an early draft of *The Lay of the Land* written before Hurricane Katrina struck, it becomes apparent that in the eventual, rewritten novel, environmental assaults and fears of terrorist attacks are newly interwoven into the text. Just as importantly, there is clear evidence that Ford has borrowed imagery both from 9/11 and from Hurricane Katrina. He has adapted those images to explore his political thesis, that the repercussions of the hurricane and the assaults of 9/11 can be attributed, in the main, to the inadequacies of President George W. Bush.

The Sportswriter trilogy is the fugal counterpoint to America's contemporary crises. It is redolent with gathering gloom, encroaching natural and man-made disaster, increasing violence and the threat of death, laced together with ever more complex and compressed prose. In fictional form, Ford is more acerbic, acute and critical than he has tended to be in his journalism. To underline the political nature of his fiction and the close links he perceives between his portrayal of Frank and his own responses to contemporary events, he told me that in order to bring Frank back to life for a fourth time, he would need to be provoked by some form of political or environmental crisis. That crisis duly arrived in the form of Hurricane Sandy, which devastated Frank's beloved Jersey Shore. The result is Ford's short story collection *Let Me Be Frank with You*.

---

[2]Richard Ford, interviewed by Charlie Lee-Potter, 27 November 2012.

Fiction's apparently diminishing capacity to adequately reflect the extreme dystopia of the new millennium is an issue I will explore in relation to realist texts like Ford's, arguing that the essential 'weakness'[3] of the realist text with its 'simulated reality',[4] as defined by Catherine Belsey, has been altered by time and by circumstance; it is no longer a 'weakness' but a potential strength, and one that Ford uses to his advantage. Belsey's argument was that 'fiction does not normally deal with "politics" directly, except in the form of history or satire, that it is ostensibly innocent and therefore ideologically effective. But in its evasion of the real also lies its weakness as "realism".'[5] However, we are arguably more familiar now with the notion that facts themselves can have a 'simulated reality' and can specifically attempt to bring about an 'evasion of the real'. The sense that what they were witnessing could surely not be happening is certainly common to those who saw the 9/11 attacks. The phrase 'it was like a movie' was repeated countless times and was, incidentally, invoked again by many of those who survived the murderous assaults in Paris in November 2015. The notion of invented reality is also strikingly similar to the phrase used by an aide to President George W. Bush, who talked of the administration being able to create 'our own reality', when it was expedient to do so. I will discuss the aide's words in detail later in the chapter. My contention is that the perceived threat of international terrorism, our sense of latent crisis, the compulsion to anticipate risk, combined with the critical erosion of trust in the veracity of factual reporting, have created a new space in which realist fiction can both evolve and resonate. In this chapter, I examine the ways in which Ford and Ian McEwan explored this new territory. While Ford complains that novelists 'jumped on 9/11 too soon', McEwans's view is more sanguine. As he put it, the novel is an 'open-ended way of looking at our own image', and since it is our 'best machine',[6] it is inevitable that we must use it.

---

[3]Catherine Belsey, *Critical Practice* (1980; London: Routledge, 2002), p. 107.
[4]Ibid.
[5]Ibid.
[6]Zadie Smith talks with Ian McEwan, *The Believer*, August 2005, http://www.believermag.com/issues/200508/?read=interview_mcewan [accessed 6 January 2016].

Part one: Ford's 9/11 novel

Given that Ford maintained he would write one book about Frank and yet went on to write three more, it is possible to argue that he had a covert epic ambition for Frank all along. Yet it does not matter. It is the fact that Frank has evolved as circumstances have evolved that makes his transactional role so important. Frank and Ford have advanced together, arms linked, each unprepared for the lives and savage circumstances they would inherit, making Frank's trajectory very different to the pre-planned paths of other twentieth-century protagonists. Jean Paul Sartre plotted his document of French political life in the trilogy of novels *The Roads to Freedom*, knowing what the *dénouement* would be. Paul Scott did not publish the first of the novels that make up the *Raj Quartet* until 1966, long after the political era with which he dealt had ended.

When Ford began writing *The Sportswriter* in the 1980s, the prevailing political wind was blowing briskly from the right. Kevin Phillips, Republican political analyst and author, defined Ronald Reagan's presidential decade as a 'second Gilded Age'[7] which saw '[t]he triumph of upper America – an ostentatious celebration of wealth, the political ascendancy of the richest third of the population and a glorification of capitalism, free markets and finance'.[8] By comparison with the political landscape that Frank would find himself inhabiting as the second and third novels evolved, *The Sportswriter* years were relatively benign and prosperous. Frank could indulge in his voyeuristic passion for mail order catalogues, seeking out the 'abundance of the purely ordinary', secure in his comfortable suburb. But as Ford told me, the suburbs do not remain consoling forever:

> They seem less redemptive and consoling as the novels add up. [...] I wanted [Frank] to be a kind of moral pragmatist and to engage the argument about the suburbs. Namely, 'Okay. We authorized the suburbs, now let's live with it, find something in it that you like. Or don't'. I was trying to articulate what made us think they were good.[9]

---

[7]Kevin Phillips, *The Politics of Rich and Poor: Wealth and the American Electorate in the Reagan Aftermath* (New York: Random House, 1990), p. xviii.
[8]Ibid., p. xvii.
[9]Richard Ford, interviewed by Charlie Lee-Potter, 31 January 2016.

Ford's insistence on changing the nature of Frank's surroundings is just one aspect of his fictional response. As real-life political events evolved, Frank himself changes too. Indeed, Frank does not so much evolve as metamorphose into someone else. Perhaps, given the bleakness of the landscape, it would be more appropriate to say that he metastasizes.

Frank's career change from seller of stories to seller of realty coincides with his growing power as a commercial man. He trades in property, occasionally buys houses back, even moves them brick by brick from one place to another. Frank does not create things any longer, but simply makes transactions, which is where his true value lies. Interviewed in 2006, Richard Ford described his desire to make Frank a 'transactive' character, a kind of universal currency-converter. 'I was determined not to write a book about a writer. But yes, I needed something to make him persuasive as the sort of transactive character I wanted him to be. With Frank's speaking voice – the intelligence that that voice implies – he is able to transact the culture for the reader.'[10] Frank's 'transactive' role means that he is a different man in each of the four books, because the world he is 'transacting' keeps changing. This is not simply character development or evolution, but wholesale character reinvention, a fact that Ford celebrates. Speaking about the creation of the character that, to use numerical rubric, we might call Frank No. 3, Ford described him as a new individual altogether, an invented fictional model of Franks 1 and 2:

> [T]he whole conception of character is something fictitious that we invent to make our lives, as they go along, begin to seem continuous and more plausible and to make sense to ourselves. Because what I was doing was I was just making another guy up in the third book. I gave him the same name as the guy in the other two books and I gave him some of the same attributes but I was inventing him wholly newly.[11]

[10] RF, interviewed by Phil Hogan, 'To Be Frank', *Observer*, 24 September 2006, http://www.guardian.co.uk/books/2006/sep/24/fiction.features [accessed 25 March 2013].
[11] RF, interviewed by Ramona Koval, *The Book Show*, Radio National, 4 June 2007, http://www.abc.net.au/radionational/programs/bookshow/richard-fords-the-lay-of-the-land/3242570#transcript [accessed 25 March 2013].

Ford asserts, too, that there is no reason why he should not be able to change characters' eye colours if he chooses, or their opinions. In his interview with me, I would argue that he went even further, asserting that when he wrote *The Lay of the Land* he had wanted to change Frank's race too:

> I did think about making Frank be an African American in some novel. Probably I lacked the nerve for that, thought people would think I was an idiot (which might be true). But the more important point is that in each succeeding book who Frank is, is entirely my choice. I can make him more or less consistent with who he was before, or I can change him. It's all artifice. The thought of making him an African American was just to stress that point, and to stress that I'm free to do what I please.[12]

The key influences that have made the fictional Frank change his nature, aside from the artistic autonomy of his creator, are of course the facts: the real-life world of America. As the three novels and collection of short stories unravel, the world in which Frank lives becomes progressively more violent, less forgiving and ultimately life-threatening. *The Lay of the Land*, written, as Ford has said, 'entirely' after 9/11 carries within it the shadow of forthcoming real-life events, as well as bearing the imprint of terrorist attacks such as the 1995 Oklahoma bombing, which was, until 9/11, the worst peacetime attack upon the United States in the country's history. Timothy McVeigh, the 33-year-old Gulf War veteran responsible for the murder of 168 people, was executed three months before the 9/11 onslaughts. Not surprisingly, the implicit threat of terrorism becomes much more direct in *The Lay of the Land*. So too does the impact of natural disaster, Nature's own terrorist force.

Frank's awareness of terrorism is vague to the point of non-existent in *The Sportswriter*. Before the attacks of 11 September 2001, America's recent experience of domestic terrorism had been limited to McVeigh's assault and to the campaign of the Unabomber. In *The Sportswriter*, Selma, Frank's lover during his disastrous term teaching at Berkshire College, admits to him that she has had a 'profound' involvement with terrorists, 'in which she'd hinted

---

[12]RF, interviewed by CLP, 31 January 2016.

she'd killed people ...'.[13] There is a delusional boastfulness to her claim, but, by the time that Frank emerges as a new character in *The Lay of the Land*, he is briefly suspected of involvement in a genuine terrorist attack on Haddam Hospital which kills one of his acquaintances. As the novel closes, we hear that the man responsible is 'A man of the Muslim faith'[14] who wanted to send a message to a fellow-Muslim whom he believed had been corrupted by American values.

Earlier in the novel we learn that Sally, Frank's second wife, has religious fundamentalist children from whom she is estranged. Frank returns home and picks up a newspaper in his office and reads about a 'CIA warning about a planned attack on our shores by Iran'.[15] In a paragraph distilled until it is no more than a concentrated jus of American millennial angst, Frank watches a threatening gang of youths standing beneath the crawling neon of a quasi-Times Square electronic billboard. In an asyndetically neurotic construct, he reads:

> Quarterlysdown 29.3...ATTdown62%...Dowclose10.462... HappyThanksgiving2000...LLBeanChinamadeslippersrecalled duetodrawstringdefectabletochoketoddlerusers...PierreSalinger testifiesreLockerbiecrashsez 'Iknowwhodidit'...Airlineblanket sandheadrestssaidnotsanitized ... Buffalostymiedunder15 lakeeffectsnow...HorrorstorieswithFlaballots: 'Whatinthe name ofGodisgoingonhere?'workersez...NJenclavesuffers mysterious bombdetolinktoelectionsuspec'd...Tropicaldepres Waynenot likelytomakeland...BigpileupontheGardenState...HappyThanks giving....[16]

Ford blends financial ruination, litigiousness, blame, threat, trash-culture, terrorism, and that monument to the all-American ideal – Thanksgiving Day – into one gigantic, choking, indigestible declaration of dependence on consumer products and the financial markets. Thanksgiving Day in *The Lay of the Land* is marked by Frank's near murder.

---

[13]Richard Ford, *The Sportswriter* (1986; London: Collins Harvill, 2006), p. 222.
[14]Richard Ford, *The Lay of the Land* (London: Bloomsbury, 2006), p. 478.
[15]Ibid., p. 228.
[16]Ibid., pp. 163–164.

Violence appears to be easier for Frank to understand than terrorism; his early experience of it is limited to being punched comically in the face by his girlfriend Vicki in *The Sportswriter*, her 'fists balled like little grapeshoots'.[17] Yet, by *Independence Day*, we learn that Frank has been mugged and a former lover Clair Devane has been raped and murdered. The inexorable drive towards violence, threat and terror is marked quite clearly in the development of the character of Paul, Frank's son. In *The Sportswriter*, Paul is an eccentric joke-teller with an interest in ornithology. By *Independence Day*, Paul has progressed to being a maladjusted, sinister teenager who kills birds, enjoys shoplifting and has been arrested for attacking the female security guard deployed to arrest him. By *The Lay of the Land*, we learn that Paul, aged seventeen, had attempted to have sex with his fifteen-year-old sister. Frank's own trajectory has taken him from a recollection of exceptional gallantry as he saved his wife Ann from a gunman, to a revelation in *Independence Day* that he had simply jumped behind her to protect himself. By the end of *The Lay of the Land*, gunmen appear once again. This time, Frank does not step aside, but in a *dénouement* that runs counter to any idea of heroic justice, he is shot and comes close to death.

Frank's acquaintance Wally, whom he meets at the Divorced Men's Club, commits suicide in *The Sportswriter*. Frank is more puzzled than distressed and wonders why Wally could not find a reason to keep going, since 'what else is the ordinary world good for except to supply reasons not to check out early?'[18] In a neat piece of synchronicity, Frank has a more important and devastating encounter with a suicidal man, also called Wally, in *The Lay of the Land*. This Wally is the first husband of Frank's second wife Sally. And to reinforce the idea of growing disharmony and discord in *The Lay of the Land*, Wally does not commit suicide once, as his alter ego does in *The Sportswriter*, but performs the apparently impossible and does it twice. Wally Mark 2 is the man who outdoes the spirit of American excess and dies twice. There is a sense of diminishing values as the three novels progress and it seems somehow incumbent on Wally 2 to go for the double in order for his statement about life to have any meaning at all. Making meaning

---

[17]Ford, *The Sportswriter*, p. 290.
[18]Ibid., p. 343.

out of death is something that preoccupies Ford. As I demonstrate later in this chapter, it is a conundrum to which he finally secures an answer when writing journalistically about 9/11.

Independence Day was written during the early 1990s, when domestically the pivotal event was the 26 February 1993 bombing of the WTC in New York that killed six people and injured more than 1,000. The van, packed with 1,500 pounds of explosives and driven to the door, brought with it a new domestic awareness of the threat of international terrorism. New York's then State Governor Mario Cuomo assessed the lack of awareness hitherto: 'We all have that feeling of being violated. No foreign people or force has ever done this to us. Until now we were invulnerable.'[19] An eyewitness quoted by the BBC at the time spoke with prescient insight: 'It felt like an airplane hit the building.'[20] In October 1995, as *Independence Day* was being published, Sheikh Omar Abdel Rahman, a blind cleric, was given a life sentence for orchestrating the bombing. Internationally, the news for Americans was dominated by Iraq's invasion of Kuwait in August 1990 and the United States' retaliation. Coverage of the relentlessly televised war of Desert Storm with its ineluctable smart bombs that seemed, impossibly, both simulated and real simultaneously was hard to avoid. But who would have imagined, Richard Ford or anyone, that by the time he would be writing the third unplanned novel in his trio of novels that the 1993 bombing of the Twin Towers would be eclipsed by the subsequent assault upon them.

In *The Lay of the Land*, Frank has reached the age of 55, the year is 2000 and the American election is in the process of being 'stolen'[21] by George W. Bush with the complicity of the American media and public. It is potentially difficult, therefore, to accept without question that *The Lay of the Land* is what Ford calls 'my 9/11 novel'. The action of this third novel takes place the year before the terrorist attacks of 11 September 2001, but Ford has confirmed that it was written 'entirely' after 2001[22] and, crucially, with those

---

[19]Mario Cuomo, New York State Governor, quoted by the BBC, 26 February 1993, http://news.bbc.co.uk/onthisday/hi/dates/stories/february/26/newsid_2516000/2516469.stm [accessed 4 May 2008].

[20]BBC News, 26 February 1993. http://news.bbc.co.uk/onthisday/hi/dates/stories/february/26/newsid_2516000/2516469.stm [accessed 4 May 2008].

[21]RF, interviewed by Chas Bowie, *Portland Mercury*, 19 October 2006.

[22]RF, interviewed by Ramona Koval, 4 June 2007.

attacks in mind. Even though he chose deliberately to write about times *before* the 9/11 assaults took place, he did so because these were the 'twilight years of perceived normalcy' when that terrible day 'is just around the corner'. This is where the novel's 'frictive power'[23] is generated:

> When I started thinking about 9/11 and its immediate aftermath, it seems to me that all the things that we thought had changed our lives forever were really going on before that. And we, because of this fierce grasp upon normalcy, were not available to it. And one of the things that realistic fiction can do – and its moral address – is to say to the reader, 'Pay attention. Pay attention. Pay attention'.[24]

Richard Ford's repeated plea that we should 'pay attention' is redolent of Arthur Miller's distant call that 'attention must be paid'. Comparisons have been drawn between Frank and Willy Loman as the quiet, insignificant but insistent voices of America's recent past.[25] But that invocation of Loman, combined with our knowledge of subsequent events, brings a mournful futility to paying attention after the tragic event.

Questioned more closely about the implicit connections between 9/11 and *The Lay of the Land*, Richard Ford has, in the past, been clear. Asked about the timeline of *The Lay of the Land*, he stressed the political outcome that the brawl between Gore and Bush had produced: 'it was the moment the Republicans stole the government and the Supreme Court acted not like a Supreme Court but a Republican court, and the aftermath is the war in Iraq'.[26] In his interview with me, Ford went further than he has done hitherto in clarifying his intentions in *The Lay of the Land*. He confirmed that the work is his 9/11 novel, but asked if he found it disappointing that so few people seemed to see that context, he said that it did not surprise him. Not entirely because of the obliqueness of his approach, but because of the inadequacies of his American audience in particular:

---

[23]RF, interviewed by Phil Hogan, *Observer*, 24 September 2006.
[24]RF, interviewed by Chas Bowie, *Portland Mercury*, 19 October 2006.
[25]RF, interviewed by Phil Hogan, *Observer*, 24 September 2006.
[26]RF, interviewed by Chas Bowie, *Portland Mercury*, 19 October 2006.

The Lay of the Land is specifically – if indirectly – a 9/11 novel. It deals with America *before* that calamity. It wants to make the point that what observers said happened *after* the Towers fell was pretty much what was going on before. Most readers didn't identify *The Lay of the Land* as a 9/11 novel – which was somewhat (though not entirely) my wish. Americans aren't very interested in politics, except every four years. They want to be left alone, not to think about politics or about government – which they're also not interested in. The inter-relationships between what we as citizens should've known *before* 9/11 and how shocked we were when it happened – those are things Americans don't want to think about because to do so implicates us in the causes of 9/11. And feeling implicated as citizens in the disaster of 9/11 is definitely not on the American menu. It would make us at least partly responsible, and that's not popular. We prefer to feel entirely, innocently outraged, betrayed.

When I started to write *The Lay of the Land* I realized I couldn't write about the specifics of 9/11 because it was too soon after the events. The details were still in the province of the journalists. For me to write about important public events, they have to sink into the ground and percolate up feelingly through my shoe soles.[27]

For Americans reading *The Lay of the Land*, the re-examination of that phase in the nation's history is potentially a resonant and painful one. The hagiography of President George W. Bush in the aftermath of the 9/11 attacks becomes highly questionable once memories are summoned of that earlier political phase in 2000, when Bush retained the presidency with fewer votes than his political opponent. In 2001, America crowned Bush as their charismatic saviour, even though his legitimacy was arguably seized rather than earned. The inadequacy of the American media in exposing the tenuousness of George W. Bush's mandate served only to underline the flaws inherent in the reporting of the so-called facts. The facts did not fit, so the American media invented a new set of them that would. Few seemed willing to 'pay attention', so the view was taken that the facts did not matter. This was how Robert W. McChesney,

---

[27]RF, interviewed by CLP, 31 January 2016.

professor in the Department of Communication at the University of Illinois at Urbana-Champaign, put it:

> [W]ho actually won the actual election in Florida seemed not to interest the press one whit. [...] If the media conceded that Gore, in fact, had won the race in Florida, it would have made people logically ask, 'why didn't the media determine this when it mattered?' ... As soon as the leaders are not the product of free and fair elections, the professional reliance on official sources – which is wobbly by democratic standards to begin with – collapses.[28]

To 'pay attention' to Richard Ford's sequence of realist fiction is to glean a different sense of the nation's history than we might from some so-called factual reports of the years that fictional Frank and his real-life contemporaries lived through. Changes in the language, tone, style and even in the character of Frank himself tell their own story. The narrative sway of Richard Ford's trilogy and short stories takes us from the 'normal applauseless life of us all'[29] to a bigger canvas, to a world threatened by terrorism, corruption and natural disaster. But it is in that narrative, in fiction and in story telling that we seek a form of verisimilitude that the so-called facts can never fully establish. Even America's most revered television news presenters who codify, organize and disseminate the apparent facts could only make sense of the events of 11 September 2001 in fictional terms. 'It looks like a movie' was the best description that one of the United States' most familiar news anchors could summon to her aid on the day that the aircraft hit. It was a more prosaic way of expressing what Susan Sontag meant when she wrote that 'a catastrophe that is experienced will often seem eerily like its representation'[30] but it nevertheless cut to the heart of Jean Baudrillard's conundrum: which one is real – the copy or the original? (The novelist Will Self, who complained about journalism's obsession with the 'continuous now', experimented with the idea of the copy and the original in his

---

[28]Robert W. McChesney, 'September 11 and the Structural Limitations of US Journalism', in *Journalism after September 11*, eds Barbie Zelizer and Stuart Allan (London: Routledge, 2002), pp. 91–100, 97.

[29]Ford, *The Sportswriter*, p. 8.

[30]Susan Sontag, *Regarding the Pain of Others* (London: Penguin, 2003), p. 19.

short story 'iAnna', published to mark the tenth anniversary of the 9/11 attacks. A psychiatrist seeks advice after seeing a number of patients who believe the world is an iPad, which they can manipulate by tapping, poking and 'tweezering' the air. The psychiatrist names the new syndrome 'iPhrenia'.) There is, of course, an obvious flaw in my argument that a fictionalized representation of the actual can render that catastrophe more real. Ford attempted to define the catastrophe of 9/11 in fiction because he felt he would be able to say so much more; yet, if his American audience failed to see that he had written a 9/11 novel, how then could fiction be more resonant than journalism? Here again is Ford's assertion that journalism is somehow 'quick and easy', but his initial point is overlaid with the assertion that journalism does not require deep knowledge. And if it does not require deep knowledge, how reliable can it genuinely be?:

> Journalism, Walter Lippman said, is there to provide a view of the world upon which citizens can act. I'm more interested in providing a view of the world which shows the reader both what causes events, and then what consequences events have in our lives. Necessarily, that's speculative and provisional.[31]

Many journalists, if they were being honest, would ruefully admit that the novelist faces the more challenging task. As Ford told me, 'You have a lot of rope to hang yourself with a novel.' Frank Bascombe, with his sometimes limited grasp on reality, is of course emblematic of the way in which fiction and facts can elide; so too are the novels, blending as they do a fictional landscape on which twentieth- and twenty-first-century realities encroach. The elision of fact and fiction is deliberate, but possibly inevitable too, given Ford's own inability to remember what is real and what is imagined. *The Lay of the Land* includes a reference to the Barnegat Bay Bridge road sign that trumpets it is 'New Jersey's Best Kept Secret'. Asked about the sign on a driving tour with a reporter from the *New York Times*, Ford attempted to find the sign, but then admitted, 'I can't remember whether I made that up or not.'[32] More crucially, the

---

[31]RF, interviewed by CLP, 31 January 2016.
[32]Charles McGrath, 'A New Jersey State of Mind', *New York Times*, 24 October 2006, http://www.nytimes.com/2006/10/25/books/25ford.html?fta=y [accessed 4 May 2008].

fictional/factional transactions come from Frank himself. After all, he begins his fictional existence working as a novelist, a purveyor of storytelling. But he finds, not in the least to his regret, that after one glorious burst of sparks, he has nothing more to say and turns himself into a sports journalist. Yet he discovers that his subjects, athletes, do not have that fictional quality which would make them interesting: 'When you look very closely, the more everybody seems just alike – unsurprising and factual. And for that reason I sometimes tell less than I know, and for my money the boys in my racket make a mistake with in-depth interviews.'[33] Ford has touched upon an aspect of 'the real' that reinforces not its strengths, but its flaws. In fact, Catherine Belsey's definition of realist fiction as suffering from an 'evasion of the real' suddenly has some currency as a definition of the factual, in which writers may evade that which is 'unsurprising' by telling 'less than' they know.

The final stage in Frank's evolution from a peddler of the imagined to a salesman of the real is represented by his eventual choice of career. What could be more intensely, concentratedly, reductively real than the big brother of the adjective 'real' – the noun 'reality' – and reality's stake-holding, commercial cousin, 'realty'? In *Independence Day*, Frank elects to become a conduit, a transactor, for those who seek their own piece of American soil, a realtor for whom prices will always be 'an index to the national well-being'.[34] Frank's new job as a barometer of 'national well-being' with reality/realty for sale allows him to spin dreams for putative customers like the Markhams from Vermont. They do not want the reality of realty, but they do want to be able to imagine it. Frank has finally walked inside one of his beloved home shopping catalogues. Smiling out of its pages, he can promise irresistible abundance for anyone who will transact with him. But in a piece of omniscient real-estate manoeuvring, he gets to seal his own violent fate by selling a house to the Feensters. The Feensters have entered into that double-edged trade-off. They have won a vast amount of money on the lottery, but have thereby lost the sense of having earned the house that they buy. Their criminal leanings will bring gunmen to Frank's door in retribution.

---

[33]Ford, *The Sportswriter*, p. 62.
[34]Richard Ford, *Independence Day* (1995; London: Bloomsbury, 2006), p. 5.

The restorative power of real estate evaporates as the three novels progress. In tandem with the increasing violence and the growing suspicion of incomers and immigrants, real estate starts to lose its 'redemptive theme in the civic drama...And realty itself – stage manager to that drama – had stopped signalling our faith in the future, our determination not to give in to dread'.[35] Worse, Haddam, the town where Frank bought his first family house, becomes the kind of place where 'someone might set a bomb off just to attract its attention'. It is Richard Ford's cry to 'pay attention' yet again, to ward off violent disaster, as the solid, reassuring heft of small town America is being eroded. Collapse is, after all, real estate's final appointment and one that Richard Ford returns to in the form of the Queen Regent at the end of *The Lay of the Land*. It is an anthropomorphic, crenellated and canopied hotel, stoically facing the Atlantic. When it is demolished, it gets an audience of camera-wielding groupies and petty criminals to see it go. The description, as it falls, is redolent of the Twin Towers as they imploded.

> Her longitude lines, rows of square windows in previously perfect vertical alignment, all go wrinkled, as if the whole idea of the building had sustained, then sought to shrug off a profound insult, a killer wind off the ocean. And then rather simply, all the way down she comes, more like a brick curtain being lowered than like a proud old building being killed. Eighteen seconds is about it.[36]

The description of the Queen Regent's collapse is one that could easily have been included in a news report from New York on 11 September 2001 and it would have been more meaningful than the news-anchor's prosaic statement that 'It looks like a movie'. Lest these assertions seem tendentious, I asked Ford if it was legitimate to suggest that his description of the Queen Regent's demise was, in fact, his way of describing the Twin Towers' demise too:

> I was aware of that. I was also very much in the grip of all the film footage I'd seen of buildings being imploded: namely, that you're

---

[35]Ford, *The Lay of the Land*, p. 90.
[36]Ibid., pp. 305–306.

looking at an intact structure, then there are these puffs of smoke from the bottom, and then the building sinks ... from the bottom up. Very profound image for me. One second everything's intact, the second it's gone. That happened to the hotel I grew up in, in Little Rock.[37]

It is possible to argue that the stage-managed quality of the Queen Regent's demolition, with its attendant audience braying for drama, brings a kind of formality and order to the hotel's collapse entirely different from the catastrophic chaos produced by the collapse of the WTC. (However, there is an air of anarchism to the Queen Regent's demise as the demolition men's organized destruction goes wrong and a young thug armed with a brick in a carrier bag vandalizes Frank's car.) More importantly perhaps, there is an intellectual engagement with the description of the hotel's collapse that has been stripped from the endlessly replayed footage of the Twin Towers' destruction, replays that turned their collapse into grotesque and macabre spectacle. As Ken Paulson pointed out, television companies were not immune to the realization that the 9/11 attacks made electrifying footage: 'there were far too many replays of the second plane hitting the World Trade Center'.[38] It is an interesting trade-off. Overuse of the footage has pushed the Twin Towers' collapse into the realms of the impossible hyperreal, while Ford's precise narrative has gone largely unrecognized and is thereby stripped of intent.

Part two: Redemption and narrative

Tony Blair, British prime minister in 2001, had to choose which reading to give at the memorial service for the British victims of the 9/11 attacks. It was deemed essential that it should be inclusive, consoling and redemptive in spirit, but not monotheistic or even covertly religious. The passage he selected was the final section

[37]RF, interviewed by CLP, 31 January 2016.
[38]Paulson, 'A Patriotic Press Is a Vigilant One', *in Crisis Journalism, A Handbook for Media Response* (Sunrise Valley, Reston, VA: American Press Institute, October 2001), pp. 46–47, p. 47.

from *The Bridge of San Luis Rey*, written by Thornton Wilder and published in 1927. The work examines whether life has any transcendent meaning, after five people die in the collapse of a bridge above a gorge. This is the section that Tony Blair read:

> But soon we will die, and all memories of those five will have left earth, and we ourselves shall be loved for a while and forgotten. But the love will have been enough; all those impulses of love return to the love that made them. Even memory is not necessary for love. There is a land of the living and a land of the dead, and the bridge is love. The only survival, the only meaning.[39]

At the same church service, the UK ambassador to the United States, Sir Christopher Meyer, extrapolating from the theme that 'love will have been enough', read a message from the Queen that included the line, 'Grief is the price we pay for love.' To underline the effectiveness of Blair's and Meyer's choice of words, Alastair Campbell, Tony Blair's director of communications, reported that they resonated powerfully with former US President Bill Clinton. Clinton, who was sitting in the front row of the church with Blair, asked Campbell afterwards if he had written Meyer's line about grief being the price we pay for love. 'I said I'd love to take credit, but no. He said find the guy who did, and hire him.'[40] It seemed that Blair and Meyer achieved something with their rhetoric that few others managed. The political commentator Andrew Rawnsley, in noting that Blair chose Wilder as his source material, suggested that the British prime minister singled himself out:

> There was [...] a unique quality to Blair's response to 9/11. This was in part simply because his public performances were so masterly. The *Washington Post* opined that he and Rudolph Giuliani, the Mayor of New York, were the two political figures 'who broke through the world's stunned disbelief'.[41]

---

[39]Thornton Wilder, *The Bridge of San Luis Rey* (1927; London: Penguin, 2006), p. 127.
[40]Alastair Campbell, *The Burden of Power: Countdown to Iraq, The Alastair Campbell Diaries* (2012; London: Arrow Books, 2013), p. 22.
[41]Andrew Rawnsley, *The End of the Party: The Rise and Fall of New Labour* (London: Penguin, 2010), p. 37.

While Blair borrowed from Wilder, Giuliani turned to Winston Churchill. Returning home late at night on 11 September 2001, he re-read the passages about the Battle of Britain in Roy Jenkins's newly released biography of Churchill:

> [D]uring the day I had been thinking about the Battle of Britain. I had been thinking, 'The English went through something worse than this. They went through being bombarded every day, bombed every night, not knowing who was going to be alive the next day'. [...] And I thought [...] I could learn some lessons from how Churchill got the people of England through something.[42]

It is interesting that both Blair and Giuliani felt they needed to borrow the prose of other exemplary rhetoricians to bring persuasive force to their actions. (That said, Senator Joe Biden later complained acerbically, 'There's only three things [Rudy Giuliani] mentions in a sentence: a noun, a verb, and 9/11.'[43]) Thornton Wilder, the author who enabled Blair to break through the 'stunned disbelief', is perhaps best known for *Our Town*, said to be the most frequently performed play in American schools. Richard Ford, too, seemed alert to the possibilities of allowing Wilder's redemptive spirit to burnish his text. In a cheeky piece of real-estate inventiveness in *The Lay of the Land*, Frank coins the epithet 'Thornton Wilders' to define all those idyllic 'Our Town' properties that people most desire in their dreams but do not necessarily intend or even wish to buy: in the published novel, Ford declares that Clare Suddruth would be 'more at home in a built-out Greek revival or a rambling California split-level. "Thornton Wilders", we call these in our trade.'[44] In an earlier draft, Ford attaches the same term, a 'Thornton Wilder', to a 'big solid Dutch Colonial or a rambling

---

[42]Rudy Giuliani, interviewed by Steve Forbes: 'Remembering 9/11: The Rudy Giuliani Interview', *Forbes*, 9 September 2011, http://www.forbes.com/sites/steveforbes/2011/09/09/remembering-911-the-rudy-giuliani-interview/#2715e4857a0b6e0504a45897 [accessed 18 January 2016].

[43]Joe Biden said this in October 2007, while competing to be the Democratic presidential candidate. Rudi Giuliani was trying to secure the Republican nomination at the time.

[44]Ford, *The Lay of the Land*, p. 273.

late-Georgian vernacular'.[45] Ford simply made the architectural term up in order to harness both the idea of American-ness and its attendant dream, as well as to invoke, possibly, the much publicized and much discussed occasion on New York's Fifth Avenue when Tony Blair deployed Thornton Wilder's words to evoke a sense of continuity and meaning. Indeed, when questioned, Ford told me why he had borrowed Wilder's name:

> That's because I once acted in *Our Town*. In high school. I played George Gibbs, and we had a stage set with a certain kind of prosaic American town architecture. It evoked small-town, cosy, fire-in-the-fireplace, steak on the table life. Something conservative and nominally redemptive. I just applied that name to houses in New Jersey that appear in the novel.[46]

This is of course an instance of elision between Ford and Frank, to the point that Ford often forgets where the divisions lie. Only two days before we spoke for the first time, Richard Ford said that he had written another episode in Frank's life, this time involving the death of his dog. It is a dog, incidentally, that Frank does not even own in the trilogy or in the later short stories. The reason he was driven to write about how Frank would feel if he lost his dog is because Ford himself had lost his dog a few days before. Once again, the elision is there:

> People ask me what Frank's 'doing now'. I tell them he isn't doing anything. There *is* no Frank except in the books where he already appears, and in raw form in my notebooks. I keep such notes in the freezer compartment of my refrigerator. I met the novelist Ali Smith in London, and one of the things we agreed about is that we keep our important papers in the freezer. If the house burns down the freezer will probably remain intact. I keep things in plastic so they won't get wet in there. At the moment, there's lots and lots of 'Frank' left in note form. I put 'F.B.' on the notes I dedicate to him.[47]

---

[45]Richard Ford, *Exclusive Extract from The Lay of The Land: Special Edition for Richard Ford's UK Tour December 2004*, produced by OSCAR (South East Literature Promoters Network), courtesy of Random House Publishers.
[46]RF, interviewed by CLP, 31 January 2016.
[47]Ibid.

Asked when he last wrote 'F.B.' in the margin he replied: 'Wednesday. My dog died so I sat down and I wrote down some notes that Frank might think if *his* dog died. It was very sad. He was old. He was 15 and a half years old. Nonetheless I wrote that down. Pirated poor Scooter's demise and gave him to Frank.'[48]

Given Ford's admission that he continues to write about Frank whether it is for publication or not, it is still puzzling that he could not, would not take Frank to the specific moment or place of 9/11. There are, at least, references to 9/11 in the much later short story collection *Let Me Be Frank with You*. Frank idly imagines that the detritus remaining after Hurricane Sandy hit the New Jersey shoreline in 2012 will be scooped up by armies of trucks 'conscripted to get destruction, pain, the memory of pain and destruction, up, out and away and into some landfill in Elizabeth like the 9/11 remains'.[49] But it is no more than casual speculation, and Frank reveals his ignorance when he wonders about a doctor he knows, Dr Zippee, who travels to Pakistan each winter to work in a madrassa, by adding 'whatever that is'. Ford was still struggling with the same conundrum: how to grant post-death meaning to the lives of those who perished, even though there was no meaning, no sense at all. The *New York Times* had found a partial solution in their 'Portraits of Grief'[50] series, assembling the fragments of life that constitute a person: what they liked to cook, the jokes they loved to tell, the furniture they wanted to buy. This was a process of turning real people into mythological figures, fictive characters, people with an *after*-life. By mythologizing the dead, meaning and redemption were grasped for, where none had been before. It has become the model for what to do when the details of a terrorist attack are universally known but in which the victims are not. After the murders in Paris in November 2015, *En Memoire* was created on Twitter: 'one tweet for every victim'. The recollections are touching for being so slight, so modest: 'Loved life even though it wasn't always easy', 'Friend said she was "shy, but not invisible"' and 'Built and repaired guitars

---

[48]RF, interviewed by CLP, 27 November 2012.
[49]Richard Ford, *Let Me Be Frank with You* (London: Bloomsbury, 2014), p. 23.
[50]*New York Times*' 'Portraits of Grief' have been widely quoted and much cited in the literature about 9/11. They also feature in DeLillo's *Falling Man* and, as 'Relatives' Rumination' in Amy Waldman's novel *The Submission*.

in Paris'. Perhaps oddly, Ford equated fiction's redemptive role in this with its capacity to distract:

> Any piece of fiction, any piece of art, has a potentially redemptive dimension and function insofar as it directs the reader's attention away from whatever he's thinking about, and implicitly asks, 'Hey, Look at this, not at that. This is better'. If nothing else it redeems a moment. There's also the implication in a piece of fiction that there will be a future in which the work will be used by the reader. That's positive. And there's also the idea that fiction is always about life (no matter its type of verisimilitude), and implicitly says that life is worth closer attention that we're giving it in the novel. It needn't be that at the end of a book the birds all be tweeting and Heidi come skipping down the mountain side. It can be redemptive and still be serious and even dour.[51]

Yet, it is still the case that fiction has the ability to impart things that journalism does not or cannot, which is in part the legacy of our growing mistrust of politicians and what they say, and journalists and what they report. The severed pact between politician and reporter which led Tony Blair to choose 'feral beasts' as his new epithet for journalists when he left office has left a vacuum in which facts, truths or falsehoods all float unchallenged or disbelieved even when they are apparently verified. The Washington-based journalist and author Ron Suskind, quoting an aide to President George W. Bush, took the question of what is true and what is not a stage further. The aide, in an audacious and much-quoted piece of *braggadocio*, suggested that there is no such thing as the truth at all, simply a new 'reality'. The aide told Suskind that journalists were wrong to believe that by studying things closely an absolute meaning would emerge:

> That's not the way the world really works anymore ... We're an empire now, and when we act, we create our own reality. And while you're studying that reality – judiciously, as you will – we'll act again, creating other new realities, which you can study too,

---

[51]RF, interviewed by CLP, 31 January 2016.

and that's how things will sort out. We're history's actors... and you, all of you, will be left to just study what we do.[52]

Marc Redfield, citing the Suskind article, suggests that such a 'dream of godlike sovereignty'[53] even manages to outdo the 'phantasmic speech act' of inventing the rhetorical impossibility of a 'war on terror'. That is, of course, quite an achievement in itself.

The impossible phrase, the 'war on terror', lived on, even after the Obama administration dropped it in 2009 and insisted on using 'overseas contingency operation' instead. In November 2015, after the Paris terrorist attacks, French President François Hollande took the phrase up. Addressing both houses of parliament, he stated that 'we are at war with Jihadist terrorism'. It is of course a logic-defying rhetorical contrivance, but it is not in the same league as the reality-inventing ambitions of George W. Bush's aide. The president was a recidivist when it came to inventing versions of reality. His speech on board an aircraft carrier in which he declared the end of major fighting in Iraq received wide coverage in May 2003. It soon emerged that Bush was flown the short distance to the ship by jet, wearing flight dress. The USS Abraham Lincoln was then turned around so that Bush could be filmed with the cinematic open sea as his backdrop, rather than the more prosaic San Diego coastline. His aides had claimed initially that he was forced to fly by jet, and therefore to wear the macho clothing, rather than by helicopter and wearing civilian clothes because the aircraft carrier was too far out to sea.[54] The distance from ship to shore turned out to be a modest thirty-nine miles.

The instability of language and its inherent unreliability have led some news organizations to demand greater precision in its use. Take for example the BBC's decision to ignore the British government's exhortations in 2015 for news outlets to abandon the

[52]Ron Suskind, 'Faith, Certainty and the Presidency of George W. Bush', *New York Times Magazine*, 17 October 2004, http://www.nytimes.com/2004/10/17/magazine/17BUSH.html [accessed 21 February 2016].

[53]Marc Redfield, *The Rhetoric of Terror: Reflections on 9/11 and the War on Terror* (New York: Fordham University Press, 2009), p. 51.

[54]John King, 'Administration Defends Bush Flight to Carrier', *CNN International*, 8 May 2003, http://edition.cnn.com/2003/ALLPOLITICS/05/07/bush.lincoln/ [accessed 4 May 2008].

terms IS or Islamic State or ISIL and use the term Daesh instead. Daesh is an Arabic acronym which, when spoken, sounds similar to the word 'dahes' which means 'one who sows discord'. The BBC's Director General Tony Hall said that to use the term would risk doing damage to the corporation's impartiality since it gave the impression of offering support to the group's enemies. The BBC continued to use the term 'Islamic State', usually prefacing it with the equivocal phrase 'so-called'. The naming of sinister ideas or organizations is fraught with difficulty, of course. Al-Qaeda seemed even more threatening once it had a formal name meaning 'the base'. Rohan Gunaratna has suggested that the name emerged from an essay by Osama bin Laden's mentor Abdullah Azzam about the concept of *Al-Qaeda al-Sulbah*, the 'solid base' that would have the 'sole purpose of creating societies founded on the strictest Islamic principles'.[55] Lawrence Wright traced the formation of Al-Qaeda to a meeting that took place in October 1988, although bin Laden appeared to place no particular significance on it at the time. It was simply the name used for a training camp: '"We called that place al-Qaeda – in the sense that it was a training base – and that is where the name came from."'[56] Whatever its origins, precision in the choice of language is clearly vital to both the writer of fiction and of fact. Take, for example, another exploration of the vexed and fraught term 'terrorism' by journalist and commentator Robert Fisk, pointed up by Karim H. Karim.[57] Fisk writes that

'terrorism' no longer means terrorism. It is not a definition; it is a political contrivance. 'Terrorists' are those who use violence against the side that is using the word. The only terrorists whom Israel acknowledges are those who oppose Israel. The only terrorists the United States acknowledges are those who oppose the United States or their allies. The only terrorists Palestinians acknowledge – for they too use the word – are those opposed to the Palestinians.[58]

[55]Rohan Gunaratna, *Inside Al Qaeda: Global Network of Terror* (New York: Columbia University Press, 2002), p. 4, ProQuest ebrary. Web. 15 December 2015.
[56]Lawrence Wright, *The Looming Tower* (London: Allen Lane, 2006), p. 134.
[57]Karim H. Karim, 'Making Sense of the "Islamic Peril"', *Journalism after September 11*, p. 102.
[58]Robert Fisk, *Pity the Nation: Lebanon at War*, 3rd Edition (Oxford: Oxford University Press. 2001), p. 441.

Choice of language is self-evidently central to the writer's art. While agreeing with that, novelist Ian McEwan has made a case for the empathetic force that is built by words in combination, in other words the overarching, salving power of narrative. In his post-9/11 essay, he appeared to link the idea of empathy inextricably with story. He decried the attempted evisceration of narrative in his journalistic essay about 9/11, explaining the terrorists' willingness to murder so many because they had eschewed all forms of human empathy. Remove that sanctifying quality, reject the unifying nature of storytelling and turn instead to attenuated fantasy, and we will be left with the mindset described so vividly by W. B. Yeats in his poem 'Meditations in Time of Civil War': 'We had fed the heart on fantasies,/The heart's grown brutal from the fare.' BBC correspondent Fergal Keane, writing about 9/11, used Yeats's words to explore 'the power of mythology in the shaping of the terrorist's consciousness'. Keane's analysis overlaps with McEwan's: 'to be able to subject [the enemy] and his loved ones to a relentless campaign of terror – a war in which the normal rules, the concept of a "warrior's honour" are abandoned – it is necessary to narrow the mind, make it subject to a very limited range of ideas and influences'.[59] Using this definition of the terrorist mind as a model, it would seem ever more important for novelists to attempt to define 9/11, to write and rewrite the narrative, however flawed and desperate the attempt, and even if, to use Rowan Williams's phrase, the best we can hope for is the 'noble failure'. In contraflow to the terrorist's drive to 'narrow the mind', the opening out of traumatic experience by writing it down would seem relevant to any writer's art.

A few days after the 9/11 attacks, Ford was asked by the *New York Times* to contribute his reflections. He began by describing his father's death more than forty years before. He was graphic in his physical description of the body, but he then moved into territory that seemed unfamiliar. He reached for the idea that love could grant those who died a form of enduring afterlife:

> [A] death's importance is measured by the significance of the life that has ended. Thus to die, as so many did on Sept.11 – their

---

[59]Fergal Keane, 'The Mind of the Terrorist', in *The Day That Shook the World*, eds Jenny Baxter and Malcolm Downing (London: BBC Worldwide, 2001), p. 56.

singular existences briefly obscured – may seem to cloud and invalidate life entirely. Yet their lives, though amazingly lost, remain indelible and will not by simple death be undone.[60]

The sentiments echo those expressed by Tony Blair at the memorial service in New York although, unlike Wilder, Ford is not prepared to concede that even memory itself is not necessary. I will reflect on Ford's choice of words later in this chapter, but in his definition of the ultimate significance of the victims' lives, he is in fact expressing a view that is *anti*-axiomatic of the novelist's grasp on reality. He is granting them 'indelible' lives despite their lives' lack of 'significance' and the pointlessness of their deaths.

The craving for empathy, permanence, indelibility is clearly not unique to Richard Ford. Ian McEwan wrote two journalistic essays immediately after 9/11: the first appeared on 12 September, the second on 15 September. The first, titled 'Beyond Belief', is dislocated by his shock, horror and disgust and, once again, the movie metaphor is deployed. McEwan ends the piece, sure that from now on the world will forever 'be worse'. (His dread at the inevitability of that fact would be grimly vindicated in the email he wrote on the day after the Paris terrorist assaults of 13 November 2015. McEwan was by now living in Paris and witnessed at first hand the 'worse' that he had so bleakly envisaged.) In his second response to 9/11, McEwan appeared to seek the indelibility that Ford craved: the idea that lives would not 'by simple death be undone'. Emerging from his first shocked response, he wrote of empathy – that quality which allows us to 'think oneself into the mind of others'. He listed amongst the hijackers' crimes their use of 'dehumanising hatred to purge themselves of the human instinct for empathy', thereby suffering from 'a failure of the imagination'. Their victims asserted their humanity, compassion and defiance in the phone messages they left, 'snatched and anguished assertions of love'. It is a variant of Wilder's and Meyer's 'bridge of love' and Ford's 'indelible lives' of course. But by the time McEwan came to write journalistically about the murder of 130 people in Paris

---

[60]Richard Ford, 'The Attack Took More than the Victims' Lives. It Took Their Deaths', *New York Times*, 23 September 2001, http://www.nytimes.com/2001/09/23/magazine/23WWLN.html [accessed 30 March 2013].

in November 2015, a new steeliness had entered his prose. Here was the 'worse' that had always been coming since 9/11, the 'bridge of love' replaced by a new fatalistic realism. Rather than defiant invocations of love, his Paris email ends with a resigned assertion of collectivist solidarity: 'The death-cult's bullets and bombs will come again, here or somewhere else, we can be sure. [...] In January we were all *Charlie Hebdo*. Now, we are all Parisians and that at least, in a dark time, is a matter of pride.'[61] The rhetorical effect is similar in both pieces of prose: each concludes with a call for unity, but his cry from Paris has a resigned pessimism at its heart.

Michel Houellebecq confessed that his 2015 novel *Soumission* (Submission) would have been far bleaker and more violent if it had been published after the *Charlie Hebdo* murders, rather than on the day itself; similarly, it seems likely that McEwan's novel *Saturday* would have been less sentimental in its *dénouement* if he had written it after the Paris massacre. McEwan's journalism from September 2001 is clearly imbricated into *Saturday*. There are the passages in the novel that read more like a newspaper editorial than fiction: 'After the ruinous experiments of the lately deceased century, after so much vile behaviour, so many deaths, a queasy agnosticism has settled around these matters of justice and redistributed wealth.'[62] There are also references in his essay to thinking 'oneself into the minds of others. These are the mechanics of compassion: you are under the bedclothes, unable to sleep, and you are crouching in the brushed-steel lavatory at the rear of the plane, whispering a final message to your loved one. There is only that one thing to say, and you say it. All else is pointless.'[63] In the novel, that episode becomes more taut, more spare, but it is the same sentiment: 'he often wonders how it might go – the screaming in the cabin partly muffled by that deadening acoustic, the fumbling in bags for phones and last words'.[64] In both the essay and the novel, McEwan echoes the sentiments of those who survived the attacks. The BBC's then North America Business Correspondent Stephen Evans, who was

---

[61]Ian McEwan, 'A Message from Paris', Edge.org, 14 November 2015 [accessed 23 May 2016].

[62] McEwan, *Saturday* (London: Jonathan Cape, 2005), p. 74.

[63]Ian McEwan, 'Only Love and Then Oblivion. Love Was All They Had to Set against Their Murderers', *Guardian*, 15 September 2001.

[64]McEwan, *Saturday*, pp. 15–16.

in the North Tower when the first plane hit, expressed exactly that sense: 'I've thought a lot since then about the terror felt by those on board the two Boeing 767s, seized after leaving Boston.'[65] In an insightful essay he described, too, the effects on him of shock in the months afterwards: 'a frisson of fear when a bus clanks over a steel sheet, or when a group of people suddenly start rushing in the street, or when thick smoke appears. For a while I couldn't go near big windows inside high-rise buildings – I kept imagining the nose of an airliner suddenly shattering the plate-glass.'[66] Years later, he told me that he still cannot tolerate big windows or being high up: 'I don't go up high buildings. I really don't like heights. If someone said, "let's go up the Empire State Building," I would say "why?" I wouldn't do it. I would certainly never work in one. Perched up there like a sitting duck, a target.'[67]

Stephen Evans was one of the thousands of journalists who reported the news that day, although he was one of very few to both experience and transact it simultaneously. McEwan was full of admiration for those who covered the crisis, going so far as to say that 'the best things written about it have been journalism, not fiction'. It is clear that McEwan allowed, encouraged even, his journalism to encroach on his fiction, but we should not be surprised, given his admiration for the form and for its capacity to bring order to the present moment, that it was journalism not fiction that he wanted to write first. His instinct seemed less that he wished to avoid writing a novel, more that he actively wished to write prose non-fiction first:

> [J]ournalists rose to the bar that day, and when I wrote I just wanted to write in that public way, expressing my immediate reaction, the same honorable tide that everyone else was on. Not to write fiction. But even as I was doing that I was thinking the human way into it this [sic] would take more than journalism, would be more intimate than that. The thought of so many of these people announcing their love down mobile phones.[68]

---

[65]Stephen Evans, 'Ground Zero', in The Day that Shook the World, eds Jenny Baxter and Malcolm Downing (London: BBC Worldwide, 2001), p. 23.
[66]Ibid., p. 33.
[67]Stephen Evans, interviewed by Charlie Lee-Potter, 13 February 2016.
[68]Zadie Smith talks with McEwan, The Believer, August 2005.

But later, when he came to write *Saturday*, he appeared to train his gaze on exactly the phobia that Stephen Evans admitted to suffering from after the attacks: the violation and invasion that comes from fear of 'the nose of an airliner suddenly shattering the plate-glass'. I do not know if McEwan read Evans's account of that day, but he has since said that in writing *Saturday* he needed to find a private scale for the sense of invasion that Evans described. McEwan found his microcosmic equivalent in Baxter, who breaks into Perowne's house and orders Daisy to strip naked in front of her family. When explaining how he wrote it, McEwan identified the image of the aircraft's nose 'shattering the plate glass', as Evans had done:

> I leave blanks in my planning, and there are bits it's best not to think about till you get there. I didn't know whether he had a knife nor did I know what he wanted. [...] I knew that he would end up being thrown down the stairs, and that the operation would happen but [...] to go back to [...] 9/11, and the sense of invasion, one can only do it on a private scale. If you say the airliner hit the side of the building, a thousand people died, nothing happens to your scalp. So I, in a sense, tried to find the private scale of that feeling.[69]

Perhaps strangely, there is an optimism that lingers in *Saturday*, a sense that by harnessing 9/11 as a narrative rather than as an event, he can bring order to it. The closing passage in which brain surgeon Henry Perowne reconstructs the crushed head of his sinister attacker Baxter takes on the air of a paean to the power of writing. As the *Goldberg Variations* play in the operating theatre, Perowne/McEwan essentially rewrites his narrative and it is as much the writer's art that McEwan is celebrating as it is the surgeon's:

> For the past two hours he's been in a dream of absorption that has dissolved all sense of time, and all awareness of the other parts of his life. Even his awareness of his own existence has vanished. He's been delivered into a pure present, free of the weight of the past or any anxieties about the future. In retrospect, though never at the time, it feels like profound happiness.[70]

---

[69]Ibid.
[70]McEwan, *Saturday*, p. 258.

While it seems to be a manifesto for the empathetic force of the writer, once again McEwan directed his praise at the journalist rather than the novelist: '9/11 was a heroic moment for journalism. [...]It happened two o'clock our time, London time. So front pages had to be clear and basically twenty-five pages set out, produced, and this much-hated profession had its sudden noble moment.'[71] It is a view that BBC reporter Stephen Evans would probably share, given his own acerbic distinction between the writing of journalists who were there that day, and the prose of those who wrote about 9/11 later:

There were a lot of reporters afterwards who were looking for that metaphor. But you don't need metaphor. There you were – and crunch! That's it. On the spot, you just described what you saw and what it sounded like. For people who were there it was easy. But three or four days later the 'writers' started arriving, to think big thoughts, to bring atmosphere. But there wasn't much more to say. Their stuff should have been the 'why', the 'what next?' But in terms of being there on the ground, it was reporting, plain reporting – the conveying of information in plain language. Just describe. I remember my language being very direct – there was no need for purple prose. The only metaphor I remember using was to say that the impact of the first plane as heard by me from the other tower was like a giant skip full of concrete falling from a great height – that's because it was and the phrase needed no composition. It's just the way it seemed.[72]

As one of the writers who arrived to 'think big thoughts', McEwan avoided the conventional metaphor that so dismayed Stephen Evans. Nevertheless, his methods were overtly literary. *Saturday* is an organizing text, bringing order to chaos by sheer force of intellectual will. In the opening chapter, Perowne reads the biography of Charles Darwin given to him by his poet daughter Daisy. (It is Daisy who recites Matthew Arnold's 'Dover Beach' to Baxter at the end of the novel, using poetry to alter the narrative's violent course.) Perowne articulates literature's power as the novel

---

[71]McEwan, *The Believer*, August 2005.
[72]Stephen Evans, interviewed by Charlie Lee-Potter, 13 February 2016.

opens, but at this point he is still ambivalent about it and is yet to appreciate its true redeeming capacity to subsume everything:

> At times this biography made him comfortably nostalgic for a verdant, horse-drawn, affectionate England; at others he was faintly depressed by the way a whole life could be contained by a few hundred pages – bottled, like homemade chutney. And by how easily an existence, its ambitions, networks of family and friends, all its cherished stuff, solidly possessed, could so entirely vanish.[73]

By the end of the novel, Perowne has been shown that literature can forge the kind of empathy that McEwan has said terrorists so demonstrably lack. Poetry forms a bridge between Daisy and Baxter, Baxter and Perowne, Daisy and her grandfather John Grammaticus, and McEwan and the reader. But Daisy's ability to distract Baxter with verse is the note that jars in the novel, although McEwan does at least prove his case that we would *like* it to be true. In thinking about the resolution and remedy provided by the salving power of verse, the phrase Zadie Smith used to disparage Joseph O'Neill's *Netherland* comes to mind: 'the bedtime story that comforts us most'. There is a sense of comfort at the end of *Saturday*, if we allow ourselves to believe it, and while McEwan's novel deploys different tactics to those used by Richard Ford, both share that redemptive drive to bring pattern to shapelessness. Unlike Frank, whom Ford has finessed for more than thirty years thereby giving him 'significance', the victims of 9/11 were largely unknown and unknowable in the immediate aftermath of the attack. Ford's attempt to make them 'indelible' merely by saying that they were is not convincing in the end. As I have demonstrated, Tony Blair's and Richard Ford's attempts focused in part on the notion of transcendence. This is why Blair turned to the unifying force of fiction for his address and why Ford argued perversely that the dead 'live still, and importantly in all but the most literal ways'. Yet Ford's reinvigoration of the victims, his salving drive to give them back their lives 'in all but the most literal ways', is inevitably destined for failure and the eternal life he attempts to grant them is no more real, no more solid than the 'life' he granted Frank Bascombe.

---

[73]McEwan, *Saturday*, p. 6.

By the time Ford came to complete the text of *The Lay of the Land*, his ideas on indelibility had moved on, shaped in part by the unleashing of another catastrophic attack on America's shores. As I have suggested, Ford's three-novel epitaph to the prosperous, comfortable, middle-class life of suburban America is incrementally more violent, more threatening and more bleak. The attacks of 9/11 clearly influenced Ford's ways of writing and thinking. But there was another devastating attack upon America's security and confidence that I believe consolidated his sense of dread, and that is equally important in terms of its effect upon his work. It was this attack, on New Orleans, which finally shaped his views on death and the meaning that a novelist can bring to it.

Part three: Hurricane Katrina's legacy

On 29 August 2005, as Richard Ford was finalizing the manuscript of *The Lay of the Land*, a natural catastrophe hit the American city of New Orleans. It was a disaster that led Ford to discard any attempt to grant eternal life to those who died in 9/11. Hurricane Katrina killed almost 2,000 people and flooded 80 per cent of New Orleans. It was an assault on an American city that resonated, Ford implied, with the attack on New York in 2001. This was a city of huge importance to Ford: he had lived in New Orleans both as a child and as an adult; he owned a house there and he wrote part of *The Lay of the Land* there.[74] His wife, Kristina, to whom all his novels are dedicated, was, for eight years, the New Orleans director of city planning.

Ford, by his own admission, struggled to find a vocabulary to express the loss of his city. This was not the noble attempt by one of America's leading novelists to give voice to a national craving for explanation: it was deeply personal. And even he, the master of the hyper-hyphenated, extravagantly redolent and meaning-crammed noun, found it impossible to express his sense of bereavement. In attempting to do so, he bound 9/11 and Hurricane Katrina together:

---

[74]McGrath, *New York Times*, 25 October 2006, http://www.nytimes.com/2006/10/25/books/25ford.html?fta=y [accessed 4 May 2008].

An attempt to advance a vocabulary for empathy and for reckoning is frustrated in a moment of sorest need by the plain terms of the tragedy that wants explaining...In America, even with our incommensurable memories of 9/11, we still do not have an exact human vocabulary for the loss of a city – our great, iconic city, so graceful, livable, insular, self-delighted, eccentric...Other peoples have experienced their cities' losses. Some bombed away (by us) .... Our inept attempts at words only run to lists, costs, to assessing blame. It's like Hiroshima a public official said. But, no. It's not like anything. It's what it is. That's the hard part. He, with all of us, lacked the words. [75]

Ford found that this time he could not grant any form of life to the victims, fictional, mythic or otherwise. Such a failure was not what had been expected of him, and I asked him how his lack of words had been greeted. It is striking that, like McEwan, it is the word 'empathy' that he reached for:

I wrote something in that essay about the aftermath of Katrina being beyond the reach of empathy. Some people complained to me about that – not that it made any sense to me. What I was trying to get across was that sometimes terrible things happen and we're taken beyond the scope of our moral vocabulary. I wasn't conceding defeat to these forces, just trying to ascribe their consequences. To write most anything good you often have to channel a certain amount of aggressiveness: you have to say to the reader, 'No, wait. Stop doing and thinking what you're doing and thinking, and do and think what I want you to'. I happen to think readers get pleasure from surrendering; but you also have to have something good and important for them to surrender to.[76]

Ford added that one of the difficulties he would always face when attempting to write about recent catastrophe is that he cannot control the material. As he told me, 'one of the things that I

---

[75]Richard Ford, 'Elegy for My City', *Observer*, 4 September 2005, http://www. guardian.co.uk/books/2005/sep/04/hurricanekatrina.features [accessed 25 March 2013].
[76]RF, interviewed by CLP, 31 January 2016.

feel I need to do when I write a novel is dominate the material, commandeer it and subordinate it to my private purposes. I didn't think I could do that to the events of 9/11 – because it's so fresh and factual.'[77] It was potentially a difficulty when it came to writing about Hurricane Katrina too. But it is my view that when Ford revised the manuscript for *The Lay of the Land*, prior to its publication in 2006, he drew on his shock about Hurricane Katrina to write about his horror of 9/11. How much more powerful it was than his journalistic attempt in 2001 to grant eternal life to those who had no such thing. A comparison between the early draft and final text of *The Lay of the Land* makes that clear. In December 2004, Ford was sent on a pre-publication UK tour by his publisher Random House. To give him something to read at the literary events they had organized, his publicists printed a small pamphlet containing an extract from an early draft of *The Lay of the Land*.[78] The extract that Ford's publicists selected for him to read came from what was to become Chapter 9 of the published novel, but is simply called *The Shore* in the pamphlet. A few pages before this section begins in the final novel, Ford sets his context, describing the 'whole deluging, undifferentiated crash-in of modern existence American-style, whose sudsy, brown tree-trunk-littered surface most of us somehow manage to keep our heads above so we can see our duty and do it'.[79] Anyone who has seen television pictures of the days after New Orleans was swallowed by water can testify to the precision of this description, although many people trying to keep their heads above the 'tree-trunk-littered surface' had succumbed to the brown, stinking water and drowned.

The 'crash-in' of modern existence American-style is the essence of *The Lay of the Land*, gloomily compressed from the wide-angle vision of *The Sportswriter* and *Independence Day*. And 'the sudsy, brown tree-trunk-littered surface' sets the scene for the extract from the pamphlet that Richard Ford read aloud on his UK tour. The scene focuses on Mr Clare Suddruth, a 65-year-old Viet vet with 'Clint Eastwood features'. Suddruth is trying to buy

---

[77]RF, interviewed by CLP.
[78]*Special edition for Richard Ford's UK Tour December 2004*, OSCAR (South East Literature Promoters Network), courtesy of Random House Publishers.
[79]Ford, *The Lay of the Land*, p. 224.

a beach house in a town called Sea-Brite, its perky, hyphenated name gleaming with the promise of white incisors and orthodontic hygiene. As Ford admitted, 'The copy editors gave me a hard time about the hyphen…They argued that very few place names in America are hyphenated. But I said that this was a town invented by land developers, and they would definitely want the hyphen'.[80] By the time of the official publication of *The Lay of the Land*, Sea-Brite's promise has contracted and it is now called Sea-Clift. The jaunty property-developer's hyphen is still there – but Brite has become Clift, bringing with it a sense of confrontation with the ocean, rather than an invigorating, cleansing pact with clear, lapping waves. Clift suggests the cracking, the cleaving of rock, of splitting, as well as a sense of division. The biblical connection with the word 'cleft' brings a sense of aggression and retribution. The topographical reference to a cliff with its high, flat rocky face set against the incoming ocean sets up an altogether more threatening and confrontational tone.

The substance of this section of both the novel and of the earlier pamphlet deals with Suddruth's suspicion that the beach chalet Frank is attempting to sell him has cracked concrete foundations and will ultimately succumb to the force of the wind and the salty waves. In both publications, Suddruth explains the dangers inherent in a house perched so unwisely on the sea front: '… because it's on the ocean, salt and moisture go to work on it. And suddenly – though it isn't sudden of course – Hurricane Frank blows up, a high tide comes in, the force of the water turns savage and Bob's your uncle.' The words are identical, save for an extra '*boom*' inserted for theatrical effect in the pamphlet but removed from the more sober final novel. The sense is clear that a 'high tide' could be devastating.

Looking to the pamphlet again, we see that the 'steely-blue, flat-surfaced Atlantic is beyond the wide low-tide beach…In the middle distance, a boatful of day fishermen is anchored, their short poles abristle off both sides.' But turn to the published novel and we find this: 'Lavender flat-surfaced ocean stretches beyond the wide high-tide beach. Breeze seems to stream straight though my ears and gives me a shiver.' The threatening *high* tide has arrived and the

---

[80]McGrath, *New York Times*, 25 October 2006, http://www.nytimes.com/2006/10/25/books/25ford.html?pagewanted=all&_r=0 [accessed 28 January 2013].

jaunty photogenic fishermen on their day trip have been excised from the scene. Both versions are heavy with suggestions of cracked foundations, of threat, of terrorism. Suddruth speculates about what might happen to the country which would 'make just normal not possible again'. Both publications were written after the 9/11 attacks and both sections contain the same references to the anxiety that New Jersey could be a 'target for some nut with a bomb', but it is only the final version, re-written after Hurricane Katrina struck, which contains the sense that *environmental* terror is not just on its way, it is virtually upon him. Ford's short story collection, published ten years after *The Lay of the Land*, returns to that same scene again and disaster has, at last, come. Suddruth turns out to have been right, but it is not fictional Hurricane Frank that has destroyed the New Jersey shoreline but the real Hurricane Sandy, which caused catastrophic damage in 2012. Just as he feared, Suddruth's house has been wiped out, its contents 'sucked up and blown away to some farmer's field in Lakehurst, to be found, possibly returned, or else put in a museum to commemorate the awesomeness of mother nature when she gets it in her head to fuck with you'.[81] Yet again, Frank is pictured in the same place on the beach, staring out to sea and this time a fisherman is back again and Frank is being watched from a ship:

> Out at sea, between the land and the fog bank, an unmeasurable distance from where I'm sitting behind the wheel, a great white cruise ship – a wallowing twelve-decker – sits motionless against the gray. [...] I have a feeling passengers are at the rails, scoping out what used to be New Jersey, taking snaps with phones [...] I'm not so certain they're empathetic to our lives ashore.[82]

Reciprocal suspicion, surveillance's cool gaze and a mood of hopelessness are what prevail this time. And, once again, it is empathy that is lacking, the quality that so preoccupies writers of post-9/11 fiction. There is also a sense of the vacuity of the distant observer, captivated by others' suffering while failing to act. It was something that President George W. Bush was accused of during the

---

[81]Ford, *Let Me Be Frank with You*, p. 33.
[82]Ibid., pp. 33–34.

acknowledged low-point of his two-term presidency when he failed to respond adequately to the crisis caused by Hurricane Katrina. The *New York Times* editorial from 1 September 2005 berated him for making one of the 'worst speeches of his life', complaining that during his Rose Garden address he had read out a 'long laundry list of supplies, grinned and promised that everything would work out in the end'.[83] The scene that has become emblematic of George W. Bush's presidency was of him, safely seated in Air Force One, flying briefly over the flooded roads and streets of the drowning city. The people trying to keep their heads above the 'sudsy, brown' water and holding up their arms in pleading distress would have looked tiny to him as he looked out of his window. Literally *over*looked. He could not know what they were enduring because he did not descend to ground level to speak to them. The White House staffer Scott McClellan famously quoted the president's breathtakingly inadequate response: 'It's devastating. It's got to be doubly devastating on the ground.'[84]

There is a long tradition of the spectator as contented survivor, not just relishing the fact that he has escaped suffering, but actively enjoying the suffering of others. The tradition was perhaps in Richard Ford's mind as he described the shipload of tourists photographing the devastated shoreline of New Jersey. Hans Blumenberg, in *Shipwreck with Spectator*, makes reference to the work of Montaigne, who argued that the spectator of a shipwreck is justified in the pleasure that he feels (described as *volupté maligne*, or malicious and sensual pleasure) by his 'successful self-preservation. By virtue of his capacity for this distance, he stands unimperiled on the solid ground of the shore. He survives through one of his useless qualities: the ability to be a spectator.'[85] President Bush had a great deal more than the 'ability' to be a spectator: he had specific instructions to be one. His staff valued his life above

[83]'Waiting for a Leader', *New York Times*, 1 September 2005, http://www.nytimes.com/2005/09/01/opinion/01thu1.html [accessed 30 March 2013].

[84]'Press Gaggle with Scott McClellan Aboard Air Force One En Route Andrews Air Force Base, MD', *The White House Archives*, 31 August 2005, http://georgewbush-whitehouse.archives.gov/news/releases/2005/08/20050831-2.html [accessed 30 March 2013].

[85]Hans Blumenberg, *Shipwreck with Spectator* (Cambridge: Massachusetts Institute of Technology, 1997), p. 17.

any other, both at the time of the 9/11 attacks, when he was ordered to fly away, and at the time of Hurricane Katrina. Blumenberg cites the fifteenth book of *Dichtung und Wahrheit*, in which Goethe uses the metaphor of the sea silkily erasing evidence of a ship's course to illustrate the way in which 'eminent minds' are able to erase any trace of previous errors made. There was a phalanx of White House staff whose job it was to erase the 'error' that President Bush made in his response to Hurricane Katrina, to the extent that they argued that a mistake had not been made at all: 'I reject outright any suggestion that President Bush was anything less than fully involved', said his homeland security adviser Frances Fragos Townsend.[86]

Arianna Huffington, the influential Washington political powerbroker and journalist, dubbed Bush's tenure in office the 'Flyover Presidency'.[87] The tactic of the 'flyover', or possibly even the 'fly *away*', is the same stratagem President Bush adopted on 11 September 2001. Bush's advisors forced him to evacuate by plane, arguing that issues of national security demanded he be kept away from Washington and New York. When he returned briefly to Washington, his words were banal at best. In a piece of cosy hometown rhetoric inadequate for the enormity of the event, he promised that he would find those 'folks' who had done this thing. I would suggest that the vision of the president first flying away and later flying above the fray is the context that Ford had in mind when he talked retrospectively about the vision he had when he was writing all three books in his trilogy:

> I guess it's my view that if you're flying over a suburb in a helicopter and see some guy down there schlumming along, he's probably a Pakistani or Chinese or an African-American. I think suburbanites are not knowable. They are only knowable as literature or art knows them, which is to say up close.[88]

---

[86]Frances Fragos Townsend quoted by Spencer S. Hsu, *Washington Post*, 14 February 2006, http://www.washingtonpost.com/wp-dyn/content/article/2006/02/13/AR2006021300679.html [accessed 4 May 2008].

[87]Arianna Huffington, 'The Flyover Presidency of George W. Bush', *Huffington Post*, 31 August 2005, http://www.huffingtonpost.com/arianna-huffington/the-flyover-presidency-of_b_6566.html [accessed 28 May 2013].

[88]RF, interviewed by Phil Hogan, *Observer*, 24 September 2006.

My sense that Ford had the president's inadequate thirty-five-minute New Orleans fly-over in mind when he said that literature can say more than the facts because it is 'up close' is underlined by Ford's words in the immediate aftermath of the hurricane:

> From the ruins, it's not easy to know what's best to think. Even the President may have felt this way in his low pass over that wide sheet of onyx water, the bobbing rooftops peeking above the surfaces, the vast collapse, the wind-riddled buildings, that little figure (could he see who she was?) standing in the water, and on those rooftops – many black, many poor. Homeless.[89]

That eyeline then, that perspective of the man above looking down on the unknowable and refusing to descend to find out for himself, is one we know for certain that Ford considered. That is why the closing page of the final novel in the trilogy is so redolent with meaning. Frank is on an aircraft, bound for the Mayo Clinic, to find out if his cancer has returned. He looks out of the window, as George W. Bush would have done, and he sees the snow-covered landscape below sliced into miniature squares and segments of land. He considers his dead son, his own near death and he recalls his return from hospital after the shooting. When he got home, he stood in the ocean, exactly as his alter ego had done at the end of *The Sportswriter*. The first time around he had the sensation of sloughing off a layer of skin and of experiencing a sense of 'nowness' and his own quiddity. But at the conclusion of *The Lay of the Land*, which Richard Ford mistakenly believed would be his last 'big book', Frank feels something more than the 'nowness' of his earlier life. This is how he puts it: '*Here* is necessity. *Here* is the extra beat – to live, to live, to live it out.' The vital point is that Frank's life does not have any transcendent meaning at all. He is no longer thinking of his quiddity or the qualities that he shares with others, but his haecceity, his own unique, isolated 'thisness'.

Frank, the transactor, is not 'everyman'[90] as interviewers so frequently like to describe him. He is *no*-man. No longer is Ford urging us to believe that Frank or even we ourselves will continue to have life

---

[89]Ford, *Observer*, 4 September 2005, http://www.guardian.co.uk/books/2005/sep/04/hurricanekatrina.features [accessed 25 March 2013].

[90]RF, interviewed by Ramona Koval, 4 June 2007.

'in all but the most literal ways'. No longer does he sign up to Thornton Wilder's, Tony Blair's or journalism's disingenuous call for meaning where there can be none. To 'live it out', Frank must adopt the eyeline shunned by President Bush as he circled above New Orleans overlooking his people. Frank's plane starts to descend. 'We are going down fast now. Sally clutches my fingers hard, smiles and encouragement. [...] A bump, a roar, a heavy thrust forward into life again, and we resume our human scale upon the land.'[91] This, then, is the redemptive power of the novel. It is to inhabit life on 'a human scale', not to view it from a safe distance as a president or a journalist might. When I asked Ford if my assessment of the effect of Hurricane Katrina on his final text was justified his response was characteristically blunt:

> Now that you've said it, maybe I will think about it a little bit. But I would also have to go and read those passages again and there's almost nothing that could make me do that. But we're not talking about my intention here. We're talking about your intelligence in trying to connect things that seem important. I don't have to take credit for it. [...] This is interesting to me. It isn't what I was thinking. It's just what I wrote.[92]

Ford's lack of consciousness about how or why he writes extends, a little comically, to *what* he wrote too. On the subject of the two Wallys in Books 1 and 3 of the trilogy, each of whom commits suicide, his response was unexpected: 'Who Is Wally in Book 3?' When I reminded him that Wally is Sally's dead husband who appears to die, reappears and then dies again, he still did not remember:

> I didn't realize I'd done that. An editor, I suppose, should've caught that. But I'm just a regular plug-along kind of writer and human being. So that kind of thing occasionally happens, although I try to avoid it. I'd have changed it if someone had pointed it out. One has an affinity for certain names. Carver's stories often re-use names. But, truthfully... this doesn't really worry me. Novels are made by humans, right. Humans aren't often perfect.[93]

---

[91] Ford, *The Lay of the Land*, p. 485.
[92] RF, interviewed by CLP, 31 January 2016.
[93] Ibid.

On one level, Ford's absent-mindedness about what he has written is amusing, but on another, it reinforces the instinctual nature of the way he writes. He is not aware that his work has become more solidly real, less dream-like, more contracted than it used to be, although I would argue that it has. However, there is a more serious point here than the simple forgetfulness of a writer who has written hundreds of thousands of words over several decades. Not only has Frank come to accept that to 'live it out' will do, so too has Ford. His novels are subtly imbued with the traumas that have faced and foiled the United States for the past three decades, but the trilogy is defined, ultimately, by the specific crises of 9/11 and Hurricane Katrina. The fact that he does not always realize how that has come about is immaterial. Ford asserted that once 9/11 'gets outside the purchase of other writers, of journalism', perhaps he will be able to write more specifically about it. In the following chapter, I assess the work of novelists Don DeLillo and Jonathan Safran Foer who, despite finding it exceptionally demanding to write about 9/11, forced themselves to do so relatively swiftly after the event.

2

Narratives of Retrogenesis and Abstraction

Introduction

Virginia Woolf's warning about current events towering over the writer 'too tremendously to be worked into fiction without a painful jolt in perspective' seemed prescient for the post-9/11 novelist.[1] Richard Ford's view that 9/11 was still in the territory of journalists was shared by many, and reviews of novels that emerged relatively swiftly raised questions about the feasibility of attempting to fictionalize the day so soon after the event. Novelist Jay McInerney confessed that fiction disgusted him. Not only did he not want to write it, he did not want to read it either:

> For a while the idea of 'invented characters' and alternate realities seemed trivial and frivolous and suddenly, horribly outdated. For a while. I abandoned the novel I was working on and didn't even think about writing fiction for the next six months. In fact, I was so traumatized and my attention span was shot to such an extent that for months I was incapable of reading a novel, or anything much longer than a standard article in the New York Times.[2]

McInerney signed up as a volunteer, working the night shift and feeding rescue workers at Ground Zero. And still he could not bear

---

[1] Virginia Woolf, 'Before Midnight', in *The Essays of Virginia Woolf Volume II: 1912–1918*, ed. Andrew McNeillie (London: Hogarth, 1987), p. 87.
[2] Jay McInerney, 'The Uses of Invention', *Guardian*, 17 September 2005, http://www.theguardian.com/books/2005/sep/17/fiction.vsnaipaul [accessed 22 January 2016].

to read anything longer than a newspaper feature. He considered retraining as a chef, because at least that seemed useful. But, over time, he realized that the novel was enticing him back, because it was only there that he could work out 'how we feel now and how we live now, to reveal emotional truths that approach the condition of music'.[3] The connection he made between a literary and a musical response seemed to hint at a desire, a duty almost, to write a mournful threnody. It also made clear that in order for his writing to approach 'the condition of music', he would have to create more than journalism.

A sense of obligation rested with Jonathan Safran Foer too, who felt he had no choice but to write: 'If you're in my position – a New Yorker who felt the event very deeply and a writer who wants to write about things he feels deeply about – I think it's risky to avoid what's right in front of you.'[4] Don DeLillo wrestled with the question of whether it was too soon and what could even be said. In a journalistic essay published two months after the attacks, he stated what lesser writers had failed to appreciate, that the catastrophe had 'no purchase on the mercies of analogy or simile'. As Andrew O'Hagan so memorably put it, novelists who acted as journalists at the time 'failed to see how their metaphors fell dead from their mouths before the astonishing live pictures'.[5] Nevertheless, DeLillo felt he had to keep trying to write it down, because the 'writer wants to understand what this day has done to us' and also because 'language is inseparable from the world that provokes it'.[6] His journalistic essay was his way of working out what the day had done. Perhaps surprisingly, his later novel *Falling Man* went back in time, returning to the small specifics of the event itself. As this chapter suggests, DeLillo's regressive step from large scale

---

[3]Ibid.
[4]Joshua Wolf Shenk, 'Living to Tell the Tale', *Mother Jones*, May/June 2005, http://www.motherjones.com/media/2005/05/jonathan-safran-foer [accessed 9 November 2015].
[5]Andrew O'Hagan, 'Racing against Reality', *New York Review of Books*, 28 June 2007, http://www.nybooks.com/articles/2007/06/28/racing-against-reality/ [accessed 26 January 2016].
[6]Don DeLillo, 'In the Ruins of the Future', *Guardian*, 22 December 2001, http://www.theguardian.com/books/2001/dec/22/fiction.dondelillo [accessed 22 January 2016].

theorizing to small-scale particulars set the metaphorical tone for a branch of fiction that could only make sense by reversing time itself.

On 11 September 2001, vast events were not 'shaping' as Virginia Woolf understood the term; they had *shaped*. Like molten metal plunged into cold water, the outrageous event set hard the moment it simultaneously happened and was witnessed. The luxury of time denoted by Woolf's languorous present participle was instantly petrified into the steeliness of the preterite tense. Given the event's simultaneity with its global distribution, it is legitimate to suggest that a different timescale now applies when it comes to the fictionalization of the news. There is no necessity or even responsibility for writers of fiction to delay their response, although there may still be reticence about immediacy. The Poundian idea of the *phanopoeia*, the verbal device by which the image is relayed to the visual imagination, takes on a new complexity; the reader needs no mediation from the writer in terms of the image because the image is not just familiar but is deeply ingrained in the psyche. The synaesthetic response of the reader to 9/11's images, sounds and even, in some cases, smells would seem to necessitate an approach from the writer that is vested more in narrative and alternative means of expression than it is in plain physical representation. Perplexity is added to 9/11 as a 'shaped' event by what we might call its aftershocks. Don DeLillo, in a new 2005 introduction to his 1988 novel *Libra* seemed to acknowledge that effect, saying that some stories 'never come to an end. Even in our time, in the sightlines of living history, in the retrieved instancy of film and videotape, there are stories waiting to be finished, open to the thrust of reasoned analysis and haunting speculation.'[7]

The writer Kenneth Goldsmith, conscious of 9/11's status as shaped but never-ending, exploited the 'retrieved instancy of film and videotape' quite literally in his work *Seven American Deaths and Disasters*. Goldsmith devised the art of 'uncreative writing' in which he appropriates the words of others. One of his experiments involved singing the text of Jean Baudrillard's *Simulacra and Simulation* in warbling, burlesque style. Like the eighteenth-century autodidact

---

[7]Don DeLillo, 'Assassination Aura', in *Introduction to Libra* [1988] (London: Penguin, 2005), p. v.

poet James Hogg, who taught himself to read from newspapers by 'beginning at the date and reading straight on, through advertisements of houses and lands, balm of Gilead, and everything', Goldsmith transcribed the entire text of the *New York Times* published in the early hours of 11 September 2001 – a newspaper that was both of the day, yet before that day. The effect was startling: 'The front page, replete with stories of airplanes crashing, kidnappings, and accounts of terrorist attacks, seemed to foretell that day's events.'[8] In *Seven American Deaths and Disasters*, Goldsmith clashed together transcribed live 9/11 broadcasts from CNN, WABC, WOR, WFAN and WNYC. Bizarrely, he had witnessed the aftermath of the attacks while standing on the corner of Sixth Avenue and Bleeker Street. He described hearing a parked car's radio blaring out news reports of what he was himself witnessing. Later, having transcribed the radio and television clips, he gave a performance of his mashed-up, appropriated scripts, putting the spoken voice back where it had once been. It was a reversed performance of sound artist William Basinski's *The Disintegration Loops* discussed in my introduction. Where Basinski took sound away to render 9/11 in eventual silence, Goldsmith put it back on. Transcribed news broadcasts, crushed end to end in a continuous narrative and then re-voiced for a public performance, bring the quality of a powerful, snarling howl-round, the sound phenomenon that every radio reporter tries to avoid.[9] Goldsmith has his detractors, but the effect of snatching fragments of broadcast news from a variety of sources in all their panic, uncertainty and terror, and effectively fictionalizing them, is powerful. Goldsmith did not make a bridge between 9/11 journalism and fiction, as Auster, DeLillo, Amis, McEwan, McInerney, Hamid, Lethem and Ford did. He made a news/story, trapped forever in the present tense and destined to repeat itself endlessly. The narrative is both real and unreal at the same time, not so much hyperreal as an uncanny *doppelgänger* of itself. In his news/story, reporters and presenters stutter and gasp: 'facts blurred with speculation as the broadcasters attempted to furiously weave convincing narratives from shards of half-truths'. The narrative is littered with ums, ers,

---

[8]Kenneth Goldsmith, 'Afterword', in *Seven American Deaths and Disasters* (New York: powerHouse Books, 2013), p. 171.
[9]Howlround occurs when sound from a loudspeaker is fed back into a nearby recording microphone, producing an echoing howl.

gaps, confusion, repeats, and 'then there was silence – the greatest
fear of broadcasters – lots of dead air. It was as if the essence of
media was being revealed whilst its skin was in tatters.'[10]

> It's just a, uh, eh, it's … it's … it's … this is a day that will live in
> infamy.
>   Yeah, you're … you're … right. That's, um, not overstating
> it … The morning of this day … the 11th of September, 2001 … will
> live in infamy. There's almost no textbook for any of us here on
> the radio to figure just what to say. There are no words at all to
> express this.[11]

There it is again: the haunting echo that there 'are no words', so
familiar from Rowan Williams's and Richard Ford's testimony, and
discussed in the introduction. Yet, as Aimee Pozorski has pointed
out, instead of treating this inability to find language as a defeated
end-stop, Goldsmith pushes the narrative forward to a park in
Chinatown later that same day. People are talking about what has
happened, while continuing to play card games, the fact that 'they
are talking about it, indicating that there is, in fact, language'.[12]

Goldsmith's reconstruction of 9/11, in reverse order to Basinski's
attempt, forms the starting point for what this chapter will assess:
how extricating themselves from the present tense and moving
backwards and forwards in time or perspective became the method
used by three writers: Don DeLillo, Mohsin Hamid and Jonathan
Safran Foer. As I suggested in the previous chapter, it swiftly became
clear after 9/11 that there was a need, a craving even, for narrative
about what had happened—not just a retelling of events, but a
form of interpretive, hermeneutical response. This chapter concerns
itself with the question of the artist's adequacy in confronting the
historical event. Part 1 examines the novel's potential for temporal
experimentation; Part 2 assesses our relative tolerance of the 'real'
in the novel by comparison with sculpture, as well as fiction's
drive to provide redemptive connections; Part 3 turns to the use of

---

[10]Goldsmith, 'Afterword', p. 172.
[11]Kenneth Goldsmith, 'World Trade Center', in *Seven American Deaths and Disasters*
(New York: powerHouse Books, 2013), p. 141.
[12]Aimee Pozorski, *Falling After 9/11: Crisis in American Art and Literature* (New
York: Bloomsbury, 2014), p. 59.

perspectivism and quotidian detail combined with abstraction to find a way to say the apparently unsayable. That is not to say that novelists have succeeded, rather that they have not failed.

Part one: Stasis, retrogenesis and retreat

One of the first writers to fictionalize 9/11 inventively, without recourse to the false haven of what Eric Santner terms 'narrative fetishism'[13] where trauma or loss is wiped away, was Jonathan Safran Foer in *Extremely Loud and Incredibly Close*. Foer was swiftly joined by Don DeLillo and Mohsin Hamid. None sought to erase the trauma but suggested imaginary microclimates in which 9/11 occurred but was then reeled back in, or reshaped, or, in Hamid's case, reinterpreted. Foer and DeLillo, in particular, envisaged a world in which the attacks took place but, on another imaginary level, could be arrested or even sent backwards in time. Foer's mission to freeze time was enabled by his use of the traumatized child narrator, naïve enough to imagine a parallel universe in which his father did not die and the towers did not fall, but precociously wise enough to take his adult audience with him in his tentative steps towards a redemptive comprehension. Similarly, DeLillo used a child, Justin, to plot a course where imagination could force things to be different. Later in this chapter, I will assess the way Justin reinvents language to construct an altered, less-threatening environment in which to live.

Hamid's trajectory was different. He created a means by which strongly held ideologies could be arrested and then reversed, in the form of a character who abandoned his American identity in favour of his hitherto submerged Pakistani heritage. By accompanying him on this retrocessive path, the reader's own reservations about the strangeness, the alien quality of his final reactions and motivations are rendered less acute. Changez starts as a known quantity and even though his responses become unfamiliar to a Western audience, the ultimate threat he poses is made no more alarming than the one

---

[13]Eric Santner, 'History Beyond the Pleasure Principle: Some Thoughts on the Representation of Trauma', in *Probing the Limits of Representation: Nazism and the 'Final Solution'*, ed. Saul Friedlander (Cambridge, MA: Harvard University Press, 1992), pp. 143–154, 144.

represented by the unnamed and unknown American with whom he shares a restaurant table.

DeLillo's experiment is with re-examined time. *Falling Man* opens and closes at the same moment, as his character Keith emerges bewildered and traumatized from the chaos of the burning Twin Towers. From that instant of beginning to the twinned moment of ending, DeLillo's impulse and imperative is to send time backwards. He appears to have drawn on two notorious news photographs: one was of the unnamed falling man photographed by Richard Drew, the other was of Marcy Borders photographed by Stan Honda. Marcy Borders lost her name that day and became known to us simply as the Dust Lady (Figure 2.1). Clothed in powdered remains of the

FIGURE 2.1 *Marcy Borders ('Dust Lady'). Photograph by Stan Honda/ AFP/Getty Images.*

buildings, she took on a hyperreal identity that was both familiar and yet shockingly strange, as uncanny as anything Freud ever envisaged. The Dust Lady struggled with depression, addiction and panic attacks after 9/11 and died of stomach cancer in 2015, believing her symptoms to have been brought on by inhaling the poisonous dust that coated her. She too had been trapped in time on 11 September 2001. Looking at her image now, caked in thick white dust, there is a frozen quality to her stasis quite separate from the inevitable stillness of a photograph. Her hands are in supplication, and she looks more like a shop mannequin than a human. DeLillo's characters emerging from the shattered towers are trapped in time too, and he makes several references to people walking backwards. The local *tai chi* group, who are, after all, expert practitioners of the martial art of slowing down time, freeze their movements entirely. Keith, estranged from his wife Lianne, feels compelled by the traumatic events to reverse events and return once again to his abandoned family:

> There were the runners who'd stopped and others veering into side streets. Some were walking backwards, looking into the core of it, all those writhing lives back there, and things kept falling, scorched objects trailing lines of fire.
>
> He saw two women sobbing in their reverse march, looking past him, both in running shorts, faces in collapse.
>
> He saw members of the tai chi group from the park nearby, standing with hands extended at roughly chest level, elbows bent, as if all of this, themselves included, might be placed in a state of abeyance.[14]

Lianne, Keith's estranged wife, extends the impulse to send events into reverse. She requests an MRI scan because she is worried about lapses in memory and wonders if this is a sign of impending Alzheimer's, the disease that afflicted her father. Lianne's desire to send events into reverse is to ensure that she heads off a potential assault by her own genetic inheritance. Lianne had always associated her father with the idea of being 'dangerously' alive, but the man who had radiated vital force, the man with energy in abundance, deliberately arrested that life and died 'by his own

---

[14]Don DeLillo, *Falling Man* (London: Picador, 2007), p. 4.

hand'. By shooting himself, Lianne's father chose the moment and the means, and he is as much an emblem of perfect stasis as the falling man himself is. Just as Lianne's father stops time dead, so too does the falling/suspended man. For both of them, 'there is no next',[15] that plaintive cry of finality from Lianne's mother. Lianne's anxiety that she too may have 'no next' drives her to request the MRI scan. To establish her brain function, she is asked to count backwards in sevens, which brings a kind of soothing release: 'It was her form of lyric verse, subjective and unrhymed, a little songlike but with a rigor, a tradition of fixed order, only backwards, to test the presence of another kind of reversal, which a doctor nicely named retrogenesis.'[16]

'Retrogenesis', the term coined by psychiatrist Barry Reisburg in 1999, defines the loss of faculties in adulthood in opposite order to their attainment in childhood, particularly in Alzheimer's patients. For Lianne's doctor, the delicately euphemistic term describes the point when the brain throws itself into reverse, the moment when it is demonstrably true that there can be 'no next', at least not in any progressive, linear sense. Ultimately, the mind regresses to the moment when it is no longer conscious of its own demise. But Lianne's retrogenesis is a different brand of regression from the kind referred to by the medical profession. Hers is a restorative state in which she counts numbers backwards in a form of 'lyric verse' and in which she can uphold a 'tradition of fixed order'. For Lianne, there *is* a 'next'. For DeLillo too, there is a sense in which retrogenesis defines something other than regression, mental atrophy or even nostalgia. It seems to represent the exploration of an alternative, salving retreat, in which there can be found 'a next' coupled with a craving for the soothing force of the 'fixed order'. The work of artist Imogen Stidworthy resonates powerfully here. Her installation *The Whisper Heard* uses sound recordings to explore the acquisition of language by a three-year-old child and the erasure of language in an elderly man with aphasia. Both were asked to respond to a narration of Jules Verne's nineteenth-century novel *Journey to the Centre of the Earth* since one had forgotten how to read and the other had not yet learned. As each

---

[15]Ibid., p. 10.
[16]Ibid., p. 188.

tries to mimic the sounds they hear, words become transmuted. 'So still' becomes 'not move', 'silence reigned' appears to become 'silence rained' and 'I could hear the beatings of my own heart' becomes 'beetles'. It is extraordinarily powerful to observe and has the uncanny effect of stripping away any sense of a 'fixed order' of language. Neither 'beatings' nor 'beetles' takes precedence in the end.

The craving for the 'fixed order' of language motivates many of DeLillo's and Foer's characters. In *Falling Man*, Keith and Lianne's son Justin develops a habit of talking in monosyllables because 'it helps me go slow when I think'. (Justin's words resonate with those of BBC journalist Kevin Marsh analysed in the introduction, who described the compulsion to move slowly in the newsroom on 9/11.) Oskar's traumatized and mute grandfather in *Extremely Loud and Incredibly Close* loses the power to speak but thereby reverts to an innocent state, that stage in life before the development of human speech brings its own corrupting complications. Oskar himself relies on a part-naïve, part-sophisticated form of communication that is built on bizarre ritual, superstition and word play. Both novels pay silent homage to Kurt Vonnegut's *Slaughterhouse Five*, in which Billy Pilgrim, an American prisoner of war who is, as Vonnegut phrased it, 'unstuck in time', survives the Dresden bombings, just as Oskar's grandfather has done. Billy cannot change the events of his life, but he is able to travel backwards and forwards in time to relive elements of his experiences. That ability allows him to acquire a fatalistic attitude to his own eventual demise.

Martin Amis's *Time's Arrow*, a book which itself pays tribute to Vonnegut, experiments with retrogenesis in a different way. By reversing the story of a Holocaust doctor, Amis is able to experiment with ideas about the Holocaust's reversal of all humanitarian impulses. While referencing Vonnegut and Amis, both Foer and DeLillo are working on subtly different planes. It is neither Vonnegut's fatalism nor Amis's moralism that they are reaching for in their work. Oskar's grandmother in *Extremely Loud and Incredibly Close* dreams that her own childhood trauma in the bombing raids of Dresden, where she lost her entire family, has been driven into backwards motion: 'all of the collapsed ceilings re-formed above us. The fire went back into the bombs, which rose up and into the bellies of planes whose propellers turned backward, like the second hands of the clocks across

Dresden, only faster.'[17] The description of her past-tense dream ends with a message to Oskar in the present: she has been trying to tell him that it is always vital to say, 'I love you'. This is what she failed to say to her sister before she died, believing there would be other opportunities. If it is neither stricture nor fatalism that he is reaching for, what is Foer doing by allowing his characters to reverse and rewrite traumatic events in their lives? Can we accuse him of the 'narrative fetishism' that Eric Santner derides? Santner distinguishes such fetishism from Freud's understanding of *Trauerarbeit*, or mourning, in which *Trauerarbeit* is the process of 'translating, troping, and figuring loss'. 'Narrative fetishism', on the other hand, is

> a strategy of undoing, in fantasy, the need for mourning by simulating a condition of intactness, typically by situating the site and origin of loss elsewhere. Narrative fetishism releases one from the burden of having to reconstitute one's self-identity under 'posttraumatic' conditions; in narrative fetishism, the 'post' is indefinitely postponed.[18]

At the very least, Foer could be said to be engaging in some form of therapeutic revisionism, to make the Dresden bombing, the Holocaust and 9/11 more manageable. Assessing those traumatic events by reversing and reshaping them appears to be an attempt by Foer to provide his characters with a fortifying modus vivendi. But the key to the grandmother's recollection of trying to tell her sister she loves her is her failure. It is a scene of non-communication. Anna falls asleep and her sister decides she will tell her another time. This cannot be regarded as an effective means of overcoming catastrophe or trauma. It is a deliberately failed attempt to overlay a new, less corrosive shape on that catastrophe. Foer's insistence on the methodology's failure removes his narrative from Santner's fetishism and places it in the category of *Trauerarbeit*. In its 'troping and figuring' is its salving retrogenesis, but once again with limitations that the text seems to acknowledge.

---

[17]Jonathan Safran Foer, *Extremely Loud and Incredibly Close* (London: Hamish Hamilton, 2005), pp. 306–307.
[18]Santner, 'History beyond the Pleasure Principle', pp. 143–154, 144.

The consoling love that Oskar's grandmother attempts to advocate with such limited success is not one that the nine-year-old boy is able to accept. His love for his father is so fundamental that redemption may never be possible. He even voices an imagined trade-off where he sacrifices his mother instead. Oskar shares that by now familiar impulse to send time backwards, although not in the complex and restorative way that his grandmother implicitly advocates. In a contentious manoeuvre, and turning to the same image that DeLillo invoked in *Falling Man*, Foer used a series of photographs of one of the two hundred or more people who jumped to their deaths from the Twin Towers. Oskar tears the pictures from a book and reverses their order to make a pitiful flick-book. The man falling to his death is forever rising to his salvation:

> [I]t looked like the man was floating up through the sky.
> And if I'd had more pictures, he would've flown through a window, back into the building, and the smoke would've poured into the hole that the plane was about to come out of.
> Dad would've left his messages backward, until the machine was empty, and the plane would've flown backward away from him, all the way to Boston.

Oskar concludes his time experiment with a verbal one. The urgency of the present tense offered by his grandmother ('Here is the point of everything I have been trying to tell you, Oskar. It's always necessary. I love you, Grandma.'[19]) is replaced by the regretful longing of Oskar's counterfactual conditional tense: 'We would have been safe.' [20]

The impulse not just to love but to *express* love is common to *Extremely Loud and Incredibly Close*, *Falling Man* and *The Reluctant Fundamentalist*. However, in Changez's case in the latter novel, his hopeless love for Erica, and his eventual rejection by her, is neither redemptive nor even retrogenetic. It is, after all, not even legitimate or 'real'. It is only by impersonating Erica's dead lover that he is able to make love to her at all. Changez attempts

---

[19]Foer, *Extremely Loud and Incredibly Close*, p. 314.
[20]Ibid., p. 326.

retrogenesis, but in disguise. His devotion to Erica has an added political dimension. It develops and recedes, along with his devotion to America and then his break with it. But as Hamid has made explicit, 'in the Muslim world, one sees love for things American co-exist with anger towards America. Which is stronger, politics or love, is like asking which is stronger exhaling or inhaling. They are two sides of the same thing.'[21] Duality of perspective is what sets Hamid's novel apart from the other two in that it alone envisages some sort of political accommodation in which two opposing halves need not be in opposition but can co-exist. It should be said, however, that the novel makes no claims that such a modus vivendi could operate in America itself, but merely amongst those for whom a rage against the United States coexists with a love for it. For all three novelists, *Trauerarbeit* is a stumbling, faltering and imperfect process.

Part two: *Falling Man, Tumbling Woman*: Visual image as taboo

The image of a falling man, reversed in Foer's novel, is the eponymous focal point of DeLillo's attempt to fictionalize 9/11 (Figure 2.2). DeLillo chose Richard Drew's notorious photograph, although he did not stray into the dangerous territory of manipulating the image or the series of images in order to represent a nine-year-old boy's melancholic cry that 'we would have been safe'. DeLillo did not need the photograph; he had no difficulty in conjuring up the vision of it in a few lines of charged prose:

> The mass of the towers filled the frame of the picture. The man falling, the towers contiguous, she thought, behind him. The enormous soaring lines, the vertical column stripes. The man with blood on his shirt, she thought, or burn marks... this picture burned a hole in her mind and heart, dear God, he was a falling angel and his beauty was horrific.[22]

---

[21]Mohsin Hamid, interviewed by Hamish Hamilton for Hamid's official website, February 2007, http://www.mohsinhamid.com/interviewhh2007.html [accessed 22 May 2013].
[22]DeLillo, *Falling Man*, pp. 221–222.

FIGURE 2.2 The Falling Man *by Richard Drew. Photograph by Richard Drew/AP/Press Association Images.*

DeLillo's clear prose evokes Drew's image perfectly. It should be noted of course that Richard Drew's single image encapsulates everything that is misleading about so-called 'factual' reporting. In an investigation by *Esquire* of who the falling man might be, it became apparent that Richard Drew had chosen one frame from a sequence of eleven. 'Photographs lie', said *Esquire*. 'Especially great photographs':

> The photograph functioned as a study of doomed verticality, a fantasia of straight lines, with a human being slivered at the center, like a spike. In truth, however, the Falling Man fell with neither the precision of an arrow nor the grace of an Olympic diver. He fell like everyone else, like all the other jumpers – trying to hold on to the life he was leaving, which is to say that he fell desperately, inelegantly.[23]

---

[23]Tom Junod, 'The Falling Man', *Esquire*, 8 September 2009, http://www.esquire.com/features/ESQ0903-SEP_FALLINGMAN [accessed 24 March 2013].

There is a particularly moving piece of testimony held at the 9/11 Museum by a woman who was watching, aghast, from the ground. She said she felt she could not turn away, because to recoil would be to refuse to recognize the scale of the jumpers' dreadful dilemma. Another spectator noted the piteous gesture of a woman who modestly tugged her skirt down before she jumped.

There was a great deal of agonized speculation online about the jumpers: should they be judged to have committed suicide? James Martin, a Catholic priest, attempted a religiously driven mission to remove the supposedly sinful term 'suicide' from the actions of those who jumped. In an interview broadcast on National Public Radio, he insisted that 'There's no way that that can be considered suicide. And I paused for a minute trying to figure out a way of expressing that. And this friend of mine … just said, "No they were trying to save their lives". And I remember thinking that was a beautiful response.'[24] It was a position that was widely endorsed, by both relatives and officials. Ellen Borakove, spokesperson for New York's medical examiner's office, was quoted widely as stating that a jumper 'is somebody who goes to the office in the morning knowing that they will commit suicide'. She went on to state that 'These people were forced out by the smoke and flames or blown out.'[25] Deaths were listed as 'homicide'. Richard Drew's image of the falling man was what James Martin and his cohorts were looking for. The apparent athletic grace and ferocity of purpose displayed by the man soaring to earth answered their prayers as well as the anxieties of those seeking redemptive explanations. The image seemed to proclaim that this was a divine mission and he was not tumbling chaotically to earth in a hideous trade-off between fire and damnation. Beneath this imagined narrative, there was a grittier, more challenging question: how were the television networks to report the terrible predicament of those forced to jump? The BBC's head of television news at the time, Roger Mosey, told me that on the day itself he could not think of 'any moments where we cut

---

[24]Father James Martin, interviewed on 'Fresh Air', National Public Radio, 12 August 2002.
[25]Dennis Cauchon and Martha Moore, 'Desperation Forced a Horrific Decision', *USA Today*, 2 September 2002, http://usatoday30.usatoday.com/news/sept11/2002-09-02-jumper_x.htm [accessed 21 February 2016].

away from what we were witnessing in the live coverage ... but then in the following hours and days you have to recognise that we were watching mass murder'.[26] How to report the plight of the jumpers was an extraordinarily hard editorial decision to make:

> I think on the day, as long shots and as part of the narrative of the horror, it was just about acceptable to show that this was happening. But this could be referred to in scripts in subsequent programming, recognising that it was distressing for everyone but especially any families or friends of those who died. As ever, the balance is between reporting what's happening; avoid sanitisation of the horrible truths of 9/11, but not going in for endless, gratuitous and upsetting re-runs of what the audience know has happened.[27]

The question of 'what the audience know has happened' seems to cut to the heart of the difficulties faced by novelists and artists in their attempts to represent 9/11 in their work. Certainly, the sculptor Eric Fischl discovered there was no stomach for an explicit work of art that turned away from the aesthetic principles of Drew's *Falling Man*. He found that what had been permissible in the news coverage of the day was deemed outrageous as a subsequent artistic representation of the event. Fischl's sculpture, *Tumbling Woman* (Figure 2.3), was placed outside the Rockefeller Center in New York. The naked, frightful figure, her plump, ungainly limbs twisted and chaotic, her head and neck at that moment taking the full shocking weight of her fall provoked outrage. Where was her divine mission? She appeared to be about to meet her death messily, with nothing to dignify her or to give her meaning. *Tumbling Woman's* reign lasted for only one week before she was first draped in a cloth, then surrounded by a curtain and finally removed altogether. Those affronted by her presence may well have approved of the quasi-paramedical treatment she received on her way to the morgue. But in an interview with the *New York Times* art critic David Rackoff, Eric Fischl expressed his regret that he capitulated to the demands for her removal so swiftly:

---

[26]Former head of BBC Television News Roger Mosey, interviewed by Charlie Lee-Potter, 7 January 2016.
[27]RM, interviewed by CLP, 7 January 2016.

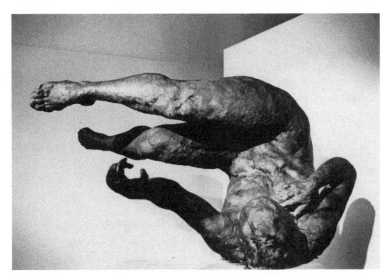

FIGURE 2.3 Tumbling Woman *(2002) by Eric Fischl. Photograph by Ralph Gibson.*

Right now we're shrinking away from truth. No one can criticize the president because we're in a very vulnerable time, even though he's doing some things that are terrifying. You can't express your personal horror and trauma at something that we all experienced. I think that what happened is that since the 60's there's been an ambition that art merge itself with pop culture. At first it was an ironic stance, and then it became actually a real thing; people wanted to have art as a playground and as entertainment. And that's fine in good times, but when something terrible or powerful or meaningful happens, you want an art that speaks to that, that embraces the language that would carry us forward, bring us together, all of that stuff. I think that 9/11 showed us that as an art world we weren't quite qualified to deal with this. Not trained enough to handle it.[28]

---

[28]David Rakoff, 'Post-9/11 Modernism', *New York Times Magazine*, 27 October 2002, http://www.nytimes.com/2002/10/27/magazine/27QUESTIONS.html [accessed 25 March 2013].

The idea that art should not be disruptive seems to run counter to twentieth-century notions of art's presentation of, indeed obsession with, the real. But it would appear that 9/11 has done something to exceptionalist sensibilities and sensitivities and made it newly necessary to produce art that is both reassuring and salving and therefore, by extension, misleading. It is possible that this requirement for dignity and reassurance is what causes the friction and tension in Foer's text. Oskar's grandmother's claim to have found a redemptive connection with her past does not sit comfortably and it does not convince.

Anxiety about being disruptive even extended to removing pre-2001 images of the Twin Towers from feature films. The gleaming buildings became abjections, deleted from the space they had once inhabited in films such as *Spider-Man* and *Zoolander*. But as Thomas Stubblefield noted, since 'these missing scenes were quickly made available online, this "removal" was inevitably incomplete and partial'.[29] To digitally excise the towers from the skyline and for them to reappear, stranded, online seemed only to reinforce their abject status. Intolerance of the 'real' in artistic expressions of 9/11 seems particular to this trauma, perhaps in part because the attacks are so recent. In 2012, fifty years after the drug Thalidomide caused such terrible damage to the limbs and organs of thousands of unborn babies, the German drug manufacturer Chemie Grunenthal apologized for the first time and unveiled a memorial statue. The apology was derided as insulting by survivors, but their fury was in large part directed at the sculpture. The impressionistic work showed a small child, sitting meekly on a chair, with vague, ill-defined damage to her arms. Survivors complained not that it lacked dignity, to use the phrase deployed by critics of *Tumbling Woman*, but that it deliberately failed to represent the true scale of the damage: 'We're all in our fifties now. We're adults who've had to endure pain and humiliation. The sculpture is of a little girl. It's saccharine and it's insulting. It infantilizes us.'[30] Thalidomiders were asking for more realism, more confrontation with the real, not less.

---

[29]Thomas Stubblefield, *9/11 and the Visual Culture of Disaster* (Bloomington: Indiana University Press, 2014), p. 8.
[30]Interview with British Thalidomide survivor by Charlie Lee-Potter, 29 January 2016.

Eric Fischl tried to present his sculpture again. Having expressed regret that he allowed *Tumbling Woman* to be removed, he made another attempt to enshrine his right to give artistic expression to 9/11. On 1 November 2008, when he reintroduced *Tumbling Woman* to the public in a solo exhibition at the Mary Boone Gallery on New York's West 24 Street, she had been subtly reinterpreted. This time *Tumbling Woman* lay forlornly on a plinth, in a giant, vaulted, cathedral-like space. The gallery said it was a 'variation' on Fischl's original bronze sculpture. *Tumbling Woman* was given 'new context in the presence of another solitary figure – the striking translucent "Ten Breaths: Falling Angel" mounted high above the floor of the Gallery'.[31] Could it be that the presence of an angel brought something of the 'divine mission' that Richard Drew's *Falling Man* represented, thereby allowing the public to find a reassuring and bolstering religiosity in their art and to accept *Tumbling Woman* in the way that they refused to do before? Fischl certainly believed that removing *Tumbling Woman* from a public space and housing her in a private gallery went some way towards making her acceptable. He told me that

> one thing I heard more than once was that it would have been okay if it had been shown in a gallery or museum. I guess they meant that art needs a context of art to make it understandable or maybe just to make it safe? I was feeling that 9/11 was a public event and a shared event. I did not want my response to be limited to an art audience. It was important for me to get the work out into a public arena.[32]

It appears that the public did not simply want a 'context'; they wanted a quasi-Christian aesthetic that the gallery's cathedral-like space provided. It is also possible that they wanted to remove her from the very 'public arena' that Fischl desired. They wanted her indoors, away from the city's streets that had reverberated with the sounds of those who really did fall that day.

---

[31]Notes from the Mary Boone Gallery, New York, http://www.maryboonegallery.com/exhibitions/2008-2009/Eric-Fischl/Eric-Fischl-2008.pdf [accessed 25 March 2013].
[32]Erich Fischl, interviewed by Charlie Lee-Potter, 25 November 2008.

FIGURE 2.4 Ten Breaths: Falling Angel *(2007) by Eric Fischl. Courtesy of the Mary Boone Gallery, New York.*

Eric Fischl blamed a great deal of the public's rage on 'journalists who wrote absurd stuff about my intentions. Their words fanned the panic/pain of the public. It was a mob mentality. They were looking for an easy target. It was ridiculous but unstoppable. There was no reasoning. It was truly hysterical.'[33] In addition to this public hysteria, Eric Fischl also identified a fundamental difficulty in attempting to interpret the event of 9/11 artistically:

> The problem with trying to confront and ultimately remember or memorialize 9/11 is that there were all these people dead and no bodies. The people simply disappeared. The only media coverage in the States that had images of people were the jumpers and that was immediately censored. The mourning turned to the loss

---

[33]Ibid.

of architecture as a way of expressing the depth of our grief. Everything focused on the Twin Towers as a symbol of our great loss. When I introduced a figure into our memorializing event it was seen as an act of selfishness, careerism and cruelty. The public was not ready to openly share and mourn the losses of human beings. I would love to see *Tumbling Woman* find its way back into the public arena. My dream would be to have it placed at the site, but I will not hold my breath on that one.[34]

Fischl believed that because the images of those jumping were inevitably censored, his introduction of a human form seemed somehow shocking. It is consistent with the ideas expressed by David Simpson that Ground Zero took on the status of 'sacred ground':

> Human relics, even the tiniest fragments of human bodies, were painstakingly excavated from the enormous piles of rubble, carefully documented, and put through DNA testing in hopes of being able to send something, however small, to the families of the dead for conventional burial. [...] It was not so. Little remained, so that bodies and body parts became absolutely precious and were accorded unprecedented levels of respect and attention.[35]

Fragments of DNA are still being sought and found. Visiting the 9/11 Museum in 2015, I was told that another victim had just been positively identified and his traces returned to his mother. The repository is held at the museum, behind a vast blue artwork by Spenser Finch made up of 2,983 squares of paper, each painted a different shade of blue to evoke the intense blue of the sky on 11 September 2001 and to represent each person killed both in 9/11 and in the World Trade bombing of 1993. The wall is marked with Virgil's words: 'No day shall erase you from the memory of time', a quotation that echoes the meaning that Richard Ford brought to his journalistic essay about 9/11 at the time, and with the words of

---

[34]Ibid.
[35]David Simpson, *9/11: The Culture of Commemoration* (Chicago: The University of Chicago Press, 2006), p. 28.

Thornton Wilder used by Tony Blair at the 2001 memorial service in New York. To reinforce the artwork's status as the guardian of the repository, each letter of Virgil's quotation was forged from steel recovered from the ruined towers.

Eric Fischl was right to be pessimistic about the possibilities of his sculpture being allowed to rest at the site. When I asked him again in 2013 if the public's revulsion had receded in any way, he said that 'nothing has changed with regards to *Tumbling Woman*'s public presence, though it has entered the lexicon through many articles and theses about censorship, art and 9/11. So it has some currency.'[36] It was not the outcome he hoped for and adds weight to the suggestion that the visual arts, and to a large degree journalism too, have been circumscribed by a return to a confining moralizing in the public sphere and to the aesthetics of tabloid outrage. But fiction has not been constrained in the same way. It appears that a novelistic approach to the post-9/11 landscape is allowed to be more explicit than other mediums, even though it too is set against the background of some of the same criticisms.

Could an evasion of the real be the reason why novelists seem less censored by the queasiness of their readers, as well as less hampered by anxieties about dealing with the very recent past? Foer and DeLillo certainly deploy children to explore 9/11 trauma, and use them to re-write the real. DeLillo's child figure, Justin, imagines that bin Laden is called Bill Lawton. Meanwhile, Foer's Oskar appears ludicrously as Yorick in his school production of *Hamlet*, having naively engineered an audience made up of people named Black who he believed could explain the circumstances of his father's death in the Twin Towers. There is both complexity and innocence here that would seem to be the twin responses of many children that day. As journalist Jay Rosen pointed out in his essay about 9/11, his four-year-old daughter held the towers as 'playful objects'[37] in her imagination because they were twins, but their loss produced a concomitant loss in her. 'September 11 was the day I lost my daughter to the news [...] By the time I got home, she had absorbed from television news images of destruction beyond

---

[36]Eric Fischl, interviewed by Charlie Lee-Potter, March 2013.
[37]Jay Rosen, 'September 11 in the Mind of American Journalism', in *Journalism after September 11*, eds Barbie Zelizer and Stuart Allan (London: Routledge, 2002), p. 27.

what I had seen in my entire life.'[38] That combination of acuity and playfulness certainly pertains to the nine-year-old boys who appear to have key status as dispensers of wisdom for both Foer and DeLillo. DeLillo has admitted that in his novel *The Names*, which ends with an excerpt from a 'novel in progress' by a nine-year-old boy, the extract was in fact written by Atticus Lish, the son of his editor and friend Gordon Lish. DeLillo said that rather than 'totally invent a piece of writing that a 9-year old boy might do, I looked at some of the work that Atticus had done when he was 9. And I used it. I used half a dozen sentences from Atticus's work. More important, the simple exuberance of his work helped me to do the last pages of the novel.'[39] In an interview that Don DeLillo gave in 1988 and in which he was asked about the way children interpret the culture in his novels, he explained his view:

> [C]hildren have a direct route to, have direct contact to the kind of natural truth that eludes us as adults. In *The Names* the father is transported by what he sees as a kind of deeper truth underlying the language his son uses in writing his stories. [...] There is something they know but can't tell us. Or there is something they remember which we've forgotten.[40]

DeLillo's words are redolent of Richard Crownshaw's when he suggested that post-catastrophe novels should find a way to memorialize, rather than indulge in commemoration. They should 'remember what a better future might look like'.[41] However, it is not convincing that children should simply be the means by which we find a direct route to 'natural truth'. The impulse to include the insights of children appears to me to have more to do with the fumbling imperative to make redemptive connections, the

---

[38]Ibid., p. 27.
[39]Robert R. Harris, 'A Talk with Don DeLillo', *New York Times Books*, 10 October 1982, http://www.nytimes.com/books/97/03/16/lifetimes/del-v-talk1982.html [accessed 25 March 2013].
[40]*Conversations with Don DeLillo*, ed. Thomas DePietro (Jackson, MS: University Press of Mississippi, 2005), p. 72.
[41]Richard Crownshaw, 'Introduction', in *The Future of Memory*, eds Richard Crownshaw, Jane Kilby and Antony Rowland (New York: Berghahn Books, 2010), p. 3.

redemptive connections incidentally that Fischl was excoriated for not providing in his sculpture. Just as DeLillo talked about a child's ability to find an 'alternate reality', it is the child in *Extremely Loud and Incredibly Close* who finds such an alternative. Early on, Oskar assumes that the endless connections he can make, just by joining up dots on his map of Manhattan, suggest they must be meaningless:

> I erased, and connected the dots in a different way, to make 'door' [...] Then I thought of porte, which is French for door, obviously. I erased and connected the dots to make 'porte'. I had the revelation that I could connect the dots to make 'cyborg', and 'platypus', and 'boobs', and even 'Oskar', if you were extremely Chinese. I could connect them to make almost anything I wanted, which meant I wasn't getting close to anything.[42]

The novelist Walter Kirn complained that Foer's eccentric writing and characterization are done in a 'nifty, Rubik's cube sort of way that gives a chilly intellectual thrill but doesn't penetrate the bosom'.[43] Admittedly, there is sentimentality present in Foer's work, as well as a typographical playfulness. But there is also intellectual rigour and an epic ambition that take this novel far beyond the sentimentality displayed by the *New York Times' Portraits of Grief*, the male-centric nationalism of films such as *Flight 93*, the bleak excursions in comic farce of novels such as Ken Kalfus's *A Disorder Peculiar to the Country* or even the quasi-religious reverence imbued by the final resting place of Eric Fischl's *Tumbling Woman*. *Extremely Loud and Incredibly Close* explores the inadequacy of language, the gaps between words and the constant struggle to say precisely what is meant – the grandfather who expresses yes with one hand and no with the other; Fo Black, who wears an 'I Love New York' t-shirt, assuming that NY means 'you' as *ny* does in Chinese; Ruth Black who believes that her husband communicated with her by shining a torch into the sky to let her know that he was there; Oskar reading 'Don't go away' on his grandmother's window

---

[42]Foer, *Extremely Loud and Incredibly Close*, p. 10.
[43]Walter Kirn, 'Extremely Loud and Incredibly Close: Everything is Included', *New York Times*, 3 April 2005, http://www.nytimes.com/2005/04/03/books/review/0403cover-kirn.html?pagewanted=all&_r=0 [accessed 25 March 2013].

and believing that it is meant for him even though we learn much later that it was a message for his unknown grandfather. The list goes on: Oskar's grandmother's long and detailed description of her attempt to stop her husband leaving her, compared to the earlier description of the same encounter by Oskar's grandfather which amounts to little more than blank pages; Oskar's father calling his mother on her mobile to say that he had escaped from the burning building, all the while knowing that she knew that he was lying to make her feel better. And finally, most poignantly of all, the final message that Oskar's father left on the answer machine at home, assuming, since no one picked up, that the apartment must be empty. Since that day Oskar has told no one that he had been there, listening, but unable to pick up the phone. But when Oskar finally meets the man to whom the mysterious key from his father's blue vase belongs, he confesses what he heard on the tape:

> Are you there? Are you there? Are you there? Are you there? Are you there?
> Are you there? Are you there? Are you there? Are you there? Are you there?
> Are you?
> And then it cut off.
> I've timed the message, and it's one minute and twenty-seven seconds. Which means it ended at 10:24. Which was when the building came down. So maybe that's how he died.[44]

But maybe not. This, in the end, is the way fiction can wrestle with the conundrums of 9/11 and this is why Oskar's use of the counterfactual conditional sits perfectly harmoniously with his grandmother's present tense. It is, after all, DeLillo's sense of 'alternate reality' and 'natural truth' that is the novelist's lingua franca. It is more in the end than the redemptive power of telling a story that I explored in the previous chapter. It is a means of conjuring a pattern out of the assortment of random dots, of finding a means of communicating between people who do not share the same language, of accepting that even though verisimilitude is sometimes difficult to achieve,

---

[44]Foer, *Extremely Loud and Incredibly Close*, pp. 301–302.

understanding is not. Fiction is unembarrassed by perspectivism, as I will now suggest.

Part three: Stopping dead

DeLillo's performance artist, the eponymous 'falling man', attempts to capture and freeze the moment after victims trapped in the towers jumped but before they reached the ground. He is, in other words, working about five seconds ahead of Eric Fischl. DeLillo is precise in his description of the technical details. His falling man does not jump on an elasticized rope as a bungee jumper would, bungee jumping being of course the epitome of 'safe', controlled danger. He does not rebound comically from his initial jump as though on a spring, or trampoline, but stops dead, when he reaches the end of his rope:

> He worked without pulleys, cables or wires. Safety harness only. And no bungee cord to absorb the shock of longer falls. Just an arrangement of straps under the dress shirt and blue suits with one strand emerging from a trouser leg and extending back to a secure structure at the top of the fall.[45]

Later, DeLillo makes clear that 'His falls were said to be painful and highly dangerous due to the rudimentary equipment he used.'[46] When the falling man's body is found, it is noted that he suffered from 'a spinal condition', his back permanently damaged by his insistence on jumping without anything to absorb the shock. He is not the 'dangling man' of Saul Bellow's creation, waiting idly for the draft that may invigorate him.[47] Bellow's Joseph, as a variant of Robert Park's 'marginal man', is lethargic and acquiescent. By contrast, the falling man is *engagé* and, in a perverse way, represents a secular Hierophant for all those traumatized by 9/11. He represents all those who jumped, while literally being a man who *has* jumped.

---

[45]DeLillo, *Falling Man*, p. 220.
[46]Ibid., p. 222.
[47]Saul Bellow, *Dangling Man* (1944; London: Penguin, 2007).

Just as the Hierophant in a pack of Tarot cards represents both heaven and earth by pointing both up and down simultaneously, the related Tarot card of the Hanged Man is suspended in mid-air, never falling and still capable of being inverted. DeLillo's falling man becomes the hero of a peculiar kind of *Schicksalstragödie*. He has not fall*en*, so cannot be The Fallen Man; neither is he fall*ing* so cannot be The Falling Man. His identity could be represented, perhaps, as The Fall Guy/Man who has juddered to a shocking and painful halt, the stark symbol of this and other 9/11 novels' attempts to stop time dead. Layered within his meaning, of course, is the totem of the hanged/dead man, whose neck is broken the instant that his fall is halted.

Mohsin Hamid's approach to arresting time is different to DeLillo's and Foer's. Hamid moves his protagonist Changez to the other side of the world, back to his native Pakistan, from where he literally and figuratively changes his perspective. Just prior to Changez's return home, he watches the attacks on television in Manila. Hamid ensures that Changez at first views the attack on the Twin Towers as fictional and then, immediately afterwards, as pleasing. It is a response that would have been unthinkable to him when he was first enjoying the successes and financial rewards of his job at Underwood Samson. His dramatic volte-face has been brought about to allow him, and therefore us, to view the scene from a radically different perspective which is, in itself, a form of temporal shift: 'I stared as one – and then the other – of the twin towers of New York's World Trade Center collapsed. And then I *smiled*. Yes, despicable as it may sound, my initial reaction was to be remarkably pleased.'[48] It may sound despicable, but it also sounds plausible, given that we have been encouraged, enticed even, to shift our perspective with him. Later, when Changez is back in Lahore and orchestrating increasingly threatening and militaristic assaults on his former US home, Hamid devises another incremental adjustment in perspective for his character. Changez has progressed from finding the attack pleasing to making a decision to abandon his 'Americanness' altogether. The employee of United Samson has evolved to the point where he neatly reverses his employer's name, so

---

[48]Mohsin Hamid, *The Reluctant Fundamentalist* (London: Hamish Hamilton, 2007), p. 72.

that it no longer throbs acronymically with the name of the nation itself or with Uncle Sam: he pits Samson against United [States]:

> I was looking about me with the eyes of a foreigner, and not just any foreigner, but that particular type of entitled and unsympathetic American who so annoyed me when I encountered him in the classrooms and workplaces of your country's elite. This realization angered me; staring at my reflection in the speckled glass of my bathroom mirror I resolved to exorcize the unwelcome sensibility by which I had become possessed.[49]

This 'different way of observing' has the equivalent effect of stopping or rewriting time. The assault of 9/11 is no longer a fundamental assault on global stability. It is something to be viewed from the other side of a two-way mirror. Changez is assisted in his attempt to 'exorcize the unwelcome sensibility' by Mohsin Hamid's choice of linguistic style which he has himself described as

> courtly and menacing, a vaguely anachronistic voice rooted in the Anglo-Indian heritage of elite Pakistani schools and suggestive of an older system of values and of an abiding historical pride. And I decided on a frame that allowed two points of view, two perspectives, to exist with only one narrator, thereby creating a double mirror for the mutual societal suspicion with which Pakistan views America and America views Pakistan.[50]

Perspectivism, the possibility of two different points of view, is scrubbed from most journalists' lexicons very early in their training. 'On the one hand and on the other hand' is usually a journalistic by-phrase for 'I have no idea'. To equivocate as a journalist is rarely encouraged, but perspectivism in the hands of a fiction writer can produce what Hamid describes as the novelist's 'core skill', empathy:

> I believe that the world is suffering from a deficit of empathy at the moment: the political positions of both Osama Bin Laden

---

[49]Ibid., p. 124.
[50]Mohsin Hamid's official website: 'Hamish Hamilton Interview with Mohsin Hamid', February 2007, http://www.mohsinhamid.com/interviewhh2007.html [accessed 9 February 2013].

and George W. Bush are founded on failures of empathy, failures of compassion towards people who seem different. By taking readers inside a man who both loves and is angered by America, and hopefully by allowing readers to feel what that man feels, I hope to show that the world is more complicated than politicians and newspapers usually have time for.[51]

Hamid's view that the novel can demonstrate the complexity of the world more effectively than newspapers is interesting. Like Jay McInerney, he told me that immediately after the 9/11 attacks he did not want to write a novel: 'I think it was mood more than anything. I just didn't feel like writing fiction for a while. Or rather, whatever fiction I wrote seemed inadequate.'[52] He went on to tell me that when it came to writing fictionally about 9/11, 'there is no "too soon" or "too late" except on an individual level', but he still found that he did not want to write about it: 'I personally resisted including 9/11 in my novel for four years, and only began to incorporate it into *The Reluctant Fundamentalist* in 2005, in part because it did feel too soon to me, personally, before that.'[53]

The Reluctant Fundamentalist questions the reader closely. According to Hamid, it 'implicates the audience; it holds up a mirror to what they are. In that process, the author establishes a conversation with the audience.'[54] In asserting its dualism, the magnetic pull of both East and West, the novel attempts the opposite of a news report. It is purposely ambivalent, deliberately misleading and relentlessly lacking in definitive answers. The inevitable consequence of the novel's refusal to be conclusive is that time is halted, albeit in a different way to that imagined by DeLillo and Foer. The reader works through *The Reluctant Fundamentalist* with a sense of insistent, low-level dread, with an expectation that a 'terrible thing is going to happen'. Yet it never does because time is arrested. The fact that something is *going* to happen sets it apart from *Falling Man* and *Extremely Loud and Incredibly Close* where

---

[51]Mohsin Hamid, interviewed by Harcourt for Hamid's official website, March 2007, http://www.mohsinhamid.com/interviewharcourt2007.html [accessed 22 May 2013].
[52]Mohsin Hamid, interviewed by Charlie Lee-Potter, 19 January 2016.
[53]Ibid.
[54]Mohsin Hamid, interviewed by Anna H. R. Khan, Stanford Daily, 23 April 2007.

the 'terrible thing' has already happened and is being coped with. As Lianne's mother Nina puts it when asked what will happen next: 'Nothing is next. There is no next. This was next. Eight years ago they planted a bomb in one of the towers. Nobody said what's next. This was next. The time to be afraid is when there's no reason to be afraid. Too late now.'[55] The landscape of *The Reluctant Fundamentalist* is a deliberately shifting one. The protagonist is a self-confessed unreliable witness and his American companion may be a benign tourist or a murderous CIA operative, but that is the whole point. It has always been the novel's virtue not its vice that it can mean many things concurrently, unconstrained as it is by factual reporting's claim to tell *the* truth.

DeLillo makes important use of this plurality of truths and the miasma of rumour and misinformation to accentuate the impossibility of ever establishing the facts entirely. The wild imaginings of Lianne's son Justin and his friends are in many ways similar to the thousands of websites that continue to peddle 9/11 conspiracy theories of the wildest kinds. Justin transmutes the name bin Laden into an innocuous sounding character called Bill Lawton:

'He was hearing Bill Lawton. They were saying bin Laden.'

Lianne considered this. It seemed to her, at first, that some important meaning might be located in the soundings of the boy's small error. She looked at Keith, searching for his concurrence, for something she might use to secure her free-floating awe. He chewed his food and shrugged.

'So, together,' he said, 'they developed the myth of Bill Lawton.'[56]

The 'myth of Bill Lawton' is emblematic of all the rumours, lies, shards of misinformation and speculative gossip that continue to litter newspapers and the Internet. But myth-making is also fiction's recourse to alternative or multiple truths. The novel can be 'a divided man's conversation with himself'[57] as described by Mohsin Hamid,

---

[55]DeLillo, *Falling Man*, p. 10.
[56]Ibid., pp. 73–74.
[57]Mohsin Hamid, 'My Reluctant Fundamentalist', in *Discontent and Its Civilizations*, 2007(London: Hamish Hamilton, 2014), p. 70.

but it can also be a divided reader's confrontation with various possibilities. If the novel can juggle different versions of the truth successfully, it follows that it must hold within it many versions of memory, with each strand in the plait being both different and yet non-oppositional.

Robert Eaglestone has explored the idea that memory is not a photographic resource from which sepia-toned pictures can be plucked at will, but rather that 'memory is akin to language'[58] and if it is a language, he argues, it is not something we simply add layer by layer to our life's experiences like new words in our lexicon; rather it is interwoven seamlessly. Eaglestone's idea of the subsumed, enveloped memory is made bizarrely literal, literally 'made flesh', by DeLillo, who physically interweaves memory into his characters' bodies. He explores the idea of what he calls 'organic shrapnel'; the fragments of flesh from the victims of a devastating explosion that catapult themselves into the bodies of those nearby. Organic shrapnel is both the representation of buried psychological trauma and its physical manifestation in the form of distinct bumps in the skin. As a medic removes splinters of glass from Keith's body, he explains how human shrapnel can enter another's flesh:

> [F]ragments of flesh and bone come flying outward with such force and velocity that they get wedged, they get trapped in the body of anyone who's in striking range. Do you believe it? A student is sitting in a café. She survives the attack. Then, months later, they find these little, like, pellets of flesh, human flesh that got driven into the skin. They call this organic shrapnel.[59]

The former Archbishop of Canterbury, Rowan Williams, who was in a building opposite the WTC that day has admitted that he finds it very difficult to read 9/11 fiction and has not read *Falling Man*. However, when I asked him if DeLillo's idea of organic shrapnel resonated with him, he found it very affecting. It was not a notion that he had encountered before, but I asked him if those who died have on a metaphorical level marked him, entered the consciousness,

---

[58]Robert Eaglestone, Keynote address at Institute of English Studies Conference *After the War*, 6 May 2009.
[59]DeLillo, *Falling Man*, p. 16.

entered the heart? Once again, a man renowned for his ability to find responses adequate to any occasion was lost for words:

> That's a very powerful metaphor I think. Very. I think it makes sense. Yes, that's right. And what I think of too, in metaphorical terms is of course the transplantation of someone else's flesh into your own is normally medically a good thing. But this isn't. Or at least … is it?[60]

The testimony of a survivor would therefore suggest that the idea of organic shrapnel does indeed resonate on the level of both the literal and the metaphorical. Dr Williams's initial uncertainty about whether such a grotesque transplant is good or bad would suggest that the idea of such shrapnel is more than simply repulsive and that there is perhaps a form of traumatic memorializing at stake here. DeLillo extrapolates further from the idea of memory being interwoven into the flesh, by using the motif of organic shrapnel in other ways. He uses the term to define the effect that exposure to television images of 9/11 had on viewers. While Lianne was not physically injured in the 9/11 attacks, nevertheless the traumatic experience has pierced her skin:

> Every time she saw a videotape of the planes she moved a finger toward the power button on the remote. Then she kept on watching. The second plane coming out of that ice blue sky, this was the footage that entered the body, that seemed to run beneath her skin, the fleeting sprint that carried lives and histories, theirs and hers, everyone's, into some other distance, out beyond the towers.[61]

In 1988, DeLillo gave an interview that effectively rehearsed the views ascribed to Lianne in *Falling Man* that the television footage of 9/11 had 'entered the body' and 'seemed to run beneath her skin'. DeLillo spoke about the life-changing experience that occurred when he watched the television coverage of the assassination of President Kennedy:

> [W]hat's been missing over these past twenty-five years is a sense of a manageable reality. Much of that feeling can be traced

---

[60]Rowan Williams, interviewed by Charlie Lee-Potter, 3 April 2013.
[61]DeLillo, *Falling Man*, p. 134.

to that one moment in Dallas. We seem much more aware of elements like randomness and ambiguity and chaos since then...It's strange that the power of television was utilized to its fullest, perhaps for the first time, as it pertained to a violent event. [...] This has become part of our consciousness. We've developed almost a sense of performance as it applies to televized events. And I think some of the people who are essential to such events...are simply carrying their performing selves out of the wings and into the theatre. Such young men have a sense of the way in which their acts will be perceived by the rest of us, even as they commit the acts.[62]

His sense that television news is a performance that has become 'part of our consciousness' has an echo in the idea of organic shrapnel entering the flesh, marking it permanently. He has admitted that without the flesh wound caused by watching the Kennedy assassination on television, he 'wouldn't have become the kind of writer I am'. The transformative effect of traumatic memory, whether displayed physically or not, is clearly stated. It is explored by DeLillo elsewhere too, in different manifestations. After the death of her mother, Lianne walks into an art gallery to look at the familiar Giorgio Morandi paintings that reminded her so strongly of the Twin Towers. DeLillo once again invokes notions of organic shrapnel; at times, Leanne absorbs the shrapnel/memory of her mother into herself; at other times, she appears to wrap herself around the shrapnel/memory in a desperate attempt to assimilate it, to *be* it. It is not a comforting idea, but rather a disturbing notion of devouring as well as being devoured:

In time she moved on to the next painting and the next, fixing each in her mind... She was passing beyond pleasure into some kind of assimilation. She was trying to absorb what she saw, take it home, wrap it around her, sleep in it... Turn it into living tissue, who you are... All the paintings and drawings carried the same title. *Natura Morta*. Even this, the term for still life, yielded her mother's last days.[63]

---

[62]DePietro, *Conversations with Don DeLillo*, p. 57.
[63]DeLillo, *Falling Man*, pp. 210–211.

DeLillo had already experimented with the idea of sitting in an art gallery and being invaded both by the art and by a fellow visitor. His 2002 short story 'Baader-Meinhof' describes a woman drawn irresistibly to a series of paintings in a New York art gallery. DeLillo is not specific, but it seems the gallery is The Museum of Modern Art, which, in February 2002, exhibited the Baader-Meinhof paintings of Gerhard Richter, the same artist who depicted 9/11 by scraping away at the brightly coloured paint he had applied, as discussed in my introduction. In DeLillo's story, the fragile and lonely woman allows a man she meets in the gallery to accompany her home. Feeling threatened, she shuts herself in the bathroom as he masturbates on the other side of the door. The devouring of or being devoured by experience and by memory seems to be linked to DeLillo's complaint that we have lacked a 'manageable reality' since JFK was murdered in 1963. He maintained that television, once the recorder of memory, is now a false witness. It has become the medium that does not so much record the event as provoke it, making us 'deeply self-referential'. There is a sense in Lianne's mind, when she sees the falling man hanging by the train track, that she should both absorb the event as she might organic shrapnel and record the event as a film camera might:

> She tried to connect this man to the moment when she'd stood beneath the elevated tracks, nearly three years ago, watching someone prepare to fall from a maintenance platform as the train went past. There were no photographs of that fall. She was the photograph, the photosensitive surface. That nameless body coming down, this was hers to record and absorb.[64]

The Morandi paintings, the video footage of the towers falling, the image of the falling man have all entered the flesh and, having done so, been transmuted into 'living tissue'. The trajectories of *Falling Man, Extremely Loud and Incredibly Close* and *The Reluctant Fundamentalist* have taken us past a craving for 'retrogenesis', via the child-like desire of Justin to make a world in which he makes 'something better than it really was, the towers, still standing …'[65] – en

---

[64] Ibid., p. 223.
[65] Ibid., p. 102.

route to a world in which the organic shrapnel of 9/11 has entered the consciousness subliminally but indelibly. Oskar lays his grandfather's letters to his unknown son inside the bodiless grave of his father. Lianne preserves the memories of her Alzheimer's patients by clipping their stories into a large file. Each is attempting to bear redemptive witness, although there is an inevitable fragility to the gestures.

As Mark Binelli and many others have noted, DeLillo was peculiarly well qualified to write about 9/11. He had, after all, 'done it already'.[66] Terrorists have been characters in his novels since *Players* in 1977, a work in which a man plots to blow up the New York Stock Exchange. The man's wife works for a firm called the Grief Management Council, which is based in the WTC, which had been formally inaugurated only four years before this novel was published. She believes at first that the WTC was 'an unlikely headquarters for an outfit such as this. But she changed her mind as time passed. Where else would you stack all this grief?'[67] Bizarrely there is a scene in which she looks out on the building from a rooftop and a neighbour notes, 'That plane looks like it's going to hit.'[68] Ten years after the publication of *Players*, DeLillo produced another novel that predicted further elements of the disaster that struck on 9/11. *White Noise* examined the notion of the 'airborne toxic event'. Then, in 1991, he published *Mao II*. The writer Toby Litt, in a critical review of *Falling Man* in which he likened the writing to that of the military thriller writer Andy McNab, said that DeLillo had no need to write a post-9/11 novel:

[F]or the truth is that, in *Mao II*, DeLillo had already written his great 9/11 novel long before the specific date and the event had happened to come around. He even identified the target: 'Out the south windows the Trade towers stood cut against the night, intensely massed and near. This is the word "loomed" in all its prolonged and impending force.'[69]

---

[66]Mark Binelli, 'Intensity of a Plot', *Guernica*, 17 July 2007, http://www.guernicamag. com/interviews/intensity_of_a_plot/ [accessed 15 May 2013].

[67]Don DeLillo, *Players* (1977; London: Vintage, 1991), p.18.

[68]Ibid., p. 84.

[69]Toby Litt, 'The Trembling Air', *Guardian*, 26 May 2007, http://www.guardian. co.uk/books/2007/may/26/fiction.dondelillo [accessed 26 March 2013].

There is a burden of expectation on DeLillo that he should be our twenty-first-century seer. Reviews of his 2003 novel *Cosmopolis* included the invocation to pay attention because 'DeLillo has always been good at telling us where we're heading…we ignore him at our peril.'[70] I don't think it is fanciful to detect the world-weariness in DeLillo's prose when the protagonist of *Cosmopolis* sees himself on screen:

> Eric watched himself on the oval screen below the spycam, running his thumb along his chinline. The car stopped and moved and he realized queerly that he'd just placed his thumb on his chinline, a second or two after he'd seen it on-screen …
> 'Shiner told me our network is secure.'
> 'Then it is'.
> 'Then why am I seeing things that haven't happened yet?'[71]

DeLillo has been seeing things 'that haven't happened yet' for thirty-five years, and in this light it is possible to see longer shadows in his character Nina's bleak statement that 'Nothing is next, there is no next. This was next.' Is this the prophet-novelist laying down his Tarot cards and saying that he is no longer in the predictions game, that his own retrogenesis is being enacted and that nothing *can* be next? In that light, DeLillo's Fallen Man resounds with echoes from his earlier incarnation as Milton's Fallen Man, who found that the glorious timelessness of his anointed state had been exchanged for the entrapping endlessness of 'nothing is next'.

DeLillo's character Bill Gray in *Mao II* complains that terrorists have taken over the role of the novelist whose purpose he says is to 'alter the inner life of the culture'.[72] DeLillo certainly appears to believe that storytelling can elevate events into territory where meaning can be found. After 9/11, DeLillo wrote an essay called 'In the Ruins of the Future', in which he neatly balanced the equation between news and storytelling, coming down firmly in favour of the power of the story. He opted to use the word 'narrative' as a

[70]Blake Morrison, 'Future Tense', *Guardian*, 17 May 2003, http://www.guardian.co.uk/books/2003/may/17/fiction.dondelillo [accessed 25 March 2013].
[71]Don DeLillo, *Cosmopolis* (2003; London: Scribner, 2004), p. 22.
[72]Don DeLillo, *Mao II* (1991; London: Vintage, 1992), p. 41.

means of defining the precise events as they occurred and elected to use the word 'counternarrative' to describe the literary edifice that elevates facts to fiction. 'The narrative ends in the rubble', he said, 'and it is left to us to create the counternarrative.' He went on to say that 'People running for their lives are part of the story that is left to us' and that is because 'they take us beyond the hard numbers of dead and missing and give us a glimpse of elevated being'. There is a subversive sense here that DeLillo is aligning himself as a freedom fighter. Just as terrorism is met by counter-terrorism, so misleading, ostensibly factual narrative that inevitably encompasses only one point of view must be met with counter-narrative.

In a powerful definition of what it means to take the events of a cataclysmic day like 9/11 and to extend them into the territory where they might be given some meaning or grant us a 'glimpse of elevated being', DeLillo said that such a day does not succumb to 'the mercies of analogy or simile'. This is a similar observation to that made by Andrew O'Hagan when he criticized novelists acting as journalists:

> It did not help us to be told by imaginative writers that the second plane was like someone posting a letter. No, it wasn't. It was like a passenger jet crashing into an office building. It gave us nothing to be told that the South Tower came down like an elevator at full speed. No, it didn't. It collapsed like a building that could no longer hold itself up.[73]

There is an overlap here with the words and tone adopted by Richard Ford, when he complained that a public official failed to capture in language what the loss of New Orleans signified. DeLillo's approach to that lack of vocabulary was to fill what he called the 'howling space' with small, seemingly inconsequential things. He argued that 'the cellphones, the lost shoes, the handkerchiefs mashed in the faces of running men and women' are more important than the big picture subjects of politics and history. 'The writer tries to give memory, tenderness and meaning to all that howling space.' It does not seem to me that Don DeLillo takes 'memory, tenderness and meaning'

---

[73]Andrew O'Hagan, 'Racing Against Reality', *New York Review of Books*, 28 June 2007, http://www.nybooks.com/articles/archives/2007/jun/28/racing-against-reality/?pagination=false [accessed 25 March 2013].

to include within it a duty to offer interpretation or explanation. 'Meaning' in DeLillo's context appears to suggest significance rather than clarification. In *Falling Man*, his character Lianne is fascinated by two still life paintings by the Italian artist Giorgio Morandi. The definition 'still life' carries within it connotations of captured life, of life brought to a halt, of time reassuringly suspended. But DeLillo is all too familiar with the Italian phrase for the 'still life'. The harmless assembly of objects, vases, pots and bowls that Morandi painted repeatedly throughout his life are *natura morta*, or dead life. As DeLillo put it, 'the Italian term for still life seemed stronger than it had to be', making it a more appropriate term for any analysis of the outrageousness of the 9/11 attacks.

Lianne looks endlessly at the two 'dead life' paintings. She is mesmerized by one of them in particular, a painting of assorted boxes and biscuit tins against a dark background. Every time she looks at them, she sees the Twin Towers, but she refuses to judge them or to give them significance. 'Let the latent meanings turn and bend in the wind, free from authoritative comment', she resolves. When Lianne's previously vibrant and vivacious mother is close to death, she views her too as she might a *natura morta*:

> It was difficult to see her fitted so steadfastly to a piece of furniture, resigned and unstirring, the energetic arbiter of her daughter's life, ever discerning, the woman who'd given birth to the word *beautiful*, for what excites admiration in art, ideas, objects, in the faces of men and women, the mind of a child. All this dwindling to a human breath.[74]

DeLillo appears to have adjusted his view about the importance of journalism over the past two decades. At the start of the 1990s, he said that he 'perceived a new level of significance for the simple news of the day, on radio, on television in the newspapers and in the magazines. The news seemed to have more force than it had in previous years. Now does that really affect the influence of novels in our time?'[75] But in writing *Falling Man* more than a decade later,

---

[74]DeLillo, *Falling Man*, p. 48.
[75]Don DeLillo, interviewed by Mark Binelli, 'Intensity of a Plot', *Guernica*, 17 July 2007, http://www.guernicamag.com/interviews/intensity_of_a_plot/ [accessed 26 March 2013].

DeLillo has changed his perspective. The giant canvas of his earlier novels on which he attempted to paint his competitive counter-blasts to the news journalism of his day has been swapped for a much smaller picture. His technique has become miniaturized as the events he has been describing have become larger in scale. It is a reversal of approach that has bemused some critics, who have complained that *Falling Man* is 'spindly'[76] or that it is 'ambitious in scope but not in scale. It is scrupulously domestic, relentlessly downbeat. If a scene can be shown in retrospect, it is; if it can have the dramatic stuffing knocked out of it in advance, all the better.'[77]

Could it be that the events themselves have become so large and so hugely publicized, theatricalized almost, that Don DeLillo is now attempting to pursue the opposite trajectory? He certainly used a theatrical metaphor when he described the new television age in which young men rushed in from the wings onto the stage to perform their self-referential acts. That is not to say that he is opting for the mundane, the trivial: far from it. As he himself put it, 'I do try to confront realities.' But crucially he went on to say that 'people would rather read about their own marriages and separations and trips to Tanglewood'.[78] After all, where do most people read about marriages and separations but in newspapers, magazines and gossip columns? But he does not reserve his criticism simply for gossip writers, complaining that there is 'an entire school of American fiction which might be called around-the-house-and-in-the-yard. And I think people like to read this kind of work because it adds a certain luster, a certain significance to their own lives.' [79] Don DeLillo's new genre is fiction in miniature, where the lost shoes, the missing briefcases and the memories of those suffering from dementia signify so much more than their material worth. These small details matter for Foer too; they are the means by which he spins a delicate and sometimes precarious confection, linking 9/11 with Dresden, Hiroshima, heredity, love

---

[76]Michiko Kakutani, 'A Man, a Woman and a Day of Terror', *New York Times*, 9 May 2007, http://www.nytimes.com/2007/05/09/books/09kaku.html [accessed 25 February 2016].

[77]Litt, *Guardian*, 26 May 2007.

[78]Robert R. Harris 'A Talk with Don DeLillo', *New York Times* 10 October 1982 [accessed 9 February 2013].

[79]Ibid.

and hope. Oskar seeks to trace every person called Black in New York as well as every lock, a cohort that he calculates numbers 472 and 162 million, respectively. With parallels to DeLillo's *The Players*, where terrorists attempt to impose order on their apparently chaotic system of operating, Oskar succeeds in creating random connections that did not exist before. He moves in the opposite direction to his incompatible grandparents whose drive to create 'nothing places' leads them to live a life where there is more nothing than something. Oskar's friend Mr. A. R. Black, who lives on the floor above, records a life of no meaning by writing out hundreds of thousands of entries for his card index, matching each name with a single word that is meant to define them. His entries, complete with tabloid exclamation marks, resemble newspaper headlines of the mono-word 'Gotcha' variety:

> Che Guevara: war!
> Jeff Bezos: money!
> Philip Guston: art!
> Mahatma Gandhi: war!
> But he was a pacifist, I said.
> Right! War!
> Arthur Ashe: tennis!
> Tom Cruise: money!
> Elie Wiesel: war!
> Arnold Schwarzenegger: war![80]

These are the celebrities of whom newspapers speak, not ordinary people like Oskar's father who, to Oskar's deep and crushing disappointment, does not have an entry. But later, when Oskar plunders Mr Black's card index, he finds that ordinary people get entries after all. There, in all its touching and redemptive glory, is a listing for one Oskar Schell, for whom the defining word is 'son', which is after all both what he is and his father was.

In shared but different ways, these three novels explore the power of little details, minutiae, the small lives set against the backdrop, just like Giorgio Morandi's mundane bottles, vases, Ovaltine tins and boxes, painted and rearranged endlessly in his Bologna

---

[80]Foer, *Extremely Loud and Incredibly Close*, pp. 157–158.

bedroom and studio. And like Morandi's props, they too are both drawn in close-up and yet are emptied of the specific too. In an interview recorded by *Voice of America* on 25 April 1957, Morandi defined the artist's creativity and inventiveness as the ability to 'get past those…conventional images which place themselves between him and things'. And asked what he thought of abstract art, he declared that 'In my opinion nothing is abstract. In fact I don't think there's anything more surreal, or more abstract than reality.'[81] Morandi was a devotee of Cézanne's and it is said that he lived by the advice that Cézanne once gave to Ambroise Vollard. Cézanne cautioned against doing things on a large and showy scale because 'the grandiose grows tiresome' (his example was that disaster epic *The Raft of the Medusa*).[82] It is a mantra that has been applied by DeLillo to *Falling Man*, and by both Foer and Hamid too. All three 9/11 novels deliver a sense of the surreal against which are set the small lives of a few characters, our view of them unobscured by the 'conventional images' so loathed by Morandi. DeLillo's vast work *Underworld* closes with a trance-like look at the Morandi-like objects on his desk, as though he can stare and then write them into meaningful reality:

> [T]he apple core going sepia in the lunch tray, and the dense measures of experience in a random glance, the monk's candle reflected in the slope of the phone, hours marked in Roman numerals, and the glaze of the wax, and the curl of the braided wick, and the chipped rim of the mug that holds your yellow pencils, skewed all crazy, and the plied lives of the simplest surface, the slabbed butter melting on the crumbled bun, and the yellow of the yellow of the pencils, and you try to imagine the word on the screen becoming a thing in the world, taking all its meanings …. [83]

As I have suggested, there is a curious smallness to DeLillo's 9/11 work by comparison with the novels that preceded it. *Falling Man*

---

[81]Giorgio Morandi, cited by Museo Morandi, Bologna http://www.museomorandi.it/index_net.htm [accessed 24 March 2013].

[82]Ambroise Vollard, *Cézanne* (New York: Dover, 1984), p. 67.

[83]Don DeLillo, *Underworld* (1997; London: Picador, 1998), p. 827.

is almost domestic in scale (although it is not 'domesticating' in the way so mistrusted and disliked by Rowan Williams); its 'braided wick' and the 'plied lives of the simplest surface', which incidentally are so redolent of Robert Eaglestone's definition of memory as being 'interwoven', are oddly affecting when set against the backdrop of 9/11. Hamid's work too is deliberately modest in scale. He wrote seven separate drafts of *The Reluctant Fundamentalist*, using a first-person narrative, a third-person narrative, an American protagonist, a Pakistani protagonist and a combination of the two. His first draft, finished in July 2001, was by his own admission vast, but the final form that he chose was miniature in scale. (Hamid described the first draft, completed two months before the 9/11 attacks, as a 'quiet fable about a man's disenchantment with corporate America and his desire to go home'. He added, a little wryly, 'it's still that'.[84]) The roughly three hours it takes to read the novel is matched by the three-hour time span of the narrative. It is, in a sense, a reply to the journalistic discourse that has consistently opted for extreme and inadequate 'common framings' decried by BBC programme editor Kevin Marsh. Hamid's text deliberately takes the opposing stance:

> [It] mimics the global media where so often you hear one side of the story. My novel is written in a form that takes the reverse side of the media; it hands the content over to the reluctant fundamentalist. It is equally biased. The reader has to realize, though, that the novel is only a version of the truth.[85]

It is a measure of the intellectual heft of these novels that they claim only to offer a small version of the truth that may alchemically transform the Ovaltine tins, the boxes and the vases into something with meaning, just as Morandi did. The braided wick and the plied lives represent a more conscious, overt attempt by writers of fiction to define 9/11 in all its complexities than Richard Ford had attempted. As DeLillo put it, 'I didn't want to write a novel in which the attacks occur over the character's right shoulder and affect a

[84]Mohsin Hamid on *Book Club*, BBC Radio 4, 4 September 2011.
[85]Mohsin Hamid, interviewed by Anna H. R. Khan, *Stanford Daily*, 23 April 2007.

few lives in a distant sort of way. I wanted to be in the towers and in the planes.'[86] The following chapter turns to the work of Paul Auster, who did not want to 'be in the towers and in the planes', but attempted to engage with the 9/11 catastrophe by envisaging a counter-historical set of verities. Like Hamid, DeLillo and Foer, he engages in temporal experimentation: the question is whether his success is any more resounding.

---

[86]Binelli, 'Intensity of a Plot', 17 July 2007.

3

After the Past

Introduction

Paul Auster, prolific in his output of novels, plays, screenplays, essays, poems, journalism and literary translations, has wrestled doggedly with the crises and conundrums of the late twentieth and early twenty-first centuries. Terrorism, war, violence, surveillance, murder, blackmail, infidelity and death have been his creative territory for so long that his harsher critics have sometimes wondered acerbically when he might stop.[1] As a resident of New York, it is not surprising that he appeared to have a sense of moral obligation to respond artistically to the 9/11 attacks. Auster wrote a short, tentative piece of prose that same day, named, appositely, 'Random Notes', which appears in an anthology about 9/11 called *110 Stories*. The hesitancy of his prose is matched by the clumsiness of the collection's title, which references both the number of fragments in the volume and the number of floors in the WTC. Auster was in New York on 9/11; it had been his teenage daughter's first day at her Manhattan high school and he and his wife, the writer Siri Hustvedt, had allowed her to travel alone on the subway for the first time:

> Less than an hour after she passed under the World Trade Center, the twin towers crumbled to the ground.
>
> From the top floor of our house, we can see the smoke filling the sky of the city. The wind is blowing toward Brooklyn today, and the smells of the fire have settled into every room of the

---

[1]James Wood, 'Shallow Graves', *The New Yorker*, 30 November 2009.

house. A terrible, stinging odor: flaming plastic, electric wire, building materials.[2]

The fragment of prose is noteworthy for being a contemporaneous response to 9/11, but it has little literary heft. It is hard to associate his threadbare assertion that 'the twin towers crumbled to the ground' with the buildings' actual collapse. Indeed it is difficult to imagine that, in choosing such a phrase, he had at the point of writing even witnessed the towers' destruction, although we must assume that he had. His attempt to describe the burning smell that permeated his house reads oddly like clumsy olfactory guesswork.

Much more acute was Richard Ford's description of the buildings' final moments, anthropomorphized as the Queen Regent Hotel in *The Lay of the Land* and analysed in my first chapter, although it is true that Ford had the advantage of time to filter and refine his prose. Martin Amis, on 18 September 2001, succeeded in finding language that was more resonant than Auster's, but his attempt evokes thoughts of Zadie Smith's complaint that the towers were 'covered in literary language when they fell':[3]

> [N]o visionary cinematic genius could hope to recreate the majestic abjection of that double surrender, with the scale of the buildings conferring its own slow motion. It was well understood that an edifice so demonstrably comprised of concrete and steel would also become an unforgettable metaphor. This moment was the apotheosis of the postmodern era – the era of images and perceptions.[4]

Amis did not so much wreathe the towers in metaphorical excess as transmute them into metaphors in their own right. Ian McEwan,

---

[2]Paul Auster, 'Random Notes – September 11, 2001, 4.00 p.m.', in *110 Stories: New York Writes after September 11*, ed. Ulrich Baer (New York: New York University Press, 2002), p. 34. All subsequent references are to this edition.

[3]Zadie Smith, 'Two Paths for the Novel', *New York Review of Books*, 20 November 2008, http://www.nybooks.com/articles/archives/2008/nov/20/two-paths-for-the-novel/?pagination=false [accessed 18 March 2013].

[4]Martin Amis, 'The Second Plane', in *The Second Plane* (London: Jonathan Cape, 2008), pp. 4–5.

three days earlier, reached for the metaphysical, once again in contrast to Auster's more pedestrian prose:

> The hijackers used fanatical certainty, misplaced religious faith, and dehumanizing hatred to purge themselves of the human instinct for empathy. Among their crimes was a failure of the imagination. As for their victims in the planes and in the towers, in their terror they would not have felt it at the time, but those snatched and anguished assertions of love were their defiance.[5]

As evidenced in the introduction to this book, McEwan's response has the anaesthetizing, consoling tendencies that could be found in Prime Minister Tony Blair's memorial service address and in Richard Ford's first journalistic attempt to contain the 9/11 attacks. The same metaphor is offered too: the bridge of love. Set against Amis's metaphors and McEwan's metaphysics, Auster's despairing prose arguably takes on a new economical rigour. Yet the difficulties that Auster faced in transacting what he experienced that day, despite having the apparent advantage of actually being there, underlines the challenges posed by the universality of the witness experience on 9/11: since the whole world saw what happened, as it happened, Auster's claim to the benefit of 'vicinity' lost its historic advantage. His prose lacks the gravitas of the deponent and reads more like the hasty testimony of the prevaricator. It was, in reality, no better at translating the moment into words than the television anchor's despairing phrase that 'it looks like a film'.

Auster, ill-equipped to 'translate the moment', has nevertheless reiterated his sense that 9/11 was a single catastrophic event that would be both defining and insurmountable:

> I've always known that there is catastrophe in the world; I've lived in the shadow of it in my mind all my life. But as a New Yorker, and as a flesh-and-blood human being, 9/11 has had an

---

[5]Ian McEwan, 'Only Love and then Oblivion', *Guardian*, 15 September 2001, http://www.guardian.co.uk/world/2001/sep/15/september11.politicsphilosophyandsociety2 [accessed 1 March 2013].

enormous effect. I'm not over it yet, and I don't think I ever will be. It was the worst day in the history of the city.[6]

Much later, he appeared to transmute that immediate sense of catastrophe into a more generalized sense of the trauma that follows disaster. The impact of a single, unexpected tragedy had wrought this effect on Auster before. When he was fourteen years old and at summer camp with a group of other children, he was caught in a severe electrical storm. It was an experience that, he has said repeatedly, 'probably formed my view of the world more than anything else that ever happened to me'. The children tried to crawl under a barbed wire fence to reach a clearing, but one boy was killed when the fence was struck by lightning:

> We pulled him through and were lying in the field with him as the storm raged – I remember holding his tongue so he wouldn't swallow it and watching his skin turn blue. If you see that when you are 14 years old, you begin to sense that the world is a lot less stable than you thought it was.
>   Life is not neatly boxed. You go into work one day, and a plane flies into the building and you're incinerated.[7]

Auster has repeated this story many times over the decades. I have chosen this version of his experience because, for the first time, he appeared to link the trauma suffered by his fourteen-year-old self with the horrors confronted by his fifty-four-year-old self on September 11. The two events – a child's experience of death and an adult's confrontation with terror – forty years apart, appear to have elided in some way, certainly in this version of his experience at least. However, because he has repeated the anecdote so many times but without initially referencing 9/11, it is hard to apply the notion of Freud's *Nachträglichkeit* to Auster's response, in its sense of the second event giving the first a retrospective meaning. The first trauma, as his repeated references to it over many years

---

[6]Paul Auster, interviewed by Andrew Van Der Vlies, 'The Tyrannies and Epiphanies of Chance', *Oxonian Review*, 15 June 2004, http://www.oxonianreview.org/wp/the-tyrannies-and-epiphanies-of-chance/ [accessed 7 May 2013].
[7]Paul Auster, interviewed by Helena de Bertodano, *Telegraph*, 16 November 2010.

demonstrate, already had meaning for him. Rather, I would suggest that, perversely, the first event gave meaning to the *second* and that, arguably, a form of beforeness rather than afterwardsness occurred when the threat to his daughter's life unfolded on 11 September. In this chapter, I assemble evidence to establish my view that 9/11 stands as a defining edifice in Auster's artistic endeavour, acting as a completion of the frame narrative to the artistic imagination that had been developing since the day his summer camp friend was killed. The despairing minimalism of Auster's journalistic response to 9/11 could potentially be explained by the events themselves acting upon his imagination as a continuum of his first childhood trauma.

Auster's insistence on repeatedly gnawing and worrying at contemporary tragedies has not won him universal praise, or even credit for trying. Indeed, some of his critics believe him guilty of a banal neuroticism. James Wood, perhaps the most stinging, has likened the novelist's productivity levels to an automated printing press: 'The pleasing, slightly facile books come out almost every year, as tidy and punctual as postage stamps, and the applauding reviewers line up like eager stamp collectors to get the latest issue.'[8] Wood drew a dotted line between Paul Auster and his identically initialled protagonist Peter Aaron from the novel *Leviathan*, and cruelly nudged us to connect the incriminating dots. Aaron, aka Auster, says that 'I have always been a plodder, a person who anguishes and struggles over each sentence, and even on my best days I do no more than inch along, crawling on my belly like a man lost in the desert. The smallest word is surrounded by acres of silence for me.' Wood's acerbic response was: 'Not enough silence, alas.'[9] While elegantly phrased, this is harsh. Auster's eventual fictional response to 9/11 does, indeed, turn to silence, although not the kind of taciturnity that Wood facetiously requested.

While examining his recourse to silence, I assessed the way that Auster exploits references to the past, the present and the future. My conclusion is that 'the worst day in the history of the city' has wrought a change in his temporal response. His is not the backwards, regressive glance of DeLillo or Foer discussed in

---

[8]Wood, *'Shallow Graves'* 30 November 2009.
[9]Ibid.

the previous chapter, or the metaphorical methodology favoured by Ford; rather it is the envisaging of an alternative counterfactual universe in which different outcomes are explored, a strategy that I term 'Auster's literary hyperparallelism'. I have chosen the hyperbolic geometrical term 'hyperparallel' because it reflects the link between Auster's imagined alternative universe and the 'real' universe, without relying on the Euclidean idea of parallels that mirror each other precisely and never intersect. Since Auster's imagined world is both the same *and* different to the real world, the notion of the hyperparallel, with its logic-defying capacity to intersect, seems more appropriate and meaningful. Using hyperbolic geometry has the added advantage of unhitching the entities it describes from any temporal classification; this is important, since 9/11 appeared to rob Auster of any sense of a continuum being, any longer, possible. His defeated prose on the day itself set in stone a kind of creative paralysis that he has yet to shake off.

As I will suggest, Auster's attempts to imagine a different American landscape start with a break from the past. Rather than DeLillo's character's plaintive cry that 'there is no next', Auster's characters proclaim that there can be no before. The three fundamental aims of this chapter are these: to examine the effect of traumatic end-stops on Auster's literary life, in other words his childhood experience and the 9/11 traumas; to assess the importance of silence in response to the politics of 9/11; and finally, in examining the three-book cycle of *The Brooklyn Follies, Man in the Dark* and *Sunset Park*, to explore the gradual adjustments Auster has made to his temporal response as a result of 9/11, from the post-past, via the pre-future and finally to the absolute present. As a cycle, there is a clear development in the treatment of temporality across the novels, but with an endeavour to avoid the kind of fictions defined by Frank Kermode as those 'whose ends are consonant with origins, and in concord, however unexpected, with their precedents, satisfy our needs'.[10] Auster's attempt to avoid the end (or to 'satisfy our needs') is however always flawed, and floored, by the domineering and intrusive end-stop of 9/11.

---

[10]Frank Kermode, *The Sense of an Ending* (1967; Oxford: Oxford University Press, 2000), p. 5.

Part one: Auster's before after and after after

Auster concluded his 'Random Notes', jotted down at 4.00 pm on the afternoon of 11 September 2001, with the words: 'And so the twenty-first century finally begins.'[11] This, then, is the break with the past and the start of something painfully new. In his first instinctive, unmediated response to 9/11, Auster is at least clear on one thing: the events of that day established Auster's sense that from now on the world is living in the 'post-past age'.[12]

The place on which Auster reflected, or rather the *absence* of place, the WTC, is territory he wrote about in very different circumstances decades before. In 1974, he described the Twin Towers in terms of rapture and awe, when his friend, the French high-wire performance artist Philippe Petit, walked between them on a steel wire rigged secretly by his accomplices (Figure 3.1). Viewing footage of that seemingly impossible experiment now, it is all the more memorable for the playful way in which Petit performed his art and appeared to dance unsupported in the air. Teasing his audience, he knelt on the wire, even lay down on it, straying flirtatiously close to the police officers standing on the roof, and then striking out into the centre again. By the time he chose to surrender, he had crossed between the buildings eight times in all. Asked afterwards why he did it, his simple answer was: 'There is no why.'[13] It was a work of artistic innocence and, if he had died, he said, 'what a beautiful death. To die in the exercise of your passion.' Auster wrote about Petit in 1982, with a postmodern appreciation of the sublime nature of the experiment:

[T]he appeal of it, finally, is its utter uselessness. No art, it seems to me, so clearly emphasizes the deep aesthetic impulse inside us all. Each time we see a man walk on the wire, a part of us is up there with him. Unlike performances in the other arts, the

---

[11]Auster, 'Random Notes', *110 Stories*, p. 35.
[12]Paul Auster, *The Brooklyn Follies* (2005; London: Faber & Faber, 2006), p. 22.
[13]Quotation taken from *Man on Wire*, film dir. by James Marsh (Wall to Wall production in association with Red Box Films, 2008).

FIGURE 3.1 *Philippe Petit (August 1974). Photo: Alan Welner/AP/Press Association Images.*

experience of the high wire is direct, unmediated, simple, and it requires no explanation whatsoever. The art is the thing itself, a life in its most naked delineation. And if there is beauty in this, it is because of the beauty we feel inside ourselves.[14]

Auster's sense of Petit's gesture being 'unmediated' is in stark contrast to the unmediated news event described by journalist Kevin Marsh in the introduction to this book, in which everyone sees but no one agrees what it means. Auster's admiration for the simple beauty of Petit's art comes from his sense that it is entirely innocent of representation or indeed *mis*representation. Writing on the afternoon of 11 September 2001, Auster revisited the location of Petit's subversive triumph, still describing his feat as an 'act of indelible beauty', but concluding that this 'same spot has been turned into a place of death'. Once again, Auster's unmediated, hastily produced prose is weak and clichéd; it is oddly similar to that used by Nathan's daughter in Auster's 2005 novel *The Brooklyn Follies*

---

[14]Paul Auster, 'On the High Wire', in *The Red Notebook* (London: Faber & Faber, 1995), pp. 91–92.

which is set, like Ford's *The Lay of the Land*, against the backdrop
of Al Gore's failure to take the presidency. To Nathan's disgust,
his daughter resorts to using hackneyed phrases like 'a living hell'.
Perhaps this suggests Auster's own prose is strongest when time
has elapsed between the experience and the telling, and it would
certainly suggest that, since Auster allows Nathan the perspicacity to
see his own daughter's inadequate prose, he must detect signs of it in
himself. Even though Petit's act may be 'indelible', asserts Auster, the
place itself is deathly. The scale both of Petit's triumph and of
the buildings themselves had made the combination sublime. But the
destruction of the buildings, from the colossus they had been to
the defeated heap they had become, stripped away any trace of the
magnificent, leaving only the 'indelible beauty' of the original act.

It is perhaps unsurprising that writers of post-9/11 fiction should
be captivated by Philippe Petit's sublime act in the air between the
towers. Novelist Colum McCann, who had read Auster's essay,
viewed Petit's walk as a spectacularly creative act in tension with
the act of supreme destruction that brought down the towers. Like
so many other New York writers, McCann wrote journalism post
9/11, but he wanted to attempt a novel. His allegorical 2009 work,
Let the Great World Spin, opened with a description of Petit's
tightrope walk, which he described in distinctive literary terms as
'scribbling' in the air:

> [W]hat was difficult for me as a writer was that everything was so
> very full of meaning that it seemed so difficult to write a sentence,
> or take a photo, or draw a picture without it having some heft
> or meaning. And it just kept getting gaining [sic] momentum,
> with Iran and Afghanistan and Madrid and London, and all that
> justice turning into revenge.[15]

McCann, like Auster, seemed fascinated by temporal experimentation:

> I thought that I could go backwards in time to talk about the
> present: that's when the tightrope walk came in. And the deeper

---

[15]Colum McCann, interviewed by Bret Anthony Johnston, 2009 National Book Award
Winner Fiction Interview, National Book Foundation, http://www.nationalbook.org/
nba2009_f_mccann_interv.html#.Vq9cBhiLQ0Q [accessed 1 February 2016].

I got into the novel the more I began to see that it was, hopefully, about an act of recovery. Because the book comes down to a very anonymous moment in the Bronx when two little kids are coming out of a very rough housing project, about to be taken away by the state, and they get rescued by an act of grace.[16]

An 'act of grace' is a striking, redemptive phrase and is precisely the one used by Auster in his earlier novel *The Brooklyn Follies* to describe being restored by flying through space, as Petit had done. Like Richard Ford, McCann stressed that 'there's hardly a line in his novel about 9/11, but it's everywhere if the reader wants it to be'.[17] By moving backwards to Petit's spectacular gesture, McCann made his interest in temporal tricks clear, and it was again laid bare when he cited the story of a man in Ireland cutting his grass on the day of 9/11, when the telephone rang and he picked it up: 'his daughter was gone, and he left the grass uncut, one half of it long, one half of it short. But the fact of the matter is that the grass will find its own level. It will grow back.'[18] The story and its capacity to render time in vivid form seems to have been the one referenced by Joseph O'Neill in his 9/11 novel *Netherland* when he explains the meaning of the word 'aftermath' as a second mowing of grass: 'You might say, if you're the type prone to general observations, that New York City insists on memory's repetitive mower – on the sort of purposeful post-mortem that has the effect, so one is told and forlornly hopes, of cutting the grassy past to manageable proportions. For it keeps growing back, of course.'[19]

As McCann used Petit to turn redemptively to the past, Auster with his sense that this was the moment when 'the twenty-first century finally begins' appeared to be making a break with it. Post-9/11, there are instances in Auster's fiction that explicitly define the human condition as a state of being in which there is no past. This is very different to his earlier fiction where the past is as much a character in his protagonists' lives as the present and future. In one of his earliest works, *Ghosts*, a man is confronted by the past in the most explicit

---

[16]Colum McCann, interviewed by Bret Anthony Johnston, 1 February 2016.
[17]Ibid.
[18]Ibid.
[19]Joseph O'Neill, *Netherland* (London: Fourth Estate, 2008), p. 2.

terms. Revisiting the Alpine landscape where his father had died in an avalanche twenty-five years before, the man finds a body:

> [H]e had the distinct and terrifying impression that he was looking at himself. Trembling with fear [...] he inspected the body more closely, all sealed away as it was in the ice, like someone on the other side of a thick window, and saw that it was his father. The dead man was still young, even younger than his son was now, and there was something awesome about it, Blue felt, something so odd and terrible about being older than your own father.[20]

There are striking similarities between this vision of a body trapped beneath the ice and the two references to frozen words trapped beneath the ice in Kamila Shamsie's 9/11 novel *Burnt Shadows*. Shamsie uses the words to establish a memorial to those who have died. In a similar way, Auster uses the image of the frozen body as a testament to the past, combining past, present and future of both father and son, each timeframe interlinked and overlapped. But by 2005, in *The Brooklyn Follies*, Auster has excised his characters' past and pushed them, untethered, into a state of past-lessness. Tom Wood is in his thirties and is stolid but thoughtful. He has discarded his aspirations for academic greatness but has failed to replace his abandoned ambitions. From this point, there is 'a new era', Tom explains to his uncle Nathan Glass. 'The post-family, post-student, post-past age of Glass and Wood, "a new era":

'Post-past?'
'The now. And also the later. But no more dwelling on the then.'

[...] Then, in a somber, mock-theatrical voice, he recited the opening lines of Raleigh's 'Farewell to Court':

> Like truthless dreams, so are my joys expired,
> And past return are all my dandled days,
> My love misled, and fancy quite retired:
> Of all which past, the sorrow only stays.[21]

---

[20]Paul Auster, 'Ghosts', in *The New York Trilogy* (1985; London: Faber & Faber, 1987), p. 153.
[21]Auster, *The Brooklyn Follies*, p. 22.

Petit's 'act of indelible beauty' has become fatally transmuted into Raleigh's weary assertion that 'the sorrow only stays'. Tom's break with the past has led him to abandon his studies at Ann Arbor and to arrive in New York, the fabulous city where a past is not required. Tom takes the job that so many rootless immigrants to the city have taken: taxi driver. Even if he does not have 'a clue as to where he was headed', he is paid to take other people where they want to go. And it is a job where human life reveals itself, in all its forms: 'You name it, Harry, and I've seen it. Masturbation, fornication, intoxication in all its forms. Puke and semen, shit and piss, blood and tears. At one time or another, every human liquid has spilled onto the backseat of my cab.'[22] But just as Philippe Petit produced a moment of 'indelible beauty' from something essentially meaningless, Tom is able to find instances of glory brought about precisely because life is so fettered by the everyday, the past-less, the future-less, the mundane and exhausting. The references here are to transcendence, flying, leaving behind the body, departing the earth, in other words to dancing in the air, as Petit did. The 'act of indelible beauty' described on the afternoon of 11 September 2001 has been altered only slightly.

In 2005, Tom describes 'indelible moments of grace', the phrase also used by Colum McCann, while performing the punishing, demeaning duties of taxi driver. In this way, the *Random Notes* written about Petit on 9/11 are the ur-text for the thoughts of Tom in 2005:

> Indelible moments of grace, tiny exaltations, unexpected miracles. Gliding through Times Square at three-thirty in the morning, and all the traffic is gone, and suddenly you're alone in the center of the world [...] Or traveling across the Brooklyn Bridge at the very moment a full moon rises into the arch [...] and you forget that you live down here on earth and imagine you're flying, that the cab has wings and you're actually flying through space.[23]

The vitality and vigour that come from the unmediated initial impulse of the ur-text are critically important to Auster. In 1983,

---

[22]Ibid., p. 29.
[23]Ibid., pp. 29–30.

he translated and published fragments and notes by Stephane Mallarmé, which were to form a four-part poem about the death of Mallarmé's beloved son Anatole at the age of eight.[24] The fragments were kept in a red box, Mallarmé's own red notebook. In his explanatory essay about the work of translating them, Auster defined his approach:

> [T]he notes are a kind of ur-text, the raw data of the poetic process... For here we find a language of immediate contact, a syntax of abrupt, lightning shifts that still manages to maintain a sense, and in their brevity, the sparse presence of their words, we are given a rare and early example of isolated words able to span the enormous mental spaces that lie between them – [...] so densely charged that these tiny particles of language could somehow leap out of themselves and catch hold of the succeeding cliff-edge of thought.[25]

The 'ur-text' Auster describes, the 'tiny particles' of language that are 'able to span the enormous mental spaces that lie between them' conjure an image of a tiny figure dressed in black, apparently dancing in mid-air and yet spanning the impossible distance between the tops of two tall towers. It is also, potentially, what Auster is attempting to find in his *Random Notes* written on 11 September 2001. The tentative quality of the prose need not necessarily be a mark of its failure, but an attempt to find words that 'leap out of themselves and catch hold of the succeeding cliff-edge of thought'. To that extent, Auster's non-fiction is a prompt, an aide-memoire for later fictional experimentation. However, the prompt is despairing and defeatist and so too is the later fiction.

Auster's daughter, on the subway beneath the Twin Towers on 11 September 2001, was saved. However, there is a connection between Mallarmé's fragments and Auster's own. In his 1982 essay, Auster said that the 'death of a child is the ultimate horror of every parent, an outrage against all we believe we can expect of life, little

---

[24]Stephane Mallarmé, *A Tomb for Anatole*, trans. Paul Auster (San Francisco: North Point Press,1983).
[25]Auster, 'Mallarmé's Son', in *The Red Notebook* (London: Faber & Faber, 1995), pp. 84–85.

though it is'.[26] It is clear that in his 'Random Notes' he is thinking about the possible 'outrage' that was so nearly his. And it is for these reasons that his fragmentary phrase 'the post-past' is not the glib aspiration that it might at first appear to be. It is Auster's manifesto for his future artistic endeavour. It is the unwritten 'raw data of the poetic process' that will become his subsequent novels. There is of course a fundamental paradox in what I am suggesting; Auster is both conditioned by and yet acting independently of the past. Yet, the apparent illogicality of the concept is held delicately within the competing words of Auster's post-past, each word dependent upon the other for relative meaning.

As Paul de Man suggested, 'modernity invests its trust in the power of the present moment as an origin, but discovers that, in severing itself from the past, it has at the same time severed itself from the present'. De Man cites the view of Nietzsche that, unlike animals who live in a state of pastlessness, man cannot escape the chain that tethers him to that past. So it is either possible, as de Man suggests, to 'resort to paradoxical formulations, such as defining the modernity of a literary period as the manner in which it discovers the impossibility of being modern',[27] or to conceive of a way in which it is possible to accept both states of post and past simultaneously. This is what Auster does. He signals his dependence on and influence by what went before – his teenage trauma at watching a friend die – at the same time as saying that a new trauma, familiar to him as a latent sensation, will determine his future modes of thought and action.

The events of 9/11, about which Auster said, 'I'm not over it yet, and I don't think I ever will be', mark a fundamental and pivotal moment in his writing, but the notion of the Miltonian before and after is a concept that he first wrote about in the 1980s. In *City of Glass*, which forms part of *The New York Trilogy*, a sense is introduced of a modus vivendi before tragedy, and an altered state of living afterwards:

> In *Paradise Lost*, for example, each key word has two meanings – one before the fall and one after the fall. To illustrate his point,

---

[26]Ibid., p. 86.
[27]Paul de Man, 'Literary History and Literary Modernity', *Daedalus*, vol. 99, no. 2, *Theory in Humanistic Studies* (Spring 1970), pp. 384–404, 385.

Stillman isolated several of those words – sinister, serpentine, delicious – and showed how their prelapsarian use was free of moral connotations, whereas their use after the fall was shaded, ambiguous, informed by a knowledge of evil. [...] The story of the Garden, therefore, not only records the fall of man, but the fall of language.[28]

Auster's sense of the fallen man/fallen language resonates with Don DeLillo's notion, examined in the previous chapter, of the falling/fallen man and the realization that 'nothing is next' because everything is now in the post-lapsarian after. The before and the after of a traumatic event is a scenario Auster revisited after *The New York Trilogy*, in his novel *Leviathan*. His character Ben Sachs does not suffer so much a metaphorical fall from grace, as a real one. On that most symbolically weighty of days, 4 July 1986, Independence Day and the 200th anniversary of the adoption of the Declaration of Independence, he falls off a fire escape at a party. (*Leviathan* is dedicated to Don DeLillo, who was to experiment so memorably with a falling man more than a decade later):

I was a dead man falling through the air, and even though I was technically still alive I was dead, as dead as a man who's been buried in his grave.[29]

Auster presented this metaphorical and literal fall as pivotal to Sachs's life, defining as it did a before and an after:

His body mended, but he was never the same after that. In those few seconds before he hit the ground, it was as if Sachs lost everything. His entire life flew apart in midair, and from that moment until his death four years later, he never put it back together again.[30]

Austerian characters who do not manage to shed their pasts need to be rescued from them. At the end of *The Locked Room*, the story

[28]Paul Auster, 'City of Glass', in *The New York Trilogy* (1985; London: Faber & Faber, 1987), p. 43.
[29]Paul Auster, *Leviathan* (London: Faber & Faber, 1992) p. 117.
[30]Ibid., p. 107.

that formed part of *The New York Trilogy*, the narrator stands in a railway station tearing out the pages of a red notebook belonging to his former friend, the writer Fanshawe. Fanshawe has pursued the narrator, who in turn had pursued him. The narrator has rescued himself and, as a consequence, Fanshawe's first wife Sophie must be rescued too:

> [B]y devoting herself to a man who was no longer there, she would be forced to live in the past, and whatever future she might want to build for herself would be tainted by the role she had to play: the official widow, the dead writer's muse, the beautiful heroine in a tragic story. No one wants to be part of a fiction, and even less so if that fiction is real.[31]

It is worth noting, in passing, that a red notebook appears many times in Auster's fiction, and *The Red Notebook* is the title of his own collection of thoughts and ideas, including the essay 'Why Write?'. As *The Locked Room* concludes, Fanshawe appears to be subsuming the narrator's own life. It is only by destroying Fanshawe's red book that the narrator is able to reclaim his own existence. In an additional literary flourish, as Malcolm Bradbury pointed out, Fanshawe is the name of an 'early fantastic novel' by Nathaniel Hawthorne,[32] a writer cited many times in Paul Auster's work. Tom's fumbling attempts to describe to Nathan (another variation on Nathaniel) and to his employer Harry those moments of transcendence, the entry into the 'fullness and thickness of the world' find new and potent force in Harry's notion of 'The Hotel Existence'. Essentially Harry's existentialist longing is for a place where anyone can go and start to live a new life 'inside your dreams'. The new existence, lived within a dream, is another variation on Auster's literary hyperparallelisms; it is where alternative trajectories to those endured in reality can be explored.

---

[31]Paul Auster, 'The Locked Room', in *The New York Trilogy* (1985; London: Faber & Faber, 1987), pp. 226–227.
[32]Malcolm Bradbury, *The Modern American Novel* (1983; Oxford: Oxford University Press, 1992), p. 259.

Part two: *The Brooklyn Follies* and *Man in the Dark* – Auster's literary hyperparallelisms

Auster has said many times that his favourite work of literature is Cervantes's *Don Quixote*. Tom's search for the post-past is oddly picaresque in that it is arguably linear, albeit in a postmodern style. So, too, is he the servant of several masters such as Harry and ultimately his wife. To that extent his quest is redolent of Don Quixote's. *The Brooklyn Follies* is, perhaps surprisingly, the most comic in tone of all Auster's novels too, even though it is the only one to focus explicitly on the events of 9/11. The title itself points to the curious, extravagant frivolity of Stephen Sondheim's *Follies*, with its existential showstopper of a number *I'm Still Here*. It is Tom, Nathan and Harry's theme too (the characters who could so easily have had the everyman names of Tom, *Dick* and Harry but for Auster's decision to include the Nathan/Nathaniel Hawthorne reference), and each of them is driven by variations on a desire to celebrate the essential pointlessness of life's quest. 'The Hotel Existence', cited by Harry, is the perfect endgame on which to focus that quest. This section of the novel is written in dramatic dialogue; in other words, it is as solidly set in the present tense as it is possible to be and comes complete with stage directions:

> HARRY (closing his eyes; pressing his forefingers against his temples): It's all coming back to me now. The Hotel Existence. [...] I had never been inside a hotel, but I had walked past enough of them on my trips downtown with my mother to know that they were special places, fortresses that protected you from the squalor and meanness of everyday life ... A hotel represented the promise of a better world, a place that was more than just a place, but an opportunity, a chance to live inside your dreams.[33]

Harry's notion of 'The Hotel Existence' is never fulfilled, indeed it is suggested that he always knew that it would not be. He dies in acute distress, running after the taxi in which his traitorous,

---

[33]Auster, *The Brooklyn Follies*, p. 101.

blackmailing lover and accomplice are escaping. But Harry leaves Tom a large bequest in his will to buy his own Hotel Existence: an airy, light-filled apartment. To that extent it is possible to argue that Tom finds his post-past, with the acquisition of his new apartment, his new wife and his soon-to-be-born child. They are the perfect accoutrements with which to soldier on in his Quixote-like mission. But there are reasons to suppose that Tom does not find a happy post-past, but merely a temporary, transitory pre-future.

The Brooklyn Follies ends as Nathan leaves hospital after suffering a suspected heart attack. For twenty-four hours he has been lying in a hospital bed, 'alone with my fear and morbid imagination as my blood gradually told the story of what had or hadn't happened to me'. As his secular dark night of the soul grinds on, three fellow patients appear and disappear one by one: Dickensian ghosts of past, present and yet-to-come, dressed in hospital gowns. First an Egyptian taxi driver, then a thirty-nine-year-old roofer and finally a seventy-eight-year-old retired carpenter. We assume that the first dies before the night is over and the second is transferred to the cardiac unit because it's 'pretty serious'. Nathan comes to view the bed next to him as 'haunted by some mysterious form of erasure, blotting out the men who had lain on it and ushering them into a realm of darkness and oblivion'.[34]

It is while thinking about the bare bed's sinister role as the conduit for death that Nathan has an epiphany, what he calls 'the single most important idea I had ever had'. His idea is that he should form a company called 'Bios Unlimited', a publishing house that will create books that resurrect the forgotten people in words, 'to rescue the stories and facts and documents before they disappeared – and shape them into a continuous narrative, the narrative of a life'.[35] It is not life insurance, the kind of work practised by Nathan in his former life, but what he thinks of as 'biography insurance'.

Nathan is discharged from hospital, so suffused with joy to be alive that he says he wants to scream:

It was eight o'clock when I stepped out onto the street, eight o'clock on the morning of September 11, 2001 – just forty-six

---

[34]Ibid., p. 300.
[35]Ibid., p. 301.

minutes before the first plane crashed into the North Tower of the World Trade Center. [...]

But for now it was still eight o'clock, and as I walked along the avenue under that brilliant blue sky, I was happy, my friends, as happy as any man who had ever lived.[36]

These are the dying moments before the 'break with the past', and the reader knows it. No Austerian plot trickery or coincidental contrivance is possible, now that a new parallelism exists: Nathan's ignorance of what will happen in forty-six minutes matched by the reader's twin awareness of his ignorance and anticipation of the catastrophe. Auster has placed the reader in a state of pre-future, along with Tom. Paul de Man's definition of the paradoxical notion of 'defining the modernity of a literary period as the manner in which it discovers the impossibility of being modern' comes to mind, for the reader if not the imaginary characters. No one can avoid what is to happen in forty-six minutes time, other of course than the characters that have yet to be invented but who will appear in the later novel *Man in the Dark*, analysed later in the chapter.

It is made very clear that *The Brooklyn Follies* is Tom's book; he is, after all, 'the long-suffering hero of these Brooklyn Follies' and, like Kafka's doll, he is changed by his experiences and choices. Auster is signalling that this book, the one we are reading, is one of the 'biography insurance' policies that Nathan was planning on that bright September morning. Tom is one of those who will die in Auster's version of the terrible events of 9/11. To support my view that Paul Auster intended that Tom should not have a future, but merely what I am terming a *pre*-future (i.e. a limited phase in which the future is envisaged but not experienced or in which a Freudian *Nachträglichkeit* is anticipated but not delivered), I would point to Auster's tradition of establishing a pattern of including books within his books, taking on either the title or the contents of work that his characters are writing or have read. In *Leviathan*, Peter Aaron names the book that we are reading after the book that his dead friend Ben Sachs was writing. 'To mark what will never exist, I have given my book the same title that Sachs was planning to use for

---

[36]Ibid., pp. 303–304.

his: Leviathan.'[37] It is the book that we have been reading, but it is also the book that Aaron has written and hands to the FBI agent to explain what Sachs has done. In Auster/Aaron's words, a book marks something that 'will never exist' and the dead can be granted a new existence by the mere fact of their story being recorded within its covers. In *City of Glass*, the slowly unravelling Quinn writes everything down in his red notebook, the same name Auster gave to his 1995 collection of interviews and essays in which he reflects upon his own work. So there is consistent evidence to support my view that if *The Brooklyn Follies* is the book of Tom's life, if he is 'the long-suffering hero of these Brooklyn Follies', as Auster tells us he is, it can be extrapolated that it is Auster's intention that *The Brooklyn Follies* is the story of someone no longer living (in as much as any fictional character can be described as 'living', of course). In other words, this is Nathan's first biography of the 'forgotten people', the invisible people whose lives are not mourned publicly. *The Brooklyn Follies* is Paul Auster's fictional 'Portrait of Grief' for solid, stolid Tom Wood by his mercurial, unpredictable, unreliable uncle, Nathan Glass.

Man in the Dark, Auster's 2008 novel, is set in a fictional future or a parallel present, but most decidedly not the past. It is Titus's book, the story of a young man kidnapped in Iraq and beheaded by his captors. Titus, like Tom, had wanted to be a writer. Both discovered that they did not have the ability. *Man in the Dark* is the book of the man who could not write his own, just as *The Brooklyn Follies* is. In *Man in the Dark*'s two hyperparallel worlds, there are two deaths, each of the protagonist. Owen Brick, the invention of Auster's similarly invented August Brill, is 'the protagonist of tonight's story'.[38] Brick is killed by Federal troops who have gathered in the street with machine guns:

> The first bullet hits him in the leg, and he falls down, clutching the wound as blood spurts onto his fingers. Before he can inspect the damage and see how badly he is hurt, a second bullet goes straight through his right eye and out the back of his head. And that is the end of Owen Brick, who leaves the world in silence with no chance to say a last word or think a last thought.[39]

[37]Auster, *Leviathan*, p. 142.
[38]Paul Auster, *Man in the Dark* (London: Faber & Faber, 2008), p. 102.
[39]Ibid., p. 118.

Owen Brick's inability to 'think a last thought' is curiously redolent of Courtney Cowart's description of being in the path of the collapsing South Tower on 9/11: 'I see it barreling toward me 1,368 feet high. [...] I think in milliseconds. I think, "When it gets to me I'll die or live. I have time for one more thought." '[40] Brick, denied that one 'last thought', has a hyperparallel counterpart in the form of August Brill; it is Brill, after all, who invents Brick as he lies, man in the dark, unable to sleep. But there is an overarching protagonist: Titus, the former boyfriend of Brill's granddaughter Katya. Titus, whose death is announced at the beginning of the novel and whose slaughter is enacted at the end, is the original man in the dark, not insomniac Brill. Titus is the man who has been forced into darkness, as 'a hood has been placed over his head'. Titus is the eponymous hero of this novel and Titus, like Brick, is murdered. Auster described the inspiration for this novel as the 2000 presidential election:

> I felt so frustrated and disgusted and outraged and angry and depressed about what happened because Al Gore won the election. He was voted President of the United States and through political and legal manoeuvrings the Republicans stole it from him and I've had this eerie sense for the past 8 years that we hopped off the tracks of reality.[41]

It is the same inspiration found by Richard Ford for *The Lay of the Land*, indeed he used a similar phrase to define the times: 'the Republicans stole the government'.[42] Ford used the events both to define a hiatus, a stalled period in history, a lacuna, a time without meaning and also as territory in which he could take refuge as a writer. Auster, however, uses it differently. His response is to create a double landscape, forming a fictional parallel time set in contradistinction to its real-world counterpart. Lou Frisk, who

[40]Courtney Cowart, *An American Awakening: From Ground Zero to Katrina: The People We Are Free to Be* (New York: Seabury Books, 2008), p. 11.

[41]Paul Auster, interviewed by George Miller, `Paul Auster: *Man in the Dark*', Faber Books SoundCloud, November 2008, https://soundcloud.com/faberbooks/paul-auster-man-in-the-dark [accessed 24 May 2016].

[42]Richard Ford, interviewed by Chas Bowie, *Portland Mercury*, 19 October 2006, http://www.portlandmercury.com/portland/richard-ford-interview/Content?oid=73912 [accessed 16 May 2013].

demands of Owen Brick that he murder the creator of his story
August Brill, defines that parallel world:

> There's no single reality, Corporal. There are many realities. [...]
> and they all run parallel to one another, worlds and anti-worlds,
> worlds and shadow-worlds, and each world is dreamed or
> imagined or written by someone in another world. Each world is
> the creation of a mind.[43]

Lou Frisk's words are startlingly similar to those expressed by the
unnamed aide to George W. Bush in 2004, in one of the keynotes
of this study, who claimed that superpowers are entitled to invent
their own realities. Indeed, I would suggest that these are the words
that Auster is referencing in his novel: 'That's not the way the world
really works anymore ... We're an empire now, and when we act, we
create our own reality.'[44]

The unnamed aide was assumed to be Karl Rove. Lou Frisk/
Karl Rove: interchangeable aggressively mono-syllabled names,
interchangeable grandiloquent views. Karl Rove notoriously
challenged reality in 2003 by arranging for President Bush to be
deposited on an aircraft carrier, with the deliberately misleading
banner declaring 'Mission Accomplished' behind his head. As I
outlined in Chapter 1, the attempts to invent new realities were just
as ambitious in real-life America as they ever were or are in Auster's
creative mind. To construct his parallel world, Auster has seventy-
two-year-old writer August Brill imagine a time when America is at
war with itself, which, in the context of America's formative history,
is not such a stretch after all. In this twin world, Owen Brick, a
professional magician, is charged with the task of killing his creator
Brill. It should be stressed that Auster believed that America really
was at war with itself, although it was a war of ideology. This, in
other words, is no idle exercise in the fantastical. Auster suggested
that his vision of a parallel world stemmed from his sense that

---

[43]Auster, *Man in the Dark*, pp. 68–69.
[44]Ron Suskind, 'Faith, Certainty and the Presidency of George W. Bush', *New York Times Magazine*, 17 October 2004. At the time the words of an unnamed aide to George W. Bush, but later attributed to Karl Rove, http://www.nytimes.com/2004/10/17/magazine/17BUSH.html?_r=0 [accessed 26 March 2013].

America was living two distinct lives. To that extent, Auster is both unhooking the United States from its past and imagining a different present and future:

> We've been living in a parallel world. The world we asked for is one in which Al Gore is now finishing his second term, the US never invaded Iraq and possibly 9/11 never happened either. And so this sense of living in a real unreal world inspired me to make this story and tell it through Brill because in a sense of course it's an exaggeration. I'm not predicting a real civil war in the US but I do think we are in a civil war of a kind. Not with bombs and bullets but with words and ideas. And the country is very divided and the two halves are not able to speak to each other anymore.[45]

Explicitly, there is no sense of a nation with a past here; Auster is dealing in Tom's 'post-past'. And since this is Titus's book, as *The Brooklyn Follies* was Tom's book, all roads lead to the section in the novel when Titus is slaughtered, forever 'live' on video. In describing the final, horrific hours of Titus, Auster reverts entirely to the present tense. The language, which is brutal and explicit, is even more sickening to read in the subsequent context of the many beheadings in Iraq and Syria carried out by the group calling itself Islamic State. In the late summer of 2014, US journalists James Foley and Steven Sotloff were murdered; British aid workers David Haines and Alan Henning were executed later that same year. In the summer of 2015, Herve Cornara was beheaded at a factory in France by a delivery driver, and in August 2015, Islamic State executed the archaeologist and historian Khaled al-Asaad, the keeper of cultural artefacts in the ancient city of Palmyra:

> When the head is finally severed from the body, the executioner lets the hatchet fall to the floor. The other man removes the hood from Titus's head, and then a third man takes hold of Titus's long red hair and carries the head closer to the camera. Blood is dripping everywhere. Titus is no longer quite human. He has

---

[45]Paul Auster, interviewed by George Miller, 'Paul Auster: *Man in the Dark*', Faber Books SoundCloud, November 2008, https://soundcloud.com/faberbooks/paul-auster-man-in-the-dark [accessed 24 May 2016].

become the idea of a person, a person and not a person, a dead bleeding thing: une nature morte.

The man holding the head backs away from the camera, and a fourth man approaches with a knife. One by one, working with great speed and precision, he stabs out the boy's eyes.[46]

It is worth noting that Auster uses the *nature morte/natura morta* motif deployed by DeLillo in *Falling Man* to signify arrested time, as well as the 'head as symbol of the whole' trope that I will go on to discuss in greater detail in Chapter 4.

It is useful to refer back to Auster's 1983 essay on Mallarmé's son at this point. In it, Auster likens the effect upon him of reading the fragments of grief written by Mallarmé to seeing the final portrait painted by Rembrandt of his son, who was of course called Titus:

[I]t is almost impossible for us to look at that last painting: the dying Titus, barely twenty years old, his face so ravaged by disease that he looks like an old man. It is important to imagine what Rembrandt must have felt as he painted that portrait; to imagine him staring into the face of his dying son and being able to keep his hand steady enough to put what he saw onto the canvas. If fully imagined, the act becomes unthinkable.[47]

Auster's Titus is introduced at the beginning of *Man in the Dark* in just those terms. Once again, Auster finds recourse in an earlier ur-text and reinvents in literary form:

His parents named him after Rembrandt's son, the little boy of the paintings, the golden-haired child in the red hat, the daydreaming pupil puzzling over his lessons, the little boy who turned into a young man ravaged by illness and who died in his twenties, just as Katya's Titus did. It's a doomed name, a name that should be banned from circulation forever.[48]

In forcing us to confront the video of Titus being butchered, sliced and dehumanized, Auster is reinventing the ordeal that he believes

---

[46]Auster, *Man in the Dark*, p. 176.

[47]Auster, 'Mallarmé's Son', p. 86.

[48]Auster, *Man in the Dark*, p. 2.

Rembrandt must have endured as he painted his dying son; his 'being able to keep his hand steady enough to put what he saw onto the canvas'.

In his use of extreme violence, his decision to have Titus's murderers stab out his eyes, Auster alludes to classical literature and Shakespearian tragedy, as well as his own numerous references over many years to eye injuries suffered by baseball stars. Richard Ford also used the image of catastrophic damage done to the eyes in baseball accidents in his *Sportswriter* trilogy, and in Chapter 4, I will analyse the use of the injured eye in novels by Kamila Shamsie and Nadeem Aslam. *Man in the Dark* extracts the motif of damage done to the eyes from its previously all-American sporting past and places it firmly in the territory of the modern-day terrorist. These injuries are no longer accidental; they are more shocking for being deliberate. *Man in the Dark* is Auster's most explicitly violent novel. Like Nadeem Aslam in his novel *The Wasted Vigil*, Auster exploits the traditional Afghani contest of 'buzkashi', polo with a goat carcass, to shockingly violent effect. In Aslam's rendition, Benedikt, the former Soviet soldier, is torn limb from limb:

> When the rifle shot comes he thinks they have fired into him, but no, he hasn't been shot, and now a dozen hands grab onto his limbs and hair and clothing and he feels himself being lifted unevenly off the ground.[49]

In *Man in the Dark*, Auster deploys the same hideous game, albeit unnamed, to bring about the death of a beautiful, left-wing 'troublemaker' in the Second World War. She was subjected to public execution because she dared disobey the guards:

> She was drawn and quartered. With long chains attached to both her wrists and both her ankles, she was led into the yard, made to stand at attention as the chains were attached to four jeeps pointing in four different directions, and then the commandant gave the order for the drivers to start their engines. [...] the woman didn't cry out, didn't make a sound as one limb after another was pulled off her body.[50]

---

[49]Nadeem Aslam, *The Wasted Vigil* (London: Faber & Faber, 2008), p. 366.
[50]Auster, *Man in the Dark*, p. 121.

As in the death of Titus, it seems important to Auster to point out that the woman 'didn't make a sound'. Neither Titus nor the woman protest or plead as they are publicly slaughtered; they come mutely to death. Perhaps, as I suggest in the following chapter with reference to Nadeem Aslam, Auster was reluctant to indulge in the descriptions of pain that must surely have resulted from the violent scenes he was describing.

Surprisingly, *Man in the Dark* ends on an oddly optimistic note, as Brill and his daughter Miriam smile together about the one line of poetry written by Rose Hawthorne that they think was any good: 'As the weird world rolls on.' In Austerian terms, the fact that the world keeps muddling along could be regarded as a victory in itself. But where *Man in the Dark* ends in its oddly jaunty way, *Sunset Park* begins in altogether bleaker, more introverted and nihilistic style. The temporal trajectory developed by Auster from the contemporaneous essay fragment on the day of 9/11 to the post-past of *The Brooklyn Follies* and the hyperparallel pre-future of the *Man in the Dark* culminates in the futureless now of *Sunset Park*.

Part three: *Sunset Park*, silence and the futureless now

Sunset Park, Auster's 2010 novel, is set in the toxic climate of sub-prime mortgage crises, evoking thoughts of refugees and the homeless. The only thriving business is in 'trashing out'; the clearing out of abandoned homes on the orders of local banks who now own the buildings and subcontract their hideously misnamed 'home preservation' services. It is another interregnum, this time between the election of Barack Obama and his inauguration. It is a world of negatives where fates are determined by things not done. Auster's character, the writer Renzo, is 'toying with' the idea of writing an essay about 'the things that don't happen, the lives not lived, the wars not fought, the shadow worlds that run parallel to the world we take to be the real world, the not-said and the not-done, the not-remembered'.[51]

---

[51]Paul Auster, *Sunset Park* (London: Faber & Faber, 2010), p. 153.

In this post-apocalyptic landscape, Miles Heller, his name as so often in Auster's work an extended embodiment of his predicament and state of mind, is one of those employed to 'trash out'. He finds himself compelled to document the detritus, to record the abandoned things on camera. His work is the bleak, dark postmodern version of Nathan Glass's nobler endeavour to produce benign biographical memorials of the forgotten dead. Miles Heller's work is to document the failure, not of the accidentally forgotten but of the wilfully vanished:

> [H]e has taken it upon himself to document the last, lingering traces of those scattered lives in order to prove that the vanished families were once here, that the ghosts of people he will never see and never know are still present in the discarded things strewn about their empty houses.[52]

Mired in other people's abandoned things, Heller tries to ration his own possessions, a job he is successful at apart from when it comes to limiting his books: 'the only luxury he allows himself is buying books, paperback books, mostly novels, American novels, British novels, foreign novels in translation, but in the end books are not luxuries so much as necessities and reading is an addiction he has no wish to be cured of'.[53] Miles's assertion that books are 'necessities' resonates with Auster's own admission in the past that, for him, writing is 'no longer an act of free will for me; it's a matter of survival'.[54] It is no accident that Miles meets his girlfriend Pilar in the park, not because they are introduced to each other but because both are reading *The Great Gatsby*.

Miles's obsessive acquisition of books is matched by a neurotic accumulation of photographs. As he clears rubbish from 'orphaned homes', Miles meticulously documents everything he finds on camera. As the novel opens, he calculates that he has already amassed thousands of these pictures:

> He understands that it is an empty pursuit, of no possible benefit to anyone, and yet each time he walks into a house, he senses

---

[52]Ibid., p. 3.
[53]Ibid., p. 7.
[54]James Campbell, 'The mighty Quinn', *Guardian*, 12 November 2005, http://www.guardian.co.uk/books/2005/nov/12/fiction.shopping [accessed 6 May 2013].

that the things are calling out to him, speaking to him in the voices of the people who are no longer there, asking him to be looked at one last time before they are carted away.[55]

It is an idea reminiscent of the objectification relentlessly and endlessly pursued by the Italian still-life artist Giorgio Morandi, detailed in the previous chapter. Morandi's obsessive assembly and reassembly of *la natura morta* or dead nature was transfigured by Don DeLillo into a representation of the Twin Towers themselves, so that, in DeLillo's imagination, the fallen towers are recreated in two of Morandi's paintings. But where DeLillo represents objects as missing towers, Auster represents them as spaces, gaps, 'people who are no longer there'. As I will explore at the end of this chapter, the idea of missing objects and empty space prefigures Auster's words at the conclusion of his memoir *Winter Journal*, when, as he walks across Brooklyn Bridge, he 'sees' empty spaces and hears voices that are no longer there.

Miles Heller, so driven by the desire to own books and to read, finds himself fatally uncommunicative. For a character both silent and oddly passive, it is important to note that Auster ensures that major decisions and actions are determined by violence, often committed by him. Miles is an intellectual and has received the best education and yet he is curiously lacking in vocabulary. He amasses not words but pictures of the 'abandoned things'; he does not make decisions for considered reasons, but is forced to act as violent deeds alter his circumstances. Miles has left home because he feels responsible for the death of his stepbrother, killed when Miles pushes him into the road. He leaves Florida when he is assaulted and threatened by his girlfriend's family:

[T]he choice was made for him by a large fist that knocked him down and commanded him to run from Florida to a place called Sunset Park. Just another roll of the dice, then, another lottery pick scooped out of the black metal urn, another fluke in a world of flukes and endless mayhem.[56]

---

[55] Auster, *Sunset Park*, p. 5.
[56] Ibid., pp. 55–56.

Finally and decisively, he destroys his chance to reinvent himself when he punches a policeman in the jaw. Once again, the man who loves to read cannot find words to communicate. There are connections to be drawn here between Miles and Herman Melville's Billy Budd; Miles, ostensibly and apparently a 'good' man, is unable to demonstrate that goodness. At the same time, in the absence of a willingness or ability to explain himself verbally, he is fatally drawn to catastrophic acts of demonstrative violence.

Miles's missing vocabulary is territory that Auster has explored before. In *The Brooklyn Follies*, Nathan's niece's young daughter Lucy refuses to speak when she arrives in New York. But Lucy's silence is a powerful silence. It allows her to exert control over those around her who cajole and exhort her to speak. But by the time Auster came to write *Sunset Park*, Miles's failure to speak has become a passive and debilitating silence. The lack of vocabulary is a conundrum that other writers have faced in attempting to write about 9/11 and twenty-first-century catastrophe. The French writer Frédéric Beigbeder in his 9/11 novel *Windows on the World* wrestled with the difficulty of finding a verb to use for 'parking a plane in a building'. As noted by Kristiaan Versluys,[57] his character finally comes up with a play on the French word 'atterrissage' which means to crash-land, and manipulates it to include the vowels 'o' and 'u' instead of 'e' so that *atterrissage* becomes *attourrissage*, trapping within it the French word for tower. In a trans-lingual reflection on the limitations of vocabulary, in the French edition, Beigbeder writes:

> Nous espérons que vous avez fait un agréable voyage en compagnie d'Air France et regrettons de ne plus jamais vous revoir sur nos lignes, ni ailleurs. Préparez-vous à l'attourrissage.[58]

But in the English edition, Beigbeder satisfies himself with a truncated version of the text and makes no play on the imagined

[57]Kristiaan Versluys, *Out of the Blue: September 11 and the Novel* (New York: Columbia University Press, 2009), p. 142.
[58]Frédéric Beigbeder, *Windows on the World*, French edition (Paris: Éditions Grasset & Fasquelle, 2003), p. 8 h.58.

verb to 'park a plane in a building'. 'Preparez-vous a l'attourrissage' is simply missing from the translation:

> We hope you've enjoyed your flight with Air France and regret that we will not have the pleasure of seeing you on our airlines, or indeed anywhere else, again.[59]

It is perhaps Auster's ability or at least willingness to try to find the words that so displeased the critic James Wood. Viewed in this light, the piercing criticism he levelled at Auster that there was 'not enough silence, alas' becomes a little petulant. His remonstration that other postmodernists, as it were, do silence better begins to sound oddly competitive:

> For Blanchot, as indeed for Beckett, language is always announcing its invalidity. Texts stutter and fragment, shred themselves around a void. Perhaps the strangest element of Auster's reputation as an American postmodernist is that his language never registers this kind of absence at the level of the sentence. The void is all too speakable in Auster's work.[60]

I am not convinced that Wood has made his case here, that Auster's silence is the void of the inadequate writer rather than the postmodernist referencer of language's own inadequacies. Auster himself has pointed to the imperative to write about the small in response to the large, such as 9/11 and, in the case of *Leviathan*, has made the connection between the small *word* and silence in the figure of Peter Aaron, the man who 'anguishes and struggles over each sentence' and for whom '... the smallest word is surrounded by acres of silence'. I would suggest that this is what Auster is reaching for in his characters' recourse to muteness: that, and focusing on the small details, gestures and words. Speaking in 2012, Auster defined explicitly how the artist must respond to 9/11:

> [H]e must continue to do his work ... Making up stories, fictions, whether films or novels or narrative poems, it's all about the

---

[59]Frédéric Beigbeder, *Windows on the World*, English edition, trans. Frank Wynne (London: Harper Perennial, 2005), p. 8 h.58.
[60]Wood, 'Shallow Graves'.

sanctity of the individual, which is what our democracies are supposedly all about, upholding the rights of the individual. And if we don't have people chronicling the lives of the individuals out there, then we become monolithic states. So therefore the job of the writer is to think small, pay attention and communicate what's out there, what people are doing.[61]

To 'think small' is Auster's drive. That is not to say that Auster registers silence by heaping up yet more words around it. And in any event, a lack of words has not always been seen as a limitation in Auster's work. *The Brooklyn Follies'* Lucy is a case in point. Silence at times appears to express a sense of solidarity with others, of shared experience and of corporate suffering. Indeed in an interview included in *The Red Notebook* and dated 1989–90, he stated that solitude is explicitly not a state of misery:

> [S]olitude is a rather complex term for me; it's not just a synonym for loneliness or isolation. Most people tend to think of solitude as a rather gloomy idea, but I don't attach any negative connotations to it. It's a simple fact, one of the conditions of being human, and even if we're surrounded by others we essentially live our lives alone: real life takes place inside us.[62]

In the notes Auster wrote on 11 September 2001, he slightly perversely included a reflection on the passengers of a subway train. He described men with briefcases, women with Bibles, children with textbooks, pan-handlers, deaf-mutes and silent men. And then the train stops:

> the lights go out, the fans stop whirring and everyone sits in silence, waiting for the train to start moving again. Never a word from anyone. Rarely even a sigh. My fellow New Yorkers sit in the dark, waiting with the patience of angels.[63]

---

[61]Paul Auster, interviewed by David Daley, Salon, 19 August 2012, http://www.salon.com/2012/08/19/paul_auster_i_think_of_the_right_wing_republicans_as_jihadists/ [accessed 26 February 2013].

[62]Paul Auster, interviewed by Larry McCaffery and Sinda Gregory, *The Red Notebook*, p. 142.

[63]Auster, 'Random Notes', p. 36.

There is something convivial, enduring, redemptive about this collegiate forbearance. New Yorkers are not renowned for either patience or angelic qualities, and why should they be? Yet, they are defined here in quasi-religious terms and their shared experience is noble. It is perhaps the one shard of redemptive light shed on his description of that day, and, briefly, the prose creeps into the sentimentalized territory occupied by McEwan, Ford, DeLillo and Lethem. But, by the time Auster came to write *Sunset Park*, the notion of shared solitude expressed in that 1989 interview and reiterated on 11 September 2001 had evaporated; Auster's aide-memoire of the 'patience of angels' had been excised and solitude no longer had its concomitant quality of solidarity. What remained was isolated despair.

Man in the Dark opens with August Brill's invented character, Owen Brick, trapped alone in a large hole, as isolated a place as it is possible to find. But Brick is released from his prison by the intervention of another character, and Brick is reunited with the world. *Man in the Dark*'s Beckettian experiment is merely a rehearsal for the figurative hole in which *Sunset Park*'s Miles Heller has tacitly agreed to be placed. His surrender is set against the backdrop of his actress mother's preparations to take on the stage role of Winnie, in Samuel Beckett's *Happy Days*. So while Owen Brick is freed from his hole, Mary-Lee, playing the part of Winnie, begins Act I, buried up to her waist, and Act II, buried up to her neck. The world of *Happy Days*, and implicitly its similarly perkily named counterpart *Sunset Park*, is, Auster writes, 'a world without darkness, a world of hot, unending light, a sort of purgatory, perhaps, a post-human wilderness of ever-diminishing possibilities, ever-diminishing movement ...'. [64] This is, of course, a description of *Sunset Park* itself, with its tragically mismatched name so full of promise, and its tragically mismatched occupants. So too is it a description of the novel's other wilderness, the savage purgatory of Florida with its 'hot, unending light' and its orphaned houses.

Sunset Park concludes with Miles's thoughts about the solider he has seen in a film, a soldier with missing hands unable to undress himself or go to bed without help. The missing, damaged eyes so familiar as a motif throughout Auster's work have become missing

---

[64] Auster, *Sunset Park*, p. 188.

hands. Miles's isolation is made ever more acute by his thought that, condemned to solitude as he is, it is a loneliness that requires the assistance of other people to allow him to live. This is absolute abandonment, not solitude with its calming, cheering, consoling spoonful of solidarity as experienced on Auster's subway train in 2001. And as Miles reflects on that absolute desolation, the two missing hands become missing buildings, the missing buildings become two, which in turn become the Twin Towers:

> [A]s the car travels across the Brooklyn Bridge and he looks at the immense buildings on the other side of the East River, he thinks about the missing buildings, the collapsed and burning buildings that no longer exist, the missing buildings and the missing hands, and he wonders if it is worth hoping for a future when there is no future, and from now on, he tells himself, he will stop hoping for anything and live only for now, this moment, this passing moment, the now that is here and then not here, the now that is gone forever.[65]

Finally, Auster has travelled from the past and the present of his earlier novels, via the post-past and pre-future of *The Brooklyn Follies*, to the futureless *now* that is *Sunset Park*. The past is not the territory of Martin Amis where it is defined as a 'huge palace in your mind, and you can go and visit all these different rooms and staircases and chambers',[66] but a past that is closed off and inaccessible. While *Man in the Dark* ended with Rose Hawthorne's invocation that the 'weird world rolls on', there is an abiding sense in *Sunset Park* that the world has finally stopped in its tracks. As I write, this remains Auster's last novel, the text which he describes as 'the first book that consciously I wrote in the now, capital N'.[67] Interviewed on the publication of *Sunset Park*, Auster confessed that the rich prolificacy of his earlier years had faded to a sense that to write another novel was no longer necessary. 'I used to have a backlog of stories', he said, 'but a few years ago I found the drawers

---

[65]Ibid., pp. 307–308.
[66]Martin Amis, 'Intoxicating, Free – the Novelist Life', *Daily Telegraph*, 15 October 2011.
[67]Auster, interviewed by David Daley, Salon, 19 August 2012.

were empty. I guess I'm getting to the point where I tell myself if I can't write another book it's not a tragedy. Does it matter if I publish 16 or 17 novels? Unless it's absolutely urgent, there's no point in writing.'[68] Auster's admission would seem to suggest that his characters' silence might become Auster's own silence. If that were true, James Wood would finally get his wish, although not for the reasons that he supposes.

Auster's description of *Sunset Park* as his first attempt to write in the absolute present tense referenced his instinct that he needed to retreat from the now into his own past:

> [*Sunset Park*] is the first book that consciously I wrote in the now, capital 'N,' and it was also immediate, all so much about our present moment, that the impulse was to go back afterwards.[69]

That impulse to 'go back' took Auster to memoir once again. *The Invention of Solitude*, the memoir about his father that launched Auster's career, now has a slightly mournful twin. *Winter Journal* is written in the second person, an odd literary indulgence that excludes the reader by its own self-absorption.

There is a sense in which *Winter Journal* is Auster's end-of-career biopsy on himself, examining narcissistically his motivations, his crises and his failures. As he put it, 'the way I seem to generate books is to bounce off the one I've done before, so to negate it, to do the opposite'.[70] Auster does indeed do the opposite and reverts from the present to the past. But, just as his childhood trauma and the trauma of 9/11 act as a frame narrative for his art, so too do *The Invention of Solitude* and *Winter Journal* (and its sequel *Report from the Interior*). And, in yet one more twinning, he offers another frame narrative as *Winter Journal* concludes: the dead of 9/11 transmuted into the dead of Bergen-Belsen. In a striking elision, Auster slides from his familiar walk across Brooklyn Bridge in which he no longer sees the towers (the precise viewpoint of the futureless Miles as he drives across the bridge in *Sunset Park*), to the day twenty-five years earlier when he visited Bergen-Belsen

---

[68] Auster, interviewed by Helena de Bertodano, *Telegraph*, 16 November 2010.
[69] Auster, interviewed by David Daley, *Salon*, 19 August 2012.
[70] Ibid.

with his German publisher Michael Naumann. The towers become a negative image of themselves, in which they exist but only in the shape of the now empty space they once occupied. The smell of smoke in his daughter's bedroom is evoked too, as it was in the ever-present non-fiction written on the day of the 9/11 attacks. But this time the prose is stronger, the tone more assertive, the faltering, formulaic note gone:

> [Y]ou can no longer make the crossing without thinking about the dead, about seeing the Towers burn from your daughter's bedroom window on the top floor of your house, about the smoke and ashes that fell onto the streets of your neighbourhood for three days following the attack, and the bitter unbreathable stench that forced you to shut all the windows of your house until the winds finally shifted away from Brooklyn on Friday [...] [T]he dead are still there, and the Towers are there as well – pulsating in memory, still present as an empty hole in the sky.[71]

Auster's sense of vanished towers still occupying the void they had left resonates with the design for the memorial that was eventually constructed at the 9/11 site. Although Michael Arad's design 'Reflecting Absence' was altered, fought over and altered again, he believed that its twin reflecting pools should express 'feelings of loss and absence' and that the two voids should be 'open and visible reminders of the absence'.[72] Still thinking about 'the dead', Auster allows the 9/11 victims to become the dead from the Second World War. It is as though, using his old defining phrase from *Mallarmé's Son*, his words 'leap out of themselves and catch hold of the succeeding cliff-edge of thought' until the dead from the towers become the dead in Belsen:

> You were standing on top of the grave of fifty thousand men. It didn't seem possible that so many dead bodies could fit into such a small space, and when you tried to imagine those bodies beneath you, the tangled corpses of fifty thousand young men

---

[71]Paul Auster, *Winter Journal* (London: Faber & Faber, 2012), p. 226.
[72]Michael Arad and Peter Walker, Extract from memorial design statement for 'Reflecting Absence', 9/11 Memorial website, http://www.911memorial.org/design-competition [accessed 23 May 2016].

packed into what must have been the deepest of deep holes, you began to grow dizzy at the thought of so much death, so much death concentrated in such a small patch of ground, and a moment later you heard the screams, a tremendous surge of voices rose up from the ground beneath you, and you heard the bones of the dead howl in anguish, howl in pain, howl in a roaring cascade of full-throated, ear-splitting torment.[73]

Auster concludes his memoir with the words, 'You have entered the winter of your life', and there is unquestionably a mournful sense that the post-past is upon him too, without any sense of a future unfolding. It is Tom's old concept of the post-past but pre-future, a time during which Freud's *Nachträglichkeit* has become detached from his past. In his attempts to define a literary hyperparallelism and to break the ties with the past, Auster has defined a bleak and unpromising landscape. He does not find refuge in the backwards glance, as Foer and DeLillo did, or seek the comfort of the individual's small life as Ford did. He has attempted something different: to unhitch himself from time altogether, and yet ultimately he fails. As Kermode put it so succinctly, 'poets think, and are of their time'.[74] Auster's attempt to make his characters 'independent of time and succession' is finally undone by Kermode's 'aevum', that is the overarching notion of duration of time which must, inevitably, lead to 9/11, which is in itself Auster's own end-stop. The peripeteia comes very late in *Sunset Park*; it is imagined in the final sentence as Nathan looks at his watch and notices, unknowingly, that it is 11 September 2001. But as Kermode pointed out, 'peripeteia depends on our confidence of the end; it is a disconfirmation followed by a consonance'.[75] Since Auster relies on the bleak consonance of his readers' knowledge of the event less than an hour after Nathan steps out into the sunshine, the absolute present tense must always dissolve into chaos and failure.

In the next chapter, I assess the way that writers from Pakistan have explored different timelines too, but in a far more politicized manner and on a much larger, broader scale. The effect in the hands

---

[73]Auster, *Winter Journal*, pp. 228–229.
[74]Kermode, *The Sense of an Ending*, p. 81.
[75]Ibid., p. 18.

of writers such as Kamila Shamsie and Nadeem Aslam is to widen our gaze beyond 9/11 and to expand the context. For Pakistani novelists, 9/11 is part of a long historical continuum, not, as in Auster's view, the defining moment for a generation and for him as an individual. For Shamsie and Aslam, 9/11 was a mid-point in history that had been developing for decades and would go on to have further drastic consequences.

4

The Long View

Introduction

The conscious myopia of novelists who focused their gaze on the day of the attacks would not do for Nadeem Aslam, Mohsin Hamid and Kamila Shamsie. By concentrating instead on 9/11's historical, social and political tributaries, they devised a form of response encapsulated by Aslam's striking aphorism: 'History is the third parent.'[1] To use journalistic shorthand, Shamsie, Hamid and Aslam were reading long-form geopolitical commentary while their American contemporaries were concentrating on the news pages. Aslam and Shamsie have pointed to failures by both Western journalists and politicians to anticipate 9/11, a consequence in part of the obsession with the 'continuous now' coined by Will Self and assessed in my introduction. (This is a different form of 'now' to Paul Auster's retreat in his late work to the 'now, capital N' which, as the previous chapter demonstrated, is highly politicized.) Shamsie, Aslam and Hamid shook their material out of the imprisoning grip of the traumatized present, so often the territory of the journalist, while at the same time eschewing the limitations of the sentimentalized past, or the alarums of dystopic prediction. Their fictions are deliberately provocative. As Mohsin Hamid told me: 'All fiction is dangerous and incendiary. That is the nature of making up tales.'[2]

Unlike other post-9/11 novelists who tried to shed journalistic methods before embarking on their fiction, Hamid and Shamsie made a virtue of them. Hamid, in particular, is conscious that his

---

[1]Nadeem Aslam, *The Blind Man's Garden* (London: Faber & Faber, 2013), p. 5.
[2]Mohsin Hamid, interviewed by Charlie Lee-Potter, 19 January 2016.

non-fiction and his fiction are starting to conflate: 'In my case the two are related. I tend to write journalism from a personal perspective, as I might a novel with myself as character. And I have grown to use the essayistic form more and more often within my novels as well.'[3] Interestingly, Hamid has admitted that he had no desire to write novels immediately after 9/11 and opted for journalism instead, but his growing sense that his fiction and non-fiction are melding seems to offer another potential route out of the confines posed by an immediate journalistic response to crisis. Hamid has spoken often about the all-important quality of empathy in his novels and his fiction/non-fiction hybrid has proved to be an effective means of reaching for it, with neither journalism nor fiction taking precedence: 'Both can [demonstrate empathy]', he told me. 'It is not a competition. Just as a song can move you and a poem can move you. And they often merge as well.'[4]

Shamsie's narrative drive has been to force the reader's gaze outwards and beyond, thereby seeking a more universal form of the empathy that Hamid described. She told me that, in her view, the United States has laid claim to the role of victimhood since 9/11, adopting an excessively narrow, narcissistic and xenophobic approach to history. It is a challenging position to take. After all, that narrow perspective is arguably the instinctive reaction in the face of attack. In microcosm, it is represented by novelist Jonathan Franzen's journalistic response to 9/11 in which he conceded the craving to 'reassert the ordinary, the trivial, and even the ridiculous in the face of instability and dread'.[5] The recourse to the quotidian was one of the methods chosen by Don DeLillo, and it would seem to be a perhaps inevitable consequence of trauma. It would certainly appear reasonable to empathize with Jonathan Lethem's admission of journalistic failure to describe the events of 11 September, when he asked, 'Can I bear to narrate this into normality, forty hours after they crumbled and fell? To craft a story: *and then, and then, and then*? [...] I'm failing and relieved to fail. I'm disgusted with myself for consenting to try.'[6] Yet Shamsie resorts to the quotidian and the

---

[3]Ibid.
[4]Ibid.
[5]Jonathan Franzen, 'Tuesday, and After', *New Yorker* (24 September 2001).
[6]Jonathan Lethem, 'To My Italian Friends', in *The Ecstasy of Influence* (2012; London: Jonathan Cape, 2013), p. 222.

personal at times too, but in a different place and with an alternative
point of view. Her short story 'Our Dead, Your Dead' takes place
at the time of the tenth anniversary of 9/11 in the Karachi offices of
StreetSmart magazine. In her story, members of staff are discussing
a new design for the magazine's cover, an image of the Twin Towers
with clusters of smoke trailing from the top containing words such
as 'Guantánamo, Drone Attacks, Waterboarding, Islamophobia,
Racial Profiling, Patriot Act'. One staff member complains that it is
an inappropriate cover, but only because it endorses the idea 'there
was something singular – something exceptional – about suffering
when it happened to Americans'.[7] Another person objects to the
cover too, but for unspoken reasons: on 9/11, her office was on
the second floor of the WTC's South Tower, a fact she has elected
to keep secret. They gather around the image on the designer's
computer screen, while a darkly comic bumper sticker on their
office wall underscores the bleakness of competing demands for
the status of victimhood: 'American had 9/11; England had 7/7;
India had 26/11; Pakistan has 24/7'. The story ends with yet more
bloodshed. Shamsie would argue that she is alerting her readers
to related tragedies being enacted elsewhere in the world, yet her
standpoint and Franzen's still seem estranged. Susan Sontag offered
a potential bridge between the two positions in her immediate
reaction to 9/11. Writing for the same edition of the *New Yorker* in
which Franzen expressed his craving for the ordinary, she suggested
a double recourse – grief *and* historical perspective in unison:

> [T]he politics of a democracy – which entails disagreement,
> which promotes candor – has been replaced by psychotherapy.
> Let's by all means grieve together. But let's not be stupid together.
> A few shreds of historical awareness might help us understand
> what has just happened, and what may continue to happen.[8]

Yet, just a 'few shreds of historical awareness' are not what Shamsie
is aiming for. She writes about 9/11 in the context of more than

---

[7]Kamila Shamsie, 'Our Dead, Your Dead', *Guardian*, 6 September 2011, http://
www.theguardian.com/books/2011/sep/06/9-11-stories-kamila-shamsie   [accessed
12 February 2016].
[8]Susan Sontag, 'Tuesday, and After', *The New Yorker* (24 September 2001).

half a century of international history, choosing as her fulcrum the physical and mental trauma suffered by victims of America's bombing of Nagasaki. Kamila Shamsie has fundamental objections to the way American writers, engulfed by the scale of the attacks, limited their scope. As Catherine Morley expressed it, they 'turned inward to depict fractured unions and broken homes'.[9] Shamsie's *Burnt Shadows* is a global novel in which the importance of connectivity is stressed and notions of American isolationism and exceptionalism are swept aside as diversions. *Burnt Shadows* forms part of the 'centrifugal literature of extraterritoriality' recommended by Michael Rothberg. Not only does it 'imagine how US citizenship looks and feels beyond the boundaries of the nation-state',[10] as Rothberg suggests that it should, but the work is placed in historical context in order to interrogate how we got to where we are now. The extraterritorial is a concept that Mohsin Hamid found very powerful when I put it to him: 'I think it's a wonderful idea. It shouldn't be a binding expectation on any particular writer of course. But it's a great notion.'[11] Shamsie believes that the extraterritorial versus what we might call the intraterritorial post-9/11 novel is creating a new literary border:

> I don't believe I have written a 9/11 novel. I have written a War on Terror novel. American and English writers seem to be more interested in the 9/11 novel and what 9/11 meant, rather than how events came to that day. There's an interesting distinction starting to form, where the United States will write about the day itself while Pakistani writers are more interested in what came before and after.[12]

When I asked Mohsin Hamid if he agreed with that demarcation, he conceded that, yes, he probably does. Given the fact that Shamsie

---

[9]Catherine Morley, 'How Do We Write about This? The domestic and the Global in the Post-9/11 Novel', *Journal of American Studies*, vol. 45, no. 4 (November 2011), pp. 717–731, p. 719.

[10]Michael Rothberg, 'A Failure of the Imagination: Diagnosing the Post-9/11 Novel: A Response to Richard Gray', *American Literary History*, vol. 21, no. 1 (Spring 2009), pp. 152–158, 158.

[11]MH, interviewed by CLP, 19 January 2016.

[12]Kamila Shamsie, interviewed by Charlie Lee-Potter, May 2009.

advocates a historicized approach to writing fiction, it is perhaps legitimate to apply that same historicized filter to writers themselves. The new Pakistani Anglophone novelists of the twenty-first-century coalesce around a distinct spur of postcolonialism's long trajectory. Fiction writers from Pakistan do not appear to be either enticed or limited by some of the expectations directed, for example, at Indian novelists writing in English, and they are providing a powerful literary voice with which to express the post-9/11 landscape. The Calcutta-born novelist Sunetra Gupta has complained that, by contrast, critics have attempted to shackle her with their continuing expectations that her novels should be 'providing a commodity, like a package holiday':[13]

> The fundamental expectation has been that a big Indian novel could be found that would somehow express the essence of India and deliver it to a Western audience. Those were essentially the terms under which Vikram Seth's *A Suitable Boy* was marketed – that it captured all of India within its covers. Trying to 'understand' India has become a global preoccupation. Indian writers in English are still seen as people who can (and should) mediate that understanding.[14]

Gupta's objection, shared by some of her contemporaries, is that Indian fiction is still the target of those beguiled by old ideas of the nation's colonial past, who define India as being post-Empire while still entrapping it. The Indian writer Amit Chaudhuri elaborated on Gupta's complaints, suggesting that it was the 9/11 attacks that provoked Pakistan's new novelists into rejecting the old pre- and post-colonial arguments and embarking on different forms of expression. Chaudhuri concluded that major contemporary novelists such as Hamid, Shamsie and Aslam 'are interestingly poised: implicated in both the unfolding and the unravelling of our age'.[15] He asserted that the old cultural context that informed the

---

[13]Sunetra Gupta, interviewed by Charlie Lee-Potter, 10 February 2016.
[14]SG, interviewed by CLP, 10 February 2016.
[15]Amit Chaudhuri, 'Qatrina and the Books', *London Review of Books*, vol. 31, no. 16 (27 August 2009), pp. 3–6, 3. http://www.lrb.co.uk/v31/n16/amit-chaudhuri/qatrina-and-the-books [accessed 22 February 2016].

early short stories of the long-established Pakistani writer Aamer Hussein came 'crashing down with the Twin Towers. [...] it's as if 9/11 has simply made a certain rehearsal of South Asian identity and history impossible, or even irrelevant'.[16]

The old 'rehearsal' of identity and history, essentially the genre of fiction that so offended Gupta, seemed irrelevant to writers such as Shamsie, Hamid and Aslam. Freed from the constraints of transacting the culture in nostalgic mode, they moved towards a new rendition of history. According to Aslam, it is not that Pakistan's Anglophone novelists have cut themselves free of history, because in some ways they are more enmeshed than they have ever been. It is simply that they are choosing to express a different version of it:

> We've lived through an extraordinary decade, beginning with 9/11 and ending with the Arab Spring. And between these two moments we had the War on Terror, the call to Jihad, Guantanamo Bay, the invasion of Iraq and Afghanistan, the murder of Benazir Bhutto, the assassination of Osama bin Laden, and a clash seems to have occurred between an incomplete understanding of the East and an incomplete understanding of the West.[17]

In many ways, Aslam's definition of global political dissonance serves perfectly as a description of the perspectivism that Mohsin Hamid was aiming for in his novel *The Reluctant Fundamentalist*. As Hamid put it, 'I decided on a frame that allowed two points of view, two perspectives, to exist with only one narrator, thereby creating a double mirror for the mutual societal suspicion with which Pakistan views America and America views Pakistan.'[18] Aslam has said that he wanted to 'use 9/11 as a hinge moment and see how much of the inadequacies of the pre-9/11 world went into making the post-9/11 world worse than it could have been. Meaning the idea of the inequality between nations, the inequalities within nations.'[19] Hamid, however, has stated that his text, which he began

---

[16]Ibid.

[17]Nadeem Aslam, interviewed on *Nightwaves*, BBC Radio 3 (6 February 2013).

[18]Mohsin Hamid's official website: 'Hamish Hamilton interview with Mohsin Hamid (February 2007)', http://www.mohsinhamid.com/interviewhh2007.html [accessed 9 February 2013].

[19]Nadeem Aslam, interviewed on *Nightwaves*, BBC Radio 3 (6 February 2013).

writing before 9/11, was the same novel before the attacks as it was after: the story of 'a divided man's conversation with himself'.[20] Later in this chapter, I assess Aslam's and Shamsie's particular interpretation of that divided conversation, as well as their response to trauma, which is often registered as a mark left on the flesh by the attritional force of history. I continue with an assessment of Pakistani novelists' reading of and response to the United States via the idea of the palimpsest or unwritten text, and, finally, in a section titled 'The Janus View', I test Hamid's, Aslam's and Shamsie's views that fiction can represent 'multiple truths' simultaneously.

Part one: Traces on the skin

The cultural historian Thomas Laqueur, reviewing Didier Fassin and Richard Rechtman's work *The Empire of Trauma: An Inquiry into the Condition of Victimhood*,[21] noted that the word 'trauma' appeared in the *New York Times* fewer than 300 times between the years 1851 and 1960, but 11,000 times since. Laqueur elaborated on the reasons for this exponential increase in its use, deducing that it lay in the reconfiguring of the term to mean not physical but psychic damage: 'today one doesn't need to have any symptoms at all to be regarded as traumatized. The "condition of victimhood" is democratically available; the past itself can lodge a "thorn in the spirit"'.[22] Laqueur added that once trauma 'expands to become the psychic and metaphorical trace of all pasts in anyone's present, [it] erases as much of a victim's life as it might recover'.[23] However, Laqueur's definition of trauma as a state that appears to erase identity rather than delineate it is not the trauma elucidated by Shamsie, Aslam or Hamid, although it does resonate with the idea of Don DeLillo's 'organic shrapnel' examined in Chapter 2.

---

[20]Mohsin Hamid, 'My Reluctant Fundamentalist', 2007, *Discontent and Its Civilizations* (London: Hamish Hamilton, 2014), p. 70.
[21]Didier Fassin and Richard Rechtman, *The Empire of Trauma: An Inquiry into the Condition of Victimhood*, trans. by Rachel Gomme (Princeton: Princeton University Press, 2009).
[22]Thomas Lacqueur, 'We Are All Victims Now', *London Review of Books*, vol. 32, no. 13 (8 July 2010), pp. 19–23, 19.
[23]Ibid., pp. 22–23.

Laqueur's definition of universal victimhood suggests that we are somehow complicit in the political process, rather than slightly naïve and feckless bystanders. Our individual identities are erased by the ubiquitous nature of our complaint that we have all suffered trauma, in a reinterpretation of Goethe's observation in 1787 that while humanity may be victorious in the end, 'I am only afraid that at the same time the world will have turned into one huge hospital where everyone is everyone else's humane nurse'.[24] It is striking that Fassin and Rechtman share this sense of the universality of victimhood and indeed co-opt the same phrase, pointing out that the expectation after 9/11 was that New York would turn into 'one huge hospital'. As a result, 9,000 mental health workers massed in the city to offer their services. However, Shamsie, Aslam and Hamid step away from the definition of victimhood for the masses, arguing essentially that it is not 'democratically available' to everyone at all, but is *un*democratically dished out to some. In their distinctive contribution to the debate, victims are not 'erased' by trauma. They may be denatured and made different by it, but they soldier on nevertheless. More than that, they are selected for that victimhood by the vagaries of twentieth- and twenty-first-century geopolitics.

Shamsie presents trauma as the grinding force of history upon the stoical, named individual, rather than Laqueur's 'psychic and metaphorical trace of all pasts in anyone's present'. Her principal character, Hiroko, is a *hibakusha*, literally 'an explosion-affected person', severely burned in the attacks on Nagasaki in 1945. In a previous chapter, I assessed Don DeLillo's attempts in *Falling Man* to use the motif of organic shrapnel to signify his own *hibakushas*, those characters who have both suffered the experience of 9/11 and who bear the marker of it in their flesh in perpetuity. But Shamsie's definition of traumatic injury is not one in which the mind and body are infiltrated, rather, it is a form of denaturing, the chemical process whereby proteins change their structure irreversibly beyond a certain temperature and thus appear to coagulate. The burns scorched into Hiroko's back take the shape of crane birds, symbol of peace and good fortune in Japan, which had been woven into her kimono. The flesh itself is transmuted, as indeed is she: 'There is

---

[24]Johann Wolfgang von Goethe, *Italian Journey* (1787; London: Penguin Classics, 1982), pp. 317, 23.

feeling, then no feeling, skin and something else. Where there is skin, there is feeling. Where there is something else there is none.'[25] And then: 'Fire and smoke and, through the smoke, nothing. Through the smoke, land that looks the way her back feels where it has no feeling. [...] How is this possible? Urakami Valley has become her flesh. Her flesh has become Urakami Valley.'[26]

Kamila Shamsie intended the attack on Nagasaki to change elements of Hiroko's character as well as her body. The atomic bomb is a genetic modifier, transmuting itself via the catastrophic power of nuclear fission. Having modified itself, it alters everything around it irreversibly, turning Hiroko into a different chemical and physical structure. As Shamsie put it, 'Hiroko is carrying Nagasaki on her back. It is both literal and metaphorical. Every time she touches her back, that's Nagasaki.'[27] Hiroko's grotesque tattoo by history forms a startling counterpoint to the elective tattoo by the unnamed American solider in Nadeem Aslam's 2013 novel, *The Blind Man's Garden*. His tattoo is a choice, the word 'infidel' inscribed in Arabic across his back as a deliberately provocative insult to Islam. Aslam's prose is characterized by its floriated style and grandiloquent imagination, but in this instance he says that he was merely relying on fact: 'Just go to the internet and type in "infidel tattoo" and American soldiers with any number of infidel tattoos will come up. And then of course he is caught and he has to keep his back covered. And then my hero has to make sure that no one sees his back.'[28] Aslam's hero, as he puts it, is Mikal, a Pakistani man who is being hunted by the Americans for killing two of their Military Police officers. Mikal protects his US adversary's back, literally and metaphorically, since the American's markings are not the manifestation of trauma, they are the provokers of it in those around him. The American is given the perverse luxury of choosing to have his skin etched and marked as an elective boast of his culture and religion. It is a triumphalist religious statement, far removed from the tattoos of early nineteenth-century sailors for

---

[25]Kamila Shamsie, *Burnt Shadows* (London: Bloomsbury, 2009), p. 26. All subsequent references are to this edition.

[26]Ibid., p. 27.

[27]KS, interviewed by CLP, May 2009.

[28]Nadeem Aslam, interviewed on *The Strand*, BBC World Service, 6 February 2013.

whom a religious marking was an indicator that they should be given a Christian burial.

Shamsie's use of the markings on Hiroko's back is very specific. To her, the dazzling light of the nuclear explosion is representative of a 'nothingness of feeling. That blinding white light, that light is an absence, it's an obliteration. [Hiroko is] without nerve endings. [...] It's an absolute loss. Your memory reminds you of what was. It's memory that draws attention to that blankness. It's like a dynamited home. It's telling you how empty it is, because you remember the house. It's an absent present.'[29] How much richer is the motif of the 'absent present' than the 'endless present' that Will Self condemned journalists for perpetuating? (It is, incidentally, also redolent of Paul Auster's sense of the absent/present towers as he continues his daily walks across Brooklyn Bridge, and Don DeLillo's representation of the absent/present towers in the paintings of Giorgio Morandi.) Shamsie's 'absent present' has the capacity to transmute still further from its first phase as scar tissue on Hiroko's back. Later in the novel it is established that those same decorative birds on Hiroko's kimono, scorched into her flesh as 'a relic of hell', have taken on a new anthropomorphic power as poisonous assailants: 'In the first years after Nagasaki, she had dreams in which she awoke to find the tattoos gone from her skin, and knew the birds were inside her now, their beaks dripping venom into her bloodstream, their charred wings engulfing her organs.'[30] The denaturing of the flesh is reinforced by the assertion that Hiroko sees herself as a creature of 'myth, a character who loses everything and is born anew in blood. In the stories these characters were always reduced to a single element: vengeance or justice. All other components of personality and past shrugged off.'[31]

Later in the novel, that alteration of the flesh extends still further, into the next generation, in the catastrophic genetic corruption of Hiroko's unborn child. But Shamsie is at pains to provide an alternative to the new creature of myth who loses all and yet is 'born anew' by the experience. The bleak alternative trajectory to the newly created being is an extreme form of the 'obliteration',

---

[29]KS, interviewed by CLP, May 2009.
[30]Shamsie, *Burnt Shadows*, p. 222.
[31]Ibid., pp. 48–49.

the 'absence' that Shamsie cited in her interview. It comes first in the form of Hiroko's father who is transformed, shockingly, into a reptilian creature by the bomb: 'Her neighbour's daughter is running towards the reptile with a bamboo spear in hand [...] The reptile raises its head and the girl drops the spear....'[32] And there is a yet more extreme stage; that of eradication, the fate suffered by Hiroko's German lover Konrad: 'Those nearest the epicentre of the blast were eradicated completely, only the fat from their bodies sticking to the walls and rocks around them like shadows. [...] I looked for Konrad's shadow. I found it. Or I found something that I believed was it. On a rock. Such a lanky shadow.'[33] Just as Jonathan Safran Foer's Oskar Schell buries his grandfather's letters in his father's grave because there is nothing else to inter, Hiroko rolls the marked rock to the International Cemetery to bury it instead of Konrad. Before the rock/man goes to its/his grave, 'she had lain down on Konrad's shadow, within Konrad's shadow, her mouth pressed against the darkness of his chest'.[34]

While Konrad's fate is to be made nothing and Hiroko's is to have her flesh made into 'an absence', Aslam in his novel *The Wasted Vigil* explores the effect of torture and trauma in a subtly different manner. He analyses the effect, both on the body and on the reader, of removing parts of the physical body under torture and persecution. It should be said however that in *The Blind Man's Garden* he depicts a scene in which two Taliban members are so brutally beaten by a crowd that they vanish altogether, just as Konrad did. But our gaze is not on the 'eaten' men so much as the crowd, people who have been made less human, less substantial by the trauma they have suffered at the hands of their Taliban tormentors. In Aslam's earlier novel, Marcus Caldwell, an English doctor living in an old perfume factory close to the Tora Bora Mountains, is literally made less than he was by the Taliban's order that his doctor wife Qatrina should amputate his left hand. Marcus's 'crime' was to be accused of theft when he was found arguing with a man about a trunk containing Qatrina's paintings, each of them bearing one of Allah's names but surrounded by forbidden images. The final act of his left hand is to

---

[32]Ibid., p. 27.
[33]Ibid., pp. 76–77.
[34]Ibid., p. 77.

stroke Quatrina's palm as she starts to cut. In the subsequent days, even though the hand was missing, it 'still hurt as though he had closed the absent fingers around a scorpion'. Qatrina, having been ordered to cut off her own husband's hand, is 'made nothing' by the disintegration of her mind and her physical body, wrapped like a parcel, is publicly stoned: 'as she lay on the ground, a man had gathered the hem of the burka and tied it into a knot and dragged her away as he would a bundle. [...] Blood was draining steadily through the holes of the embroidered eye-grille.'[35] In the same novel, the fate of Benedikt, the Soviet solider who disappeared after his country invaded Afghanistan in 1979, is no less gruesome and it is similarly symbolically charged. He is used for the traditional Afghan contest of 'buzkashi', where limbs are torn from the body of a goat. First, he is crippled by having his Achilles tendons cut, and then the signal for the start of the game begins: 'When the rifle shot comes he thinks they have fired into him, but no, he hasn't been shot, and now a dozen hands grab onto his limbs and hair and clothing and he feels himself being lifted unevenly off the ground.'[36]

In his subsequent novel, *The Blind Man's Garden*, Aslam continues to experiment with the idea that torture should make someone 'less than' they were. Rohan, traumatized by his wife's death as an apostate and by his son's murder, is blinded by an Afghan warlord who rubs dust from a pulverized ruby into his eyes. (It is typical of Aslam's byzantine imagination that the ruby crushed to dust by the warlord should have been swallowed by Rohan's son as a child but offered back, bizarrely, by his corpse.) The blinding-by-ruby echoes the removal of the radical Muslim youth Casa's left eye by the former CIA operative James Palantine in *The Wasted Vigil*. A CIA torturer in one novel, an Afghan warlord in another, a bizarre trans-novel eye for an eye ritual by two opposing sides – Aslam is nothing if not even-handed and it is startling how uncomplaining, how silent, how accepting he insists his characters must be, even under the most gruesome physical duress. Like Oroonoko, the eponymous Royal Slave of Aphra Behn's prototype seventeenth-century novel, who stood silently smoking a pipe as his tormentors cut limbs, flesh and organs from his body and face,

---

[35]Nadeem Aslam, *The Wasted Vigil* (London: Faber & Faber, 2008), p. 135.
[36]Ibid., p. 366.

Mikal endures torture from both American and Afghani adversaries without making a sound, as far as we know. Indeed, Aslam, whose prose is at times overburdened by adjectival richness, is noticeably parsimonious when it comes to the evocation of responses to pain. Aslam appears to be drawing on Hannah Arendt's assertion that sound, rage or rebellion can only emerge under torture if there is a possibility 'that conditions could be changed':

> Rage is by no means an automatic reaction to misery and suffering as such; no one reacts with rage to an incurable disease or to an earthquake or, for that matter, to social conditions that seem to be unchangeable. Only where there is reason to suspect that conditions could be changed and are not does rage arise.[37]

If Aslam's characters are indeed unconsciously accepting of the idea that conditions cannot be changed, it would suggest that the long view of history taken by Aslam, Shamsie and, to an extent, Hamid has a more pernicious force to it than simply offering a different historical and global perspective to that deployed by American novelists. Aslam's phrase that 'History is the third parent' takes on new heft. I could perhaps add, a little facetiously, that history is the third child too, given Aslam's apparent belief that not only are his characters governed by what went before but their silence suggests they will acquiesce with what comes after, too.

The concept of 'locked-in suffering' explored by Tim Armstrong resonates here, the slave figure of his work exchanged for Aslam's beleaguered and oppressed Pakistani characters; Armstrong's argument that the 'central demand of slavery itself was that slaves contain their feelings, remaining mute in their suffering'[38] is an alternative interpretation to that proposed by Arendt, that disobedience or dissent will only arise if conditions for change seem possible. But Armstrong's assessment is that the call for silence is an expectation by the oppressor rather than a choice by the oppressed, a view that is apparently imbricated more neatly into

---

[37]Hannah Arendt, *Crises of the Republic* (New York: Harcourt Brace & Co., 1969), Kindle edition, p. 160.
[38]Tim Armstrong, *The Logic of Slavery* (Cambridge: Cambridge University Press, 2012).

Aslam's apparent definition than Arendt's is. Armstrong points, too, to the 'amputation metaphor', in which the 'slave is "fractured" by the encounter with white America' and in which 'the metaphorical "body" so created carries its history as a visible cut, bespeaking an identity of self and history'.[39] The bearing of history in the form of an amputation or a mutilation, perhaps yet another rendition of Shamsie's 'absent present', is used consistently by Aslam and Shamsie, where body parts are ritualistically sliced, severed and mutilated. 'Self and history' are on parade as metaphors but within actual amputated flesh.

Aslam attempts to reshape 'self and history' in *The Wasted Vigil*, rewriting that colonial history as it were, by, impossibly, restoring post-death totemic power to the decapitated head of his character Benedikt. It is perhaps not an entirely successful or coherent gesture, but, nevertheless, it is a bold attempt. Before Casa's eye is incinerated by blowtorch, he finds Benedikt's head locked inside the box of Qatrina's paintings, the same box over which Marcus had argued and for which his hand was amputated. When Casa finds the box, it is being held in the compound of the Muslim warlord Gul Rasool, who is in turn being protected by former CIA man Palantine. After the grotesque game of *buzkashi* in which Benedikt's body is wrenched apart, all that remains is his withered head: 'It's something spherical wrapped in a dark torn shirt, and when he sees that it is a man's head he lets it drop in shock, the desiccated skin, the empty eye sockets, the dried-up nerves and blood vessels issuing from the torn neck.'[40] Aslam's description of Benedikt's desiccated head coalesces with Shamsie's efforts to represent Hiroko as a 'creature of myth', a being 'reduced to a single element: vengeance or justice. All other components of personality and past shrugged off.'[41] Benedikt is nothing *but* head. He is the dried, grotesque, miniature replica of the giant stone head of Buddha that lies in Marcus's perfume factory; stoical, enduring, the synecdoche of human suffering, and there is power and resonance to that idea. Before death and during his torture, Benedikt is co-opted as the embodiment of his tormentors' power.

---

[39]Ibid., p. 179.
[40]Aslam, *The Wasted Vigil*, p. 407.
[41]Shamsie, *Burnt Shadows*, p. 49.

But *after* death, when his head is placed inside the box that once held Qatrina's banned paintings, the power held by his torturers is at least partially wrested back by their victim. There is a dialogic force at play here. As the reductionist symbol of his own identity, Benedikt's severed head does expose the power of the regime for what it was: 'a fiction', since the Samsonite head, that essence of self, is a hideous recriminatory taunt at his torturers' inhumanity, as well as a reminder (as the banned paintings were), of their intolerance. Just as, in one reading of Charles Dickens's text, Sydney Carton's severed head 'looked sublime and prophetic'[42] as it was held up to the watching crowd, Benedikt's head is both the metonymical emblem of all those who have been persecuted and a politically charged totem with which to condemn the torturer. Charles Dickens's wish to offer redemptive meaning after death seemed to find its echo in Nadeem Aslam's desire 150 years later.

In 'The Beheading', a 2010 short story by Mohsin Hamid, the writer uses the motif of the severed head as a political imperative, as a way to admonish not the torturer but himself, should he ever find himself lacking the will or courage to speak out against injustice or inhumanity. It is an affecting piece of prose, which wrests power away from the torturer. After publication, Hamid stated that he wrote it because 'it expressed a pernicious fear, a fear that gives rise to self-censorship. I thought in writing it I would become, if not braver, then at least more questioning of my silences and those of others.'[43] As he told me, it is not an absolute position because he does 'not entirely avoid self-censorship. I simply try to be conscious of it, so that I can find ways to not be undermined by it.'[44] But as events later proved, this was no technical exercise in the speculative: in September 2015, Pakistani journalist Aftab Alam was murdered outside his house in Karachi; twenty-four hours earlier a journalist for Pakistan's largest satellite channel GEO TV was murdered. In 2014, one of GEO's anchors, Hamid

---

[42]Charles Dickens, *A Tale of Two Cities* (1859; London: Penguin Classics, 2003), p. 389.
[43]Mohsin Hamid, 'Silencing Pakistan', *Express Tribune with the International Herald Tribune*, 4 June 2011, http://tribune.com.pk/story/181760/silencing-pakistan/ [accessed 21 February 2013].
[44]MH, interviewed by CLP, 19 January 2016.

Mir, was shot and injured, and in 2015 four Bangladeshi bloggers –
Avijit Roy, Washiqur Rahman, Ananta Bijoy Das and Niloy Neel –
were all hacked to death in separate attacks. Roy's wife and fellow
blogger Bonya Ahmed was badly injured in the attack. Before his
murder, Avijit Roy had written in his blog: 'We risk our lives the
moment we started wielding our pens against religious bigotry and
fundamentalism.' Months after the attacks, in July 2015, Bonya
Ahmed, delivering the 2015 Voltaire Lecture in London, and like
Roy, invoked ideas similar to those expressed by Mohsin Hamid in
'The Beheading': 'In Bangladesh, they are fighting machetes with
pens and this is the only way we can celebrate Avijit's, Ananta's
life.'[45] In October 2015, a Bangladeshi publisher of secular books
was hacked to death in his office in the capital Dhaka. Hours earlier
another Bangladeshi publisher and two writers were injured in an
attack. Both were publishers of Avijit Roy's work. In November
2015, Pakistani journalist Zaman Mehsud was shot dead as he
rode his motorbike. The Taliban's Qari Saif Ullah Saif told Reuters
that they had killed him 'because he was writing against us'. In
Hamid's short story, his narratively challenging concept is to write
from the point of view of the beheaded man, concluding the story
at the point of death:

> I can see the long knife in his hand. He's speaking into the camera.
> I don't want to watch. I shut my eyes. I want to do something
> to make my heart explode so I can be gone now. I don't want to
> stay.
>   Then I hear it. I hear the sound of my blood rushing out and
> I open my eyes to see it on the floor like ink and I watch as I end
> before I am empty.[46]

Like Aslam and Shamsie, Hamid is generous with detail, but scant
with pain, thereby dodging some of Roger Luckhurst's admonitions
about the use of 'torture porn' in the context of the artistic
response to 9/11. Tim Armstrong's idea of the 'locked-in suffering'

---

[45]Bonya Ahmed, Voltaire Lecture 2015, The British Humanist Association, 2 July
2015.
[46]Mohsin Hamid, 'A Beheading', *Granta 112: Pakistan*, Autumn 2010.

of the slave is framed here by the withholding of the detail that would make that suffering pornographic. It is as though Hamid, Shamsie and Aslam have an unspoken pact to keep the reader on the ascetic path of ideology and politics rather than be distracted by the more baroque grotesqueries of tortured flesh. That is, until Aslam describes the torture of his character Casa in *The Wasted Vigil*; at this point, any gesture towards asceticism is dissipated. An unnamed American directs a blowtorch into Casa's left eye, in a nod towards the religious justice of 'eye for an eye, a tooth for a tooth'. In this case, it is a left eye in exchange for the left hand of Marcus: 'Casa's mouth is open in a twisted soundless scream, that eye erupting black blood. The boy with the blowtorch stands up with a glance towards James, the blue fang-like flame briefly touching Casa's hair so that a patch of it catches fire with a crackle.'[47] Aslam strays close to 'torture porn' here. Casa's scream may be 'soundless' but it is a scream nevertheless, and the 'crackle' of his burning hair adds a grotesque soundtrack. Casa's body has been co-opted by his novelist creator. In contradistinction to the power symbolically wrested back by Benedikt post-death, in Casa's case the torturer's power is retained. Why Aslam has elected to do this is an intriguing question. It is possible that he is weighting the scales to ensure that we inhabit Casa's space more fully and more sympathetically. Casa is the man, after all, who contemplates raping a woman before his martyr's death and who goes to that death willingly, taking someone else with him as he goes. The counterweights needed are substantial indeed.

In *The Reluctant Fundamentalist*, Mohsin Hamid focuses his attentions on mental rather than physical torment. His American character Erica loses all sense of herself in the world, as does Aslam's Qatrina, of course, although Aslam inflicts a violent murder on his character too. And yet there is a sense in Hamid's work that Erica is perhaps not entitled to this fate, that she has not suffered sufficiently, and certainly not on any comparable scale to Qatrina, who has been forced to amputate her own husband's hand and is publicly stoned before dying in prison, spitting maggots from the festering wounds in her mouth and nose. There is implicit puzzlement that Erica, her name a truncated form of her homeland's, should be so mentally

---

[47]Aslam, *The Wasted Vigil*, p. 410.

depleted by her experiences. Like Qatrina, Erica is 'made less', and not simply in name alone; she is gradually erased. 'Erasure' is a term cited by Laqueur, but it is expressly not used by Shamsie, Aslam or Hamid to describe trauma in their non-American characters. As I suggested earlier, characters such as Hiroko may be denatured by their torments, but they do, nevertheless, prevail.

As the first signs of Erica's anxiety begin to manifest themselves, Hamid states that this was a 'diminished Erica, not the vivid, confident woman I knew but a pale, nervous creature who could almost have been a stranger. She seemed to have lost weight.'[48] Later, Erica is described as 'emaciated, detached and so lacking in life'.[49] Changez speculates about the nature of Erica's illness and what had triggered it: 'was it the trauma of the attack on her city? [...] but I think I knew even then that she was disappearing into a powerful nostalgia, one from which only she could choose whether or not to return'.[50] Indeed she does not return, completing her self-effacement by leaving her clothes on a 'rocky bluff overlooking the Hudson, neatly folded in a pile'. Technically, from that moment she is a 'missing person', but the reality is that she has been missing for a long time already.

A dichotomy emerges between American and non-American definitions of trauma. Trauma is defined in Shamsie and Aslam's work as a national wound endured over many decades, with countless examples of extreme and routine violence. This deviates from the definition of trauma exposed in Hamid's analysis of Erica's fragile psyche, but perhaps more importantly it differs too from the sense of trauma suffered by the United States as a result of the shocking assaults on a single day in 2001. Just as Shamsie stated that 'the US is so used to seeing itself largely as a country different on September 12th 2001', so too does Hamid's character Changez believe that exceptionalism has enticed the United States into creating its own mythic status:

America was engaged only in posturing. As a society, you were unwilling to reflect upon the shared pain that united you with those who attacked you. You retreated into myths of your own

---

[48]Mohsin Hamid, *The Reluctant Fundamentalist* (London: Hamish Hamilton, 2007), p. 102.
[49]Ibid., p. 140.
[50]Ibid., p. 113.

difference, assumptions of your own superiority. And you acted out these beliefs on the stage of the world, so that the entire planet was rocked by the repercussions of your tantrums.[51]

The 'tantrums' and hints that Erica lacks entitlement to mental collapse have echoes in the scenes that examine Erica's unfinished and unpublished novel. When Changez finally reads her manuscript, given to him by Erica's mother after her breakdown, he finds not a 'tortured, obviously autobiographical affair' but 'simply a tale of adventure, of a girl on an island who learns to make do'. There is a strong sense of inadequacy, that this 'spare' tale which is full of little details such as 'the texture of the skin of a piece of fallen fruit, for example, or [...] the swaying antennae of crayfish in a stream' expressly avoids engaging with the complexities or travails of life.

Mohsin Hamid wrote seven separate drafts of *The Reluctant Fundamentalist*. He tried a first-person narrative, a third-person narrative, an American protagonist, a Pakistani principal character and then a combination of the two. His final choice of the dramatic monologue gave him certain freedoms: '[it] allowed me to capture the way in which the world sees itself today, in a sense of mutual suspicion. It almost mimics the global media where so often you hear one side of the story. My novel is written in a form that takes the reverse side of the media; it hands the content over to the "reluctant fundamentalist." It is equally biased.'[52] Hamid has been trying to give voice to the neglected 'reverse side of the media' for years in his own journalism as well as his fiction. In a 2011 essay, he described the treatment meted out to Pakistani civilians entering the United States. It was a subject he had written about fictionally already, when Changez attempted to fly back to New York after 9/11. The trajectory here is not journalism evolving into fiction, but the other way around: 'To enter the US as a Pakistani civilian "ally" now (a Herculean task, given ever-tighter visa restrictions) is to be subjected to hours of inane secondary screening upon arrival ("Have you ever had combat training, sir?").'[53] In another essay written after *The Reluctant Fundamentalist*, Hamid described a

---

[51]Ibid., pp. 167–168.
[52]Mohsin Hamid's official website.
[53]Mohsin Hamid, 'Why They Get Pakistan Wrong', 2011, *Discontent and Its Civilizations* (London: Hamish Hamilton, 2014), p. 139.

similar incident in more personal terms. Yet again, he had been subjected to a secondary inspection at JFK airport, but this time he was with his wife and daughter:

> I waited my turn to be investigated. Eventually it came, the officer questioning me about such things as whether I had ever been to Mexico or received combat training. As a result, we were the last passengers on our flight to claim our luggage, a lonely set of suitcases and a foldable playpen on a now-stationary baggage carousel. And until we stepped out of the terminal, my heart kept pounding in a way incongruent with my status as a visitor with papers in order.[54]

The 'mutual suspicion' between Pakistan and the United States, which Hamid said formed the genesis of *The Reluctant Fundamentalist*, emerged later in journalistic form too. The quality he has described of journalism being 'related' to fiction seems to have extended into a powerful intertextuality, which plays back and forth between one form of his writing and the other. In the following essay, his sense of 'mutual suspicion' was applied to political and diplomatic relations between the United States and Pakistan after the killing of the Al Qaeda leader in 2011:

> The killing of Osama bin Laden by US special forces this May in Abbottabad, Pakistan, has incensed officials on both sides: on the American side because Bin Laden's hiding place appears to suggest Pakistani perfidy; and on the Pakistani side because the US raid humiliatingly violated Pakistan's sovereignty.[55]

An additional driving force behind Mohsin Hamid's post-fictional journalism may well be his need to be specific, clear and unequivocal, in a way that a novel expressly cannot be. As Rowan Williams so shrewdly put it, a 'good novel shouldn't leave you with more conclusions, but with more room in your mind'.[56] There is a despairing, infuriated tone to Hamid's journalistic accounts of public appearances to talk about his novel. Despite the fact that

---

[54]Mohsin Hamid, 'Discontent and Its Civilizations', In 2010, *Discontent and Its Civilizations* (London: Hamish Hamilton, 2014), p. 123.
[55]Hamid, 'Why They Get Pakistan Wrong', p. 137.
[56]RW, interviewed by CLP, 3 April 2013.

there is no evidence in the text, readers persist in believing that *The Reluctant Fundamentalist* is simply a novel about a man who becomes an Islamic fundamentalist. Hamid described in an essay one particularly maddening encounter while on tour in Germany:

> Again and again, people posed queries relating to how 'we Europeans see things, in contrast to how 'you Muslims' do. Eventually I was so exasperated that I pulled my British passport out of my jacket and started waving it around my head. 'While it's true the UK hasn't yet joined the eurozone', I said, 'I hope we can all agree the country is in fact in Europe'.[57]

Writing from the 'reverse side of the media', as Hamid has so resolutely done in both fiction and non-fiction, is a tactic that resonates powerfully with Kamila Shamsie. In electing to use the dramatic monologue, Hamid took a specific stylistic path, yet even though their methods differ, his geopolitical concerns and Shamsie's overlap. As Shamsie observed, the dramatic monologue reverses 'the old colonial narrative in which the colonial voice represented the characters from the sub continent. It's playful because the narrator is so unreliable. It's conscious of the fact that we're so used to hearing and accepting just one voice. It's drawing attention to the limitations of only listening to one voice.'[58] Hamid's novel is more experimental in form than Shamsie's are, but this may be because Hamid's double perspective is more arcane. As Shamsie put it, 'Mohsin seems to feel more American than me'. So while she believes that *The Reluctant Fundamentalist* draws 'attention to the limitations of listening to one voice', some of the equivocation and openness in his text seems absent in hers. Their two approaches coalesce however in what Shamsie calls 'the old colonial narrative'. Her character Kim, daughter of Harry Burton, holds within her name the echo of Rudyard Kipling's eponymous character. Shamsie consistently evokes the colonial voice of E. M. Forster too:

> [Y]ou're right about the connections to Kipling's *Kim* and to *A Passage to India*. But it isn't explicit. I don't need to offer

---

[57]Mohsin Hamid, 'Islam Is Not a Monolith', In 2013, *Discontent and Its Civilizations* (London: Hamish Hamilton, 2014), p. 181.
[58]KS, interviewed by CLP, May 2009.

guidance to the reader. When I was writing about James and Sajjad, *A Passage to India* was just lurking there and I decided to make use of it. With Kim, I was quite genuinely thinking that Kim would do as the name for quite a while before Kipling came into my mind. Then it made it perfect.[59]

Just as past trauma leaves its trace on these writers' characters, so too do earlier novels make their marks on the texts. The Bakhtinian idea of the dialogic nature of the novel is writ large in all three writers' work, each deploying echoing intertextual references to powerful effect. The ability to talk in more than one voice is, after all, both a function and a virtue of fiction, as I will go on to discuss, and all three writers summon the motif of the palimpsest to explore their responses to history's trace.

Part two: History's palimpsest

There are many instances in these novels when the multiple voices of fiction are rendered in physical form. When Nadeem Aslam's character Lara in *The Wasted Vigil* returns to Russia after her mother's death, she visits her former home and finds her mother's notebooks scattered on the pavement. In each book only one page was filled, written on repeatedly, 'so that the feelings and ideas were juxtaposed onto each other, indecipherable, the way a book of glass would be, the eye having access to its depth through the overlapping layers of contents'.[60] This passage makes reference to multiple voices, but also to the notion that we have 'access' to a host of 'layers of contents' simultaneously. There are echoes here of Gerhard Richter's 9/11 scraped and scored painting *September*, examined in the introduction, as well as of Freud's Mystic Writing Pad, in which 'the permanent trace of what was written is retained upon the wax slab itself and is legible in certain lights'.[61] It also evokes

---

[59]Ibid.

[60]Aslam, *The Wasted Vigil*, p. 313.

[61]Sigmund Freud, 'A Note upon the "Mystic Writing Pad"', *General Psychological Theory, Chapter XIII*, 1925), p. 211, http://home.uchicago.edu/~awinter/mystic.pdf [accessed 20 May 2013].

thoughts of Balzac's 1837 story 'The Unknown Masterpiece', in which the painter Frenhofer struggles to represent the irrecoverable on his canvas. These ideas of the overwritten, irretrievable and unreliable run counter to the more familiar view expressed by Peter Middleton and Tim Woods that 'With the technology of writing, a vastly extended social memory becomes possible, enabling a society to extend its control over large areas of space and time, and to ensure its posterity by transmitting records of its achievements to descendants on whom its future integrity depends.'[62] This, they argue, is summarized by Paul Connerton, who said that 'everyone who can subsequently read that writing has potentially a share in its meanings'.[63] How uncomfortable the phrase 'a share in its meanings' must now seem to the producers of the post-9/11 American television drama *Homeland*. They commissioned artists to 'decorate' the set with Arabic graffiti, to make the scene they were shooting in a refugee camp 'look more authentic'. But as one of the Arabic-speaking artists they employed said, 'It was our moment to make our point by subverting the message using the show itself.'[64] To those who could read the manufactured graffiti, the messages aired on television read: 'Homeland is racist' and 'Homeland is rubbish'. There were multiple voices that is for certain, but not ones that the programme makers knew that they were speaking. Mohsin Hamid's phrase about 'taking the reverse side of the media' springs to mind, but rarely has the reverse side been folded into the official version so succinctly or so audaciously.

The comforting weight of journalistic record in which everyone can share and in which posterity can be ensured does not seem to interest Aslam. His is a less literal approach to the recording of memory, since he appears to be explicitly suggesting that the vagueness, the inexactitude, the failings of memory are its virtues, rather than its proscriptive, definitive, posterity-ensuring qualities. Aslam's loose approach to memory applies an entirely different interpretation to the concept of the overlapping word than that

---

[62]Peter Middleton and Tim Woods, *Literatures of Memory: History, Time and Space in Postwar Writing* (Manchester: Manchester University Press, 2000), p. 5.
[63]Paul Connerton, *How Societies Remember* (Cambridge: Cambridge University Press, 1989), p. 96.
[64]Artist quoted by BBC News, 15 October, 2015, http://www.bbc.co.uk/news/world-us-canada-34536434 [accessed 4 February 2016].

conjured from an American perspective by Don DeLillo's 'braided wick' in his novel *Underworld*, assessed in Chapter 2, or by Jonathan Safran Foer in *Extremely Loud and Incredibly Close*. DeLillo attempts to stare an assembly of objects into meaningful reality. Foer, meanwhile, invoking the palimpsest, appears to despair of bringing meaning at all. We learn that Oskar's grandfather has written over and over again on the same sheet of paper and to render that image explicit, Foer embeds in the text a photograph of the over-scored, blackened sheet made illegible by the density of ink upon it. The overwritten sheet is a representation of the 'conversations we weren't having' and with 'all the things we couldn't share'.[65] The heaped up words are a mournful rendition of the impossibility of saying what we mean, rather than a physical embodiment of memory's idiosyncrasies, as envisaged by Aslam. Asla's counter-gesture is to question whether it even matters if the words are written at all; to his mind, it is the gesture that counts. The overwritten sheets produced by Lara's mother later exude their meaning when Lara and Marcus talk about them: 'A dependable clarity dissolved out of him. An aura. It was as though she had been able to make out each of the pages her mother thought she was filling her notebooks with in her last days.'[66] In a syntactically interleaved sentence that is almost palimpsestic in itself, Aslam invokes ideas not just of 'an aura', but of Marcus *acting* as an aura, a medium. Lara's mother is somehow present in her over-scored sheets; the medium really is the message. So, far from seeing the multiple voice or the multiple word as a barrier to understanding, Aslam celebrates its depth and its mystic power.

The motif of the blank as opposed to the overwritten page is commandeered towards the close of Aslam's novel. Casa, contemplating the rape of Dania before he goes to his martyr's death, starts to record the events of his life. We assume that he would be writing in Pashto and would therefore start writing at the top right of the right-hand side and finish at the bottom left, but Aslam takes surprising care to underline the point. He reinforces the impression that Casa is looking back on his life and that he is,

---

[65] Jonathan Safran Foer, *Extremely Loud and Incredibly Close* (London: Hamish Hamilton, 2005), p. 278.
[66] Aslam, *The Wasted Vigil*, p. 417.

perhaps for the first time, attempting to record the truth or even to re-write his life by spooling backwards. The scene resonates with the passage in Foer's novel in which Oskar's grandfather strips the ribbon from his typewriter and unwinds 'the negative it held', but again, in Foer's work, it is defined as a futile gesture. This is not how Aslam sees it. Casa finds that he can only write in the dark, with his eyes shut: '[I]t is difficult to write like this, and so, after only half a dozen lines, he moves towards the lamp that rests higher up, against the top rim of the large stone ear. When he lights it, he sees that the pages are still blank, that for some reason the pen had held onto its ink.'[67] Casa's interpretation is that the words have not made an imprint on the page because it is not Allah's wish and this puts an immediate end to his attempts to go back over his life. The instinct is applauded nevertheless and once again Aslam invokes the Freudian notion of the Mystic Writing Pad, where an impression is always left, even if the words can no longer be detected (or were indeed never there). A strong sense emanates from the paragraph that the mere act of recording is enough, that it does not matter if the words are invisible because they are there in the form of the pressure that has been applied to the blank page or because, for a moment, the man holding the pen wished them to be.

Aslam returns again and again in his work to the idea of blindness and what can be seen without eyes. Indeed when writing about Rohan in *The Blind Man's Garden*, Aslam deliberately made himself sightless, to explore the idea that blindness does not necessarily mean lack of vision:

> I thought to myself that I will just have to tape up my eyes and do it myself. So that is what I did for a week, and for a week for each of the following three years. [...] I noticed when I was editing the book that everyone is reaching out their hands, trying to touch things, to smell things, trying to memorize things or looking at things as though for the first time. It was the first thing I noticed when I took the tape off my eyes. The first thing I noticed when I was standing in front of the mirror was that I was covered in bruises.[68]

---

[67]Ibid., pp. 377–378.
[68]Nadeem Aslam, interviewed on *Nightwaves*, BBC Radio 3, 6 February 2013.

It stretches the notion of the palimpsest, but not too far, to suggest that in 'trying to memorize things or looking at things as though for the first time', Aslam is using the body itself as the re-written manuscript, layers of text marked in the form of the bruises it sustains. To that extent the notion of the body as palimpsest reconnects with the idea of trauma's trace left on the body by the attritional force of history, assessed in the first section of this chapter.

There is no hierarchy apparent between the legible and illegible word in Hamid, Shamsie and Aslam's work. For example, in the case of Casa's confession, it does not matter if it is read or not. He places the folded-up blank sheet inside the giant stone Buddha's ear, the Buddha that at the end of the novel is airlifted by helicopter and taken to the National Museum in Kabul. Presumably, Casa's seen or unseen confession will be an official, albeit hidden, exhibit in perpetuity. What appears to count is the act of writing, not whether the text is legible or read. The dialogic riposte to Erica's unfinished novel in *The Reluctant Fundamentalist* is of course the trio of completed novels analysed here; in a fugal rejoinder to the suggestion that it is unimportant if a word is 'witnessed' or not, the word itself is given sacred status and heroic efforts are made to safeguard it if possible. In *Burnt Shadows*, Konrad constructs a wire mobile to hang his precious eight notebooks from. The notebooks are depicted as winged birds, splayed open, hanging from a tree:

> The wind twirled the purple-winged birds in the moonlight.
>
> He remains certain that no-one will think to enter the deserted garden to search for treachery amidst the leaves. The people who would willingly sift through every particle of dust in a house for signs of anti-state activity can always be deceived by a simple act of imagination.[69]

When Hiroko attempts to buy a replacement copy of *War and Peace* in Karachi, she is ordered to put it down by an unknown man who warns that Western books are 'the enemy of Islam'. The bookseller apologizes, saying that recently 'a group of young men with fresh beards came in and started to pull all the books off their shelves,

---

[69]Shamsie, *Burnt Shadows*, p. 9.

looking at the covers for which were unIslamic'.[70] But the 'simple act of imagination' in hanging his bird-books from a tree is identified by Konrad as the final defence against tyranny and injustice. Qatrina too, despite her mental collapse, still has the enduring sense that the written word can be defended and her solution is ingenious:

> Marcus's wife had nailed the books overhead in these rooms and corridors. Original thought was heresy to the Taliban and they would have burned the books. And this was the only way that suggested itself to the woman, she whose mental deterioration was complete by then, to save them, to put them out of harm's reach.[71]

At the start of *Burnt Shadows*, Konrad describes to Hiroko seeing a name in the river. The name has been 'written in red ink by someone – either a skilled artist or an obsessed lover – who knew how to paint on the water in the instant the ice froze the characters into place'.[72] Much later, that frozen writing is invoked once again. Hiroko is thinking about her stillborn daughter, damaged in terrible ways by the effects of radiation. 'She would have been thirty-five now. [...] If the first had been born – Hiroko thought of her as Hana after the bright-red name Konrad had seen frozen beneath the ice – there would have been no Raza. Somehow she knew that to be true.'[73] The frozen writing has become more than letters, it has become a testament to a life too, albeit a traumatized one. But there is always a rivalry between the act of imagination in the written word and the symbol of tyranny represented by the cranes that were first scorched into her skin by the Nagasaki bomb. The birds entered her body, 'their beaks dripping venom into her bloodstream, their charred wings engulfing her organs. But then her daughter died, and the dreams stopped. The birds had their prey.'[74] There is an overbearing sense of a contest between the sanctity of the written word, and the birds.

---

[70]Ibid., p. 142.
[71]Aslam, *The Wasted Vigil*, p. 11.
[72]Shamsie, *Burnt Shadows*, p. 17.
[73]Ibid., p. 205.
[74]Ibid., p. 222.

A more sophisticated, subtle contest emerges too, between the proscriptive tendency to insist upon absolute meanings and the multi-faceted interpretations offered by the palimpsest. As Aslam has said, the 'advantage of being a novelist is that novels don't tell you what to think, they tell you what to think about'.[75] (There are echoes here again of Rowan Williams's assertion that the best fiction refuses to draw conclusions.) I would also argue that in his quest to provoke thought, Aslam appears to have a sense in which he is himself a palimpsest; the text on the manuscript may be the same, but the reading of it will be different, dependent upon the beholder. He appeared to have no particular complaints about this, when noting how he and his intentions were rewritten at two consecutive public readings of his novel in New York and Lahore:

> [I]n New York [...] somebody stood up and said you are a pro-Jihadi, you approve of the 9/11 attacks from what you are saying and from what you have just read. It is clear that you approve of terrorism. The following week I went to Lahore and somebody stood up and said from what you are saying and from what you have read it is clear that you are a CIA agent and that you have been paid by Western governments to malign Islam and Pakistan.[76]

In a reworking of Hamid's idea that his novel is a 'divided man's conversation with himself', Aslam can be viewed as a man in conversation with his divided audience. In the concluding section of this chapter, I analyse the extent to which these writers are successful in representing two points of view simultaneously. Do they succeed, like Janus, in looking both ways at once, unlike Aslam's readers in Lahore and New York whose gaze was in one direction only?

Part three: The Janus view

Carson McCullers' definition of the divided self seems relevant to the divisions expressed by Hamid, Shamsie and Aslam. McCullers described a form of homesickness that was 'not simply longing

---

[75]Nadeem Aslam, interviewed on *Nightwaves*, BBC Radio 3, 6 February 2013.
[76]Ibid.

for the home town of the country of our birth', but was a 'Janus-faced' emotion in which 'we are torn between a nostalgia for the familiar and an urge for the foreign and strange. As often as not, we are homesick most for the places we have never known.'[77] That particular view of Janus, with its simultaneous yearning for both the *heimlich* and the *unheimlich*, captures some of the contradictions at the heart of Hamid's, Shamsie's and Aslam's responses. It is yet more complicated for Aslam because the Janus view has had implications for his faith:

> Before 9/11 if someone had asked me are you a Muslim I would have said not really in that I don't pray, I don't fast and I can't imagine a time in my life when I would need the idea of God in my life. [...] But after 9/11 [...] I would say yes I am [...] [T]his message is not just directed at the bigots in the West, it is directed also at people like Al Qaeda. It is me saying to them that I refuse to accept that you are the one who will define what a Muslim is.[78]

Mohsin Hamid, meanwhile, has spoken of being a divided man having a conversation with himself, while Shamsie spoke to me of being able to see 'two Americas'. The pluralism that all three writers embrace is combined with a sense that they would like to adjust the weights in the scale:

> The United States is so used to seeing itself largely as a country that was different on September 12th 2001.[79] Americans were asking themselves 'why do they hate us?' The fact that they don't have an answer to that question is a failure of fiction writers. Where was the novel putting the United States in the world? Growing up in Pakistan in the 1980s as I did, I was much more aware of America's place in the world than the US itself was. When I went to an American university, there was a blindness to what the US was doing to nations like mine.[80]

---

[77]Carson McCullers, 'Look Homeward, Americans', In 1940, *The Mortgaged Heart* (London: Penguin Classics, 1985), p. 217.
[78]Nadeem Aslam, interviewed on *The Strand*, BBC World Service, 6 February 2013.
[79]An example of this can be found in the title of the award-winning television documentary *102 minutes That Changed America*.
[80]KS, interviewed by CLP, May 2009.

Shamsie's work is, in part, an attempt to see through the mist of US national political rhetoric. To that extent her novels are highly politicized and act as both journalistic essay and fiction. She is conscious, when writing fictionally, that somehow the odds must be evened up, as it were, in favour of the non-American. She appears to believe that, in some ways, America itself must be transcended. It is a complex battle of wills which was exacerbated, according to Shamsie, when the United States constructed a notional ideology of a War on Terror, in order to invent the necessity to respond to it:

> The War on Terror was a terrible phrase. It was wide ranging enough for them to place any nation within that context and therefore to say 'we have the right to attack you because of 9/11'. 9/11 was used as carte blanche whenever and wherever we see enemies. The irony was that no nation state actually did it.[81]

Aslam, and to an extent Hamid, make repeated references to the abuses of human rights and contraventions of the Geneva Convention indulged in by the West in order to facilitate their right to that 'carte blanche'. In *Burnt Shadows*, America is responsible for extreme violence in Nagasaki, certainly. The CIA agent Harry Burton admits to torturing Gul Rasool using the technique of water-boarding, to elicit information about Zameen. These instances certainly fit the model. However, it is also legitimate to make the assumption that one of the Third Country Nationals, as they are called in Shamsie's novel, is responsible for assassinating American Harry Burton. Harry's corrupt American colleague Steve has already warned that this will happen. This does not fit Shamsie's model, but when I asked her why she had allowed such an ambiguity to creep into her text, she firmly denied that a Third Country National had committed the crime: 'Is Steve correct? No. It's not one of Harry's guys who kills him. The Third Country Nationals who come to work in Afghanistan, they do not turn on the Americans. Steve's whole prejudice is that if they are Muslim they are inevitably on the other side.'[82] I asked her if she found it risky to have the Third Country Nationals at least implicated in the death of Harry. She

---

[81]Ibid.
[82]Ibid.

paused to think but was unequivocal in her answer and indeed was at pains to correct any impression that the reader might have that such a character was responsible: 'Do I have anxieties about Harry being shot? Well, I certainly wouldn't want one of the Third Country Nationals to turn their guns on him. They are there because of economic necessity.'[83] Unusual though it may seem that Shamsie appears to be speculating about her own plot to the extent that in retrospect she enters into a conversation with herself about it, she is quite clear in admitting to being selective in her choice of culprits. The balance is deliberately stacked against nationalistic Americans in the novel. Sajjad is somehow deemed to be entitled to say that 'atrocities committed on Muslims touched him far more deeply than atrocities committed by Muslims'.[84] But Harry appears to be implicitly criticized as he rages about 9/11:

> He was in the Democratic Republic of the Congo at the time [...] and was well aware of how disproportionate his attitude must seem in a country which had lost more than two and a half million people in a war which seemed to have pauses rather than an end. He sat down with a calculator on 12 September, and worked it out to more than two thousand deaths a day, each day, for over three years – but he couldn't find any way to connect those numbers to his emotions.[85]

Earlier in the novel, Hiroko breaks away from the Americans she has been working for as a translator. The explicit statement from one of them that Hiroko's injuries in the Nagasaki bombing were effectively 'worth it' is what provokes the schism: 'near the end of '46 – the American with the gentle face said the bomb was a terrible thing, but it had to be done to save American lives. I knew straight away I couldn't keep working for them.'[86] That distinction between the American view and the voice of reason is reiterated at the close of the novel. Kim, Harry's daughter, argues with Hiroko, claiming that the only reason Nagasaki is significant is because it 'happened' to Hiroko. Hiroko's furious response, which makes an

---

[83]Ibid.
[84]Shamsie, *Burnt Shadows*, p. 88.
[85]Ibid., p. 271.
[86]Ibid., p. 62.

unconvincing apologia for Kim at the same time, follows the same trajectory as the earlier reference to the Nagasaki attack:

> In the big picture of the Second World War, what was seventy-five thousand more Japanese dead? Acceptable, that's what it was. In the big picture of threats to America, what is one Afghan? Expendable. Maybe he's guilty, maybe not. Why risk it? Kim, you are the kindest, most generous woman I know. But right now, because of you, I understand for the first time how nations can applaud when their governments drop a second nuclear bomb.[87]

There is no evidence in the text that Kim has displayed either kindness or generosity. Possibly, Shamsie asserts those qualities in order to temper her suggestion that America is willing to sacrifice countless lives for its own pragmatic reasons. Interestingly, the idea that 'nations can applaud when their governments drop a second nuclear bomb' is a nod, conscious or otherwise, towards Hamid's character Changez, who smiles when he hears for the first time that New York has been assaulted by the attacks of 9/11.

All three novels share similar approaches to the depiction and characterization of the man from the CIA (that is, if we accept that Hamid's unnamed café companion is indeed an undercover operative). In Shamsie's and Aslam's novels, there are two variants: the bad CIA man and the not-quite-so-bad. Harry Burton falls into the not-so-bad category, unlike Shamsie's Steve and Aslam's James Palantine and David Town. Put simply, Harry Burton and David Town could walk into each other's novels and exchange places. Indeed, David Town literally does walk out of one novel and into another. Rather like the different renditions of the character Wally who make repeated entrances in Richard Ford's *Sportswriter* trilogy, David Town appears in Aslam's work twice. He is the US government employee who orders the torture of Mikal in *The Blind Man's Garden* and he is the CIA operative who dies in *The Wasted Vigil*. His resolutely American name and his metronomic dialogue are evidence enough of what we might at the very least call a lack of imagination in characterization from Aslam – and this from a writer whose elaborate imagination could benefit, at times, from being

---

[87]Ibid., p. 362.

reined in. Shamsie's Steve too, who frames Raza for the murder of Harry, could quite easily stray from *Burnt Shadows* and stroll into *The Wasted Vigil*, taking the place of the torturer James Palantine. Their sanctimony, names (James even shares his name with Harry's own father), their machismo and their distorted view of the world order are interchangeable.

David Town of *The Wasted Vigil*, who claims to be a dealer in gems, was in New York in 1993, when Islamic terrorists attempted to blow up the WTC for the first time. David was brought up at a time when 'a hatred and fear of Communism was in the air an American child breathed'. And there was also the issue of his older brother Jonathan's death in Vietnam. We are told that because the Soviet Union had supported Vietnamese guerrillas, David believed that the Soviets bore responsibility for Jonathan's death:

> [F]or the rest of my life I am going to do everything I can to fuck up the Reds.
>
> But that was then. By the time he came to Peshawar as an employee of the CIA his opposition to Communism was the result of study and contemplation. Not something that grew out of a personal wound.
>
> He was in Peshawar as a believer.[88]

Much ground is covered here. David is both an ideological and a pragmatic CIA man, with personal and public reasons for what is presented as his prejudices, and he has the burning irrationalism of a 'believer'. Kamila Shamsie's Harry Burton is a David Town clone. The market scene, when fatefully Harry is witnessed giving his shoes to Raza, is a moment for Shamsie to state that 'of course, every Pakistani assumed that all Americans in their country were CIA operatives'.[89] The unintentional irony of course is that in Kamila Shamsie's fictional landscape, all Americans in Pakistan are indeed CIA operatives.

We never learn the name of Hamid's character, but named or unnamed, he is neither more nor less of a character than Harry/ David1/David2/James/Steve. Hamid's statement that 'It seems an

---

[88] Aslam, *The Wasted Vigil*, p. 153.
[89] Shamsie, *Burnt Shadows*, p. 162.

obvious thing to say but you should not imagine that we Pakistanis are all potential terrorists, just as we should not imagine that you Americans are all undercover assassins'[90] is the perfect rejoinder to Shamsie's inclusion of the line that 'of course, every Pakistani assumed that all Americans in their country were CIA operatives'. However, by this stage of the novel, not only do we assume that Changez believes he is talking to a man from the CIA, so too may we. So when Changez asks 'why are you reaching into your jacket sir? I detect a glint of metal. Given that you and I are now bound by a certain shared intimacy, I trust it is from the holder of your business cards',[91] it is more than possible that it is a gun that he sees. If it is, then Changez and his listener's fates are likely to be similar to those of Aslam's David and Casa. Just as it is possible that Changez and his listener die as intransigently opposed to each other's views but still attempting to effect a conversion, David Number 2 dies, still trying to bend Casa to his will:

> David's mouth is next to Casa's ear, and he is whispering something fast. He is hoping to win over his murderer with an embrace.
>
> They have fallen backwards on the earth. Managing to free his right hand from David's grip, Casa feels along the belt tied to the waist. Through gritted teeth he says something, his face parallel with the sky visible through a gap in the foliage. The last words David hears.
>
> The blast opens a shared grave for them on the ground.[92]

Shamsie's Harry Burton dies too, shot by someone whose views he loathes.

I interviewed Kamila Shamsie after Barack Obama signed an executive order to shut down the US detention centre in Guantanamo Bay on 22 January 2009, two days after he was inaugurated as president. He announced that it 'will be closed no later than one year from now'. When I asked Shamsie what impact that would have on her character Raza, falsely imprisoned in Guantanamo, she

---

[90]Hamid, *The Reluctant Fundamentalist*, p. 183.
[91]Ibid., p. 184.
[92]Aslam, *The Wasted Vigil*, pp. 422–423.

said that she experienced 'a sense of relief' when she heard the news and that her 'response was to the real world, not to the fictional world':

> The day Barack Obama announced that he would be closing Guantanamo, my father said to me 'well, that changes the end of your novel, doesn't it?' But the thing is that I didn't know that it would end that way. There was going to be a deus ex machina and it was all going to be OK. I wrote the end of the chapter when Kim and Hiroko get the phone call and I realized that it was the end. And it was a very disturbing moment for me. Really, what was Kim going to be able to do? The possibility is that people are going to be released from Guantanamo, but one option is that he is going to stay there.[93]

The irony is that as Barack Obama was ending his presidency more than seven years later, he was still fighting to close Guantanamo. Shamsie had been misled in her 'sense of relief' and in her 'response to the real world'. Her character Raza was still there.

All three writers have a shared, slightly unusual relationship with the real and with real-life events. There is a sense in which they engage in a literary tug of war with contemporary history. When I asked Shamsie what results she hoped for in publishing such a highly politicized novel, her answer was unequivocal. She said she had no great ambitions for her prose in terms of its power to alter the facts, but she does have a mission to reinterpret and to add complexity to the narrative, by corralling the history of the second half of the twentieth century and redefining it. In other words, she is providing her own palimpsest of history and news journalism, the endlessly rewritten and imprecise manuscripts so mistrusted by Foer but embraced by Aslam. Shamsie has taken a very particular route in her writing. Rather than attempting to shrug off earlier journalistic attempts at transacting contemporary politics, she has imbricated that non-fiction into her novels:

> I don't write because it changes things but because it bears witness. News journalism by its very nature can only report what

---

[93]KS, interviewed by CLP, May 2009.

happened yesterday. How can it reflect 50 years? It does a very different thing. Look at *The Wasted Vigil* for example. It says 'here are the layers, the complexities and the inter-twinings', so that it's no longer possible to say that 9/11 is when it started. Let's see if 1979 and the presence of the Soviets in Afghanistan is when it started. Fiction creates stories which add nuance. News journalism fulfils one function and novels which are powered by circumstances and empathy, do something else. Novels allow you to imagine yourself on other sides of history.[94]

It is a powerful manifesto for writers of fiction who wish to fix the novelist's gaze on the unexamined consequences of twentieth- and twenty-first-century *realpolitik*:

The point about being a fiction writer is that we are making up stuff all the time, but it's not the truth. The real problem comes with the idea of the singular truth anyway. There are multiple, multiple, multiple truths. But now we have a situation where different truths are colliding with each other.[95]

It cannot be said that the 'real world' of news journalism, if such a thing exists, has defended a corner of territory where the facts will be examined, protected and above all will be unambiguous. Certainly, Aslam sees it as his fictional duty to examine the facts, in other words to act as a journalist should:

I always say that the news is the most emotional programme on TV. I don't know how people who are not writers can sit down and watch the news and not be disturbed by what they are seeing. So for me, to see something on the news, one way for me not to be completely destroyed by the injustice that I see is to say that I will write about this.[96]

This free flow of methods and material between novelist and journalist continues to be productive for fiction, although rarely

---

[94]Ibid.
[95]Ibid.
[96]Nadeem Aslam, interviewed on *Nightwaves*, BBC Radio 3, 6 February 2013.

for journalism which is sentimentalized and trivialized by its dalliances with fiction. There is still, however, the difficulty for the novelist of seeming to offer false comfort when no such comfort should be given. Possibly, Aslam has found a method of surmounting that barrier. He concludes the final paragraph of *The Blind Man's Garden* by returning to the mythic lexicon settled upon by Shamsie in her depiction of Hiroko. Mikal who returned from the dead once, surely cannot do it a second time, despite Naheed's longing:

> She looks up from the page she has been reading just as the gate opens to admit Mikal. Perhaps it is his ghost, here to convince her to continue with life without him. He raises his hand slowly and she stands up and walks towards him, her own hand held out. The insects weave a gauze of sound in the air. She moves towards him and her eyes are full of a still intensity – as though aware of the unnamed, unseen forces in the world, and attempting in her mind to name and see them.[97]

It is Aslam's triumph that he does not coax the reader into thinking that Mikal really has come back to life. Yet, he finally invigorates Richard Ford's tentative phrase that it is possible to 'live on in all but the most literal ways'. Once again, Sydney Carton comes to mind and there is an aura of post-death life in Aslam's words. The writer so avowedly enmeshed by history and for whom 'history is the third parent' appears to have liberated his characters Naheed and Mikal from some of its worst entrapments, at least.

Aslam, Hamid and Shamsie bring a great deal of the journalist to their fiction, but in my fifth chapter, I assess a different form of factual/fictional contract. In an intriguing triangular motion, Amy Waldman, former newspaper reporter, set aside journalism and interpreted the events that followed 9/11 in a work of fiction – about a newspaper reporter. Exactly ten years after the 9/11 attacks, Waldman attempted to demonstrate a new accommodation with history, heralding a forward-looking trajectory for the post-9/11 novel, complete with a proleptic gaze on the future. Her escape to the future was an attempt to bring a liberated, less neurotic note

---

[97]Aslam, *The Blind Man's Garden*, p. 409.

to the post-9/11 novel. But Waldman was not the only novelist to look beyond the now, and neither was she the only one to select *Submission* as a title. French novelist Michel Houellebecq's *Soumission* (Submission) would be infinitely bleaker, as my subsequent coda will show.

5

The End of the Decade

Introduction

Novelist Ian McEwan said of 9/11 that 'the best things written about it have been journalism, not fiction'.[1] Many of the thousands of journalists who reported the news that day showed extreme courage. Photojournalist Bill Biggart was killed while taking pictures as the North Tower fell. His camera bag was found four days later and some of his remarkable photographs were recovered. Injured journalists tried to continue working. Allison Gilbert from WNBC-TV described being hit by glass and falling debris and being taken to hospital by ambulance. Once there, she continued live broadcasts from her bed. The effect on the mental health of many journalists and photographers was severe, and some continue to suffer to this day. BBC correspondent Stephen Evans, who was in the North Tower when the first plane struck and broadcast from the scene for many hours afterwards, told me that there was a specific difference between journalists who managed to deal with the effects afterwards and those who did not:

A crucial thing for the mental health of journalists covering the story was whether or not they saw the jumpers. A photographer from one of the New York papers was taking pictures, and jumpers landed near him. He was very, very damaged by it. He had nightmares, imagined demons under the bed for a long time

---

[1]Zadie Smith talks with Ian McEwan, *The Believer*, August 2005, http://www.believermag.com/issues/200508/?read=interview_mcewan [accessed 6 January 2016].

after. He was affected very differently. My immediate task was to find a phone. The first one I found was in a newsagent's shop just across the road from the South Tower. When the second plane went in just above, I didn't see it because I was just inside the shop. It had an open front but in those days phones still had leads and that kept me inside. When the plane hit the tower, the owner of the shop insisted on closing, so I went in search of another phone. I went to a hotel and hired a room for the phone, so again, I never saw the jumpers.[2]

The families of those reporting on and broadcasting the catastrophe had their own anxieties. They were watching in real time as events unfolded, knowing that their relatives were not trying to escape from the maelstrom, but to get closer to it. Stephen Evans told me that, although he did not realize at the time, his family believed that they had witnessed his death on live television:

When the South Tower collapsed, I was on the air in the Embassy Suites Hotel. I was on the air, out of vision, when the South Tower collapsed and my phone went dead. I remember being very angry, in a mad journalist's panic, because I couldn't broadcast. But watching it in Britain, I later realized, the live pictures were of the South Tower collapsing and my phone going dead. My wife was watching back in Britain and she thought I had been killed. My mother was watching and she assumed the same thing. I found it very moving afterwards. I find it very moving talking about it now. Thinking about it afterwards, it made me realize the importance of family and love.[3]

Evans disliked the use of elaborate language to report this or any other catastrophe, and he took care to be precise and direct in what he said. Nevertheless, despite the clarity of his reports, he was frustrated to find himself misinterpreted: 'I did say "explosion" in one report to describe the sound and feeling of the direct impact on the North Tower when I was at the bottom of the South Tower. Conspiracist nutters take that to mean that

---

[2]Stephens Evans, interviewed by Charlie Lee-Potter, 13 February 2016.
[3]Ibid.

the BBC said there was an explosion – in other words a bomb – and therefore, it was an inside job. It wasn't.[4] His exasperation at others' wilful manipulation of his language underscores the fraught nature of the reporter's trade and the fragility of language itself. Lionel Shriver explored the mutability of words in her short story 'Prepositions', published to mark the tenth anniversary of the attacks. In her powerful exploration of private grief and public memorialization, a woman writes with some bitterness to a former close friend. Her husband died in New York *on* 9/11 while her friend's husband died *in* 9/11. One was killed helping a family whose car had broken down, the other died in the Twin Towers simply going to work.

Given the fundamental role that journalists, and their choice of words, played in interpreting what they had seen, it is perhaps not surprising that a reporter moved from news to fiction to create a novel about 9/11. Almost ten years to the day since the attacks, American journalist Amy Waldman published her début novel, *The Submission*, exploring the grotesque repercussions of a competition to design a 9/11 memorial garden. Rather than write a novel that attempted to free itself from earlier journalistic rhetoric, her work became instead an analysis of the journalist's role in memorializing a traumatic event. The novel opens as the selection committee jury settles on the winning design for the memorial garden. The jury member most wedded to the anonymous winning entry is a 9/11 widow. When the name of the winner is finally plucked from the sealed envelope, the jury discovers that he is an architect called Mohammad Khan. His name alone establishes him in their minds not as victor but as political catastrophe. The ensuing recriminations, arguments and fatal violence are both fuelled and distorted by the fictional journalists who cover the story.

As a former reporter for the *New York Times* and its one-time New Delhi bureau co-chief, Amy Waldman was the first news journalist to chronicle in fiction the explicit role that journalism played, not at the time, but in the aftermath of the tragedy. Testimony from journalists who reported the news on the day would suggest that a remarkable mood descended on New York over the ensuing weeks. Stephen Evans described it as a privilege

---

[4]Ibid.

to witness the new solidarity: 'A big, hard-nosed city became quiet and thoughtful. It seemed gentler. It seemed human, in the best sense of the world.'[5] Inevitably, that solidarity faded with time, and the tone of the journalism changed to become more judgemental, more recriminatory, and, at times, less thoughtful. It was at this point that Amy Waldman began writing her novel. The fact that she was a journalist writing counter factually about a political drama reported by fictional journalists, who themselves inflamed the exigencies of that crisis, brings a bleak acuity to the narrative. Waldman's *détournement*, in which the journalist unpicks the tropes of journalism, has echoes of Nathaniel West's 1933 novel *Miss Lonelyhearts*, and Waugh's 1938 work *Scoop*. However, it is not just the daily trade of the reporter that becomes such an ugly spectacle, but that of the historian, the politician, the political activist and the professional committee member too. By consistently underscoring the apparent limitations of the alternative narratives, in particular that of 'authentic' history, Waldman spreads the weight of her attacks. In her view, not only is the quasi-reality of established history as flawed and inadequate as the versions of the facts promulgated by news journalists, it has, in its illusion of reliability, even greater risks. Waldman places fiction above those quasi-facts: 'One of the values of fiction is that it can hint at, or force us to imagine, the history that exists outside the official record, to make us see how partial and occluded our sense of any history is',[6] she told me. Waldman's suspicion of official histories is perhaps not surprising given her experience as a journalist. She appears to extrapolate from Robert Eaglestone's view of the potentially homogenizing effect of establishment thinking: 'The metaphysics of comprehension can be understood as both the desire for and the methods by and through which Western thought, in many different ways, comprehends, seizes, or consumes what is other to it and so reduces the other to itself, to the same.'[7]

---

[5]Stephen Evans, 'Ground Zero', in *The Day That Shook the World: Understanding September 11th*, eds Jenny Baxter and Malcolm Downing (London: BBC Worldwide, 2001), p. 34.
[6]Amy Waldman, interviewed by Charlie Lee-Potter, 29 February 2016.
[7]Robert Eaglestone, *The Holocaust and the Postmodern* (Oxford: Oxford University Press, 2004), p. 4.

Waldman's and Eaglestone's views are variations on some of the keynotes of this book: Kevin Marsh's complaint about the centripetal tendency of daily journalism; Kamila Shamsie's sense that contemporary journalism is often limited in scope both politically and geographically; and Will Self's argument that journalism is trapped in the endless now. Waldman's argument seems to be that fiction has the potential to offer something more than historical or journalistic record, yet it is a contentious claim. Why should fiction escape what Eaglestone calls the 'metaphysics of comprehension'? Can it not, like journalism and prose non-fiction, suffer from the same tendency to compress, to limit, to trap itself inside a geopolitical lasso of its own making? Proof that Waldman has escaped that lasso is a little flimsy initially, since her writing has a schematic quality at times. Few, if any, of her characters are free from ambition, hubris or vanity and, as a result, their contesting claims set up classically oppositional positions so characteristic of the tabloid news reporter's trade. Intersecting demands and expectations propel the action: one character desires something, another attempts to prevent it; one argues he is right, another demonstrates he is wrong. On the periphery of these debates, there are personalities capable of acting dispassionately, but most, if not all, are depicted programmatically as motivated by desire for personal gain, fame or their place in history. Since Waldman's characters are obeying the journalist's classic imperative to counter right with wrong or pitch guilt against innocence, it is possible to see her intricate interplay of binary forces as uncomfortably close to the kind of 'us against them' novel reviled by Kristiaan Versluys in his analysis of 9/11 fiction. Versluys argues that 'us-versus-them' fiction (what Eric Santner called 'narrative fetishism' or what Rowan Williams described to me as proselytizing fiction) is a betrayal of the art of the novel itself, providing only the 'occasion for a conversion: from a sinful or worldly attitude to a religious and pious one or from lukewarm citizenship to flag-waving patriotism. The terrorist attacks... are shamelessly recuperated for ideological and propaganda purposes'.[8] This 'us against them' literary response could be viewed as a microcosmic version of the binary, polarized

---

[8]Kristiaan Versluys, *Out of the Blue* (New York: Columbia University Press, 2009), p. 13.

vision promulgated by the Bush administration at the time of the
9/11 attacks: you are either with us or against us, 'us-versus-them'
being an acronymic double-entendre of the homeland against the
world. Versluys commends, instead, those works that abandon
the 'bland polarity' of the binary and seek instead 'a triangulating
discourse':

> The novelistic practice of viewing a situation in its full complexity
> entails the denial of the reductive logic of terrorism, the black-
> and-white ideological view that legitimates indiscriminate
> violence. [...] In embracing the viewpoint of the Other (including
> the terrorist, the ultimate Other), novelists employ an ethics that
> gainsays binary thinking.[9]

This itself seems a little black and white, to use Versluys's own
phrase, since the novel may incorporate, as Bakhtin taught us,
competing discourses and ideologies, without resorting to the
'bland polarity' that Versluys complains of. But must we, inevitably,
place Waldman's novel in the category of the binary, replete with
the triumphalist call and response of wrong versus right? In fact, we
can define Waldman's narrative as more than simply binary, as well
as subtly different from 'triangulating'. Instead, it sets up a third
way. Much like a hypotrochoid or a child's game of Spirograph,
The Submission is an oscillating geometric work, endlessly pairing
each statement, each viewpoint with a counter version, thus
offering an analysis of competing claims. 'Us-versus-them' becomes
in Waldman's hands something more interesting and subtle than
Versluys's 'bland polarity'. It is not dialectical, since its clear intent
is to avoid any verifiable 'truth'. Rather, her oscillatory approach
leads to an intricate web of responses to 9/11 that explicitly finds
no victor and no vanquished. This geometric pattern is itself an
aspect of Waldman's 9/11 thesis that no single character should be
allowed to take precedence over another in terms of motivations or
justifications. In counterpoint to the forceful, rectilinear geometry of
Mohammad Khan's memorial garden design that divides everything
and everyone before it, Waldman has devised a series of encounters

---

[9]Ibid., p. 17.

that deliver not harmony or consensus, but what she described to me as a quest to bring 'chaos to order'.

The delivery of chaos is achieved in part by the narrative's ambivalence about the process of memorialization. On the one hand, the novel focuses on the process of soothing relatives of the dead by choosing an appropriate design for a memorial garden, while, on the other hand, it reminds us that the process of reaching consensus allows discord and confrontation to reassert itself. The garden in *The Submission* is therefore both a narrative provocateur and the source of restraint and harmony. A garden's soothing, ordering qualities have been familiar from the seventeenth century onwards and have always been prominent in Islamic aesthetic tradition. These traditions were deployed by Nadeem Aslam in his 2013 novel *The Blind Man's Garden* in which a traditional Islamic garden becomes a metaphor for Pakistan's past. In depicting a beautiful outside space, he attempted to wrest back some of 'the glorious moments of Islam's past' and to bring a sense of order via the garden's topography:

> [T]o me the garden is Pakistan. At one point I say 'the boundary wall is draped by poets' jasmine' and that is Pakistan's national flower. So if you know these things, you can pick it up and in a way the book traces the history of Pakistan, a country based on the notions of having an Islamic state and then what happened to it – how Islam was hijacked ... Towards the end of that novel we are [...] in the garden again but the garden is now full of children. We can't tell you who those children belong to but I think it is enough.[10]

The order of the garden, as envisaged by Aslam, would appear to cut across Waldman's idea that fiction should bring chaos to order. But in a deliberate conflation of garden and novel, each after all a fictional construct, Waldman told me that in her view each brings order and chaos simultaneously. 'I was very interested in the way gardens came to represent both philosophical and practical order, even as their inherent wildness keeps asserting itself. There are parallels, perhaps, to the novel, which also imposes an artificial

---

[10]Nadeem Aslam, interviewed on *Night Waves*, BBC Radio 3, 6 February 2013.

order on reality. Except that the novel should also, on some level, introduce chaos to order – it should unsettle you.'[11]

I will explore in this chapter how Waldman has used the notion of bringing 'chaos to order' to construct her own memorial to 9/11, since that is, in part, what her novel turns out to be. Arguably, the most important distinction between this novel and others I have analysed thus far is to be found in its temporal focus. Amy Waldman does not deny time, reverse it, freeze it or reinvent it. Instead, she concludes her novel twenty years in the future. However, despite her attempt to envisage a future in which the crisis has been surmounted, Waldman is still not immune to the lure of what Richard Gray has called 'the seductive pieties of home, hearth and family and, related to them, the equally seductive myth of American exceptionalism'.[12] The novel is indifferent to the allure of neuroticized reportage, but it seeks other forms of comfort, nevertheless. This chapter, then, will assess the journalistic response to 9/11 as represented in *The Submission*, the process of memorialization and finally, Waldman's temporal approach. In examining her attitude to time and her conclusion that we have moved on, I will assess whether *The Submission* is the opening novel for the next decade or a work that repairs and reinstates old myths.

Part one: Journalism and history

There is a defining hierarchy in newspapers made up of reporters of information at the bottom to definers of information at the top: the news reporter versus the columnist or leader writer. As one might expect of a reporter-turned-novelist, Waldman draws narrative meaning from these distinctions. One of her novel's principal characters, journalist Alyssa Spier, is propelled from the ranks of reporter to columnist as a reward for breaking the news that the hitherto secret winner of the memorial contest is a Muslim. Alyssa, we are told, 'had no ideology, believed only in information, which she obtained, traded, peddled, packaged, and published, and she

---

[11] AW, interviewed by CLP, 29 February 2016.
[12] Richard Gray, *After the Fall: American Literature since 9/11* (Malden, MA: John Wiley & Sons, 2011), p. 17.

opposed any effort to doctor her product'.[13] Her change of status from reporter to columnist gives her the right to be even more inventive with that information.

Having won the prized column, Alyssa Spier receives instructions from Chaz, her new editor, on what she must now do in exchange for her prize: tell people what to believe or repeat what they already think. Spier is one of the most reprehensible characters in the novel, and yet, in the ambivalent, sometimes bizarre moral landscape of the tabloid journalist, she is horrified by a fellow reporter's suggestion that if she cannot find an exclusive she should make something up. She deploys the language of the playground to express her disapproval: '"That would be cheating," she said. "It's no fun, you know that. And once you start doing that, what's the point of doing this at all?"'[14]

If proof were needed that Amy Waldman equates the territory of the news reporter with the no-less disreputable realms of the lawyer, the politician and the historian, one need only examine the words of a member of the memorial jury. Bob Wilner is a lawyer and politician combined and has no anxieties about manipulating the competition result, now that the winner is, inconveniently, Muslim. 'The record of our proceedings is a fungible thing, Claire, and you know it'.[15] The historian on the panel is implicated, too, in the bid to rewrite the truth. In a striking nod towards the notorious words of Karl Rove examined in a previous chapter, he argues that it is irrelevant whether Claire's dead husband would be appalled by the committee's desire to retract their decision: 'History makes its own truths, new truths.'[16]

I asked Waldman why she had so deliberately matched journalists' equivocal view of the truth with historians' similarly fluid attitude towards it. The source of her anxiety appears to be her sense that writing, either of news or of history, has an authoritarian quality that denies other points of view. To that extent, she appears to be offering a deterritorialized manifesto that admits the possibility of other versions of events: 'The problem is that history doesn't exist

---

[13]Amy Waldman, *The Submission* (London: William Heinemann, 2011), p. 60.
[14]Ibid., pp. 158–159.
[15]Ibid., p. 18.
[16]Ibid., p. 21.

outside of our record of it; or rather, the record made of history is the only way we can access it.'[17] She is seemingly of the view that the nuanced, layered approach that fiction is able to take, untrammelled by its need to be 'official', grants it greater authority. This is inevitably problematic, since Waldman demonstrates in the novel that information itself is unreliable, whoever is distributing it. Yet, she is certainly trying to dismantle monopolies when she finds them, and to that extent she is once again deterritorializing the moral landscape:

> For all her moral reprehensibility, Alyssa has a democratic aspect to her – she's battling the 'gatekeepers' deciding what is important, or newsworthy, or proper for public consumption. In this aspect she is kind of an allegorical character – standing in, on some level, for blogs, etc. that have challenged elite power brokers – whether newspaper editors or those who have access to them – who historically have exercised control over the news.[18]

Waldman is not only building a hierarchy in which fiction trumps history, but she is also making a distinction between traditional and new forms of journalism. Her view that Spier, for all her manipulative skills, is at least challenging the 'elite power brokers' is open to question, however. Exchanging newspaper editors, who, historically, have controlled the news, for a new breed of oligarch, seems a pyrrhic victory. Yet she is shrewd in her observations about the way journalism is implicated in the creating of historical record, while ordering chaotic and disparate elements into a form of coherent narrative:

> I wasn't interested in indicting all of journalism. I was interested in showing how the media itself is an actor in history, not just a recorder of it. I think reporters are inventing rules all the time – they have to. To report is itself a distortion, since you are choosing what to include, and exclude – any neat narrative is false, by definition, because it tries to make sense of a reality that often doesn't make sense itself. (Subjects of stories, incidentally, also

---

[17]AW, interviewed by CLP, 29 February 2016.
[18]Ibid.

embroider and embellish and exclude, making them complicit in whatever narrative gets constructed.) I also think reporters are engaged in a constant process of rationalizing about how they get subjects or sources to open up, what they promise about how information will be used versus how it is used in practice, and so on.[19]

The collating and ordering of information is inevitably subjective, made more complicated by the embroidered testimony of interviewees and by unethical deals struck between journalists and subjects in order to secure their testimony. NBC Nightly News anchor Brian Williams added an extra twist to the complex relationship between journalist and subject, by acting as both reporter and embellisher simultaneously. He fictionalized his journalistic experiences in the Iraq invasion of 2003, claiming that the helicopter he was travelling in had been hit by a rocket-propelled grenade. It was untrue. There have been instances, too, of people inventing roles for themselves in the 9/11 tragedy, including the comedian Steve Rannazzisi, who claimed to have been in one of the towers that day. He later asked for people's forgiveness and admitted that he had been working in a building midtown. Even for those genuinely caught up in the catastrophe, there have been temptations to embellish the experience. Two months after the attacks, BBC journalist Stephen Evans attended a meeting of people who, like him, had been in the towers. It was an encounter he told me that he recoiled from: 'I didn't like the atmosphere there. There was a sense of self-importance. There was something I didn't like. People were describing themselves as suffering victims, just by witnessing the event. The real victims were those trapped and killed in a horrible way. I never tell anyone about it. I don't make anything of it. I don't dine out on it.'[20]

The compulsion to misrepresent or distort is captured most vividly in *The Submission* by Waldman's command of news reporters' language. Oscar and Alyssa speak a 'callous patois peculiar to reporters'.[21] It is a vocabulary that all journalists are familiar with,

---

[19]Ibid.
[20]Stephen Evans, interviewed by Charlie Lee-Potter, 13 February 2016.
[21]Waldman, *The Submission*, p. 106.

sometimes to our subsequent shame or embarrassment. Instead of talking about a catastrophic fire, Waldman's characters describe it as 'the most fun they ever had'. A building collapse becomes, instead, a 'great story'. Perspicaciously, Waldman describes these news stories not as 'tragedies' but as the reporters' 'quarries'. So is that 'callous patois' morally culpable or does Waldman view it as simply an efficient way of dealing with daily news – grading it, classing, prioritising it, but above all getting it first? Waldman's view is shrewd: 'My own experience in reporting on death, tragedy, etc. was that you have to shut down a part of yourself – you can't allow yourself to feel everything or you can't operate. Over time that hardening can become a permanent state – and the 'callous patois' many reporters speak in is a reflection of that.'[22]

It is a permanent state that many journalists would recognize. Often, it was that 'shutting down' which fortified reporters sufficiently to conduct the so-called 'death-knock', turning up at the homes of the bereaved and asking for quotes. In some ways, too, it gave reporters the steel to ask for information about the dead to include in accounts such as the *Portraits of Grief* series in the *New York Times*. Waldman's fictional version of *Portraits of Grief* is named *Relatives' Rumination*, the alliterated, deliberately cosy name standing in ironic contrast to its more cynical purpose:

> Every reporter had a digital Rolodex of widows and widowers, parents and siblings of the dead, who could be called for a quote on the issue of the day: the state of the site, the capture of an attack suspect, the torture of said suspect, compensation, conspiracy theories, the anniversaries of the attack (first one month, then six months, then yearly), the selling of offensive knickknacks depicting the destruction. Somehow the relatives always found something to say.[23]

It is beyond doubt that a journalist's version of someone's life can be unreliable, even willfully incorrect. However, just because victims sometimes write their own tragedies or recount their own grief does not mean these accounts are always reliable either. This is why, in

---

[22]AW, interviewed by CLP, 29 February 2016.
[23]Waldman, *The Submission*, p. 61.

Waldman's view, the idea of 'bringing chaos to order' via fiction is so resonant. 'Almost all storytelling about the dead is sanitized. That's going to be true whether a reporter (bound by convention, or propriety, or fear of offending) or a relative tells the story. That's where fiction can come in – by presenting the messiness of imagined lives, it reminds you that real lives are pretty messy, too.'[24] Waldman's reminder of life's 'messiness' and 'chaos' is apposite, since it takes the debate back to the earliest writing about 9/11 and its sanctified tone. Writing ten years after the attacks, Waldman has inevitably been freed from some of the obligations placed upon the first literary responders. It is important to note that she is not setting up a false contest between journalism and the novel, in which she suggests implausibly that the novel has the trump card: 'When it comes to the facts, fiction is less reliable, and should be. But when it comes to what facts mean, or suggest, or elide, when it comes to what goes unspoken when facts are recorded, or to the emotional tenor of a piece of history – yes, I would argue that fiction is more reliable.'[25]

An illustration of what Waldman is gesturing towards here comes in the path she traces from Mohammad Khan's victory in the competition, to the point when people are misled into believing he has created a 'martyrs' paradise'. The false trajectory begins with a report by the *Times'* architecture critic and an insidiously inflective headline. '"A lovely Garden – and an Islamic One?"' The critic establishes that the four quadrants of Khan's garden, along with its walls, its 'pavilion-paralleled gardens', its water features, are in fact marks of the gardens built 'across the Islamic world, from Spain to Iran, to India to Afghanistan, over a dozen or more centuries'.[26] The apparently docile interrogative of the headline transmutes into a series of devastating insinuations as the article continues, each one more incrementally damning than the last:

One does not know, of course, if these parallels are exact or even intentional – only Mr. Khan can answer that, and perhaps even he was unaware of the influences that acted upon him. But

[24]AW, interviewed by CLP, 29 February 2016.
[25]Ibid.
[26]Waldman, *The Submission*, p. 115.

the possible allusions may be controversial. Some might say the designer is mocking us, or playing with his religious heritage. Yet could he be trying to say something larger about the relationship between Islam and the West? Would these questions, this possible influence, even be raised if he were not a Muslim?[27]

To assess the impact of these words, their accretive impact must be noted. (In many ways, it is a slightly exasperating exercise given the escalatory nature of the prose, but its limitations are Waldman's point.) 'One does not know' is the safe haven for the journalist who wishes to implicitly suggest something potentially damaging; 'only Mr. Khan can answer that' insinuates that if Khan fails to respond, he must be hiding something; 'perhaps even he was unaware of the influences that acted upon him' takes the journalist, once again, into the comparatively safe legal ground of apparently hinting at something, while not explicitly stating it. 'Some might say' is the classic and much-used recourse for the journalist, sometimes expressed as 'it has been said that' or 'some have claimed that'.

Later in the novel, an explicit instance of this accretive technique appears again. Claire is duped into speaking to Alyssa and the resultant news story declares that 'Friends say Claire Burwell is concerned by Mohammad Khan's evasiveness'.[28] 'Friends' is a euphemism for Claire herself, a fact that everyone on the jury realizes instinctively. On the day the article appears, Claire meets the jury chairman, Paul Rubin, for lunch and concedes immediately that she 'screwed up'. In an ironic nod towards another method of coaxing information from an unwilling source, Paul says acerbically that 'I thought I was going to have to waterboard you to get the truth'.[29]

Once the information has been distorted by newspapers, transmuted by Fox News, and further exaggerated by a right-wing shock-jock, it is seized upon by Governor Geraldine Bitman and given a final twist for political gain: '"It's disturbing that a jury of so-called experts could miss that this is an Islamic garden," she

---

[27]Ibid., p. 115.
[28]Ibid., p. 165.
[29]Ibid., pp. 165–166.

said.... "If it turns out to be true, it would be unconstitutional to allow the establishment of any religion on public land," the governor continued. "I'm going to seek legal advice."[30] And so, on its labyrinthine path from the *Times* to Governor Bitman, who we learn at the end of the novel is rewarded with the post of US vice president, the suggestion that Mohammad Khan's garden is Islamic in inspiration has been transformed into a constitutional issue. Above all, it has become a matter for a public hearing 'even if the report isn't true'. Its complete detachment from the restraining force of the factual and the verifiable is the final triumph of Alyssa Spier and her journalist colleagues.

Part two: Textual toponymy

On the tenth anniversary of the attacks, the world watched as relatives of the dead, members of the rescue services, first responders, dignitaries and presidents paid their respects at the newly finished National 9/11 Memorial (Figure 5.1). The centrepiece of the ceremony was the controlled, rhythmic reading of the names of nearly 3,000 dead. After the speeches, the music and the marching, relatives were drawn towards the other, visual incarnation of those names: the letters inscribed in bronze around the pools where the Twin Towers had once stood. The designer of the memorial, Michael Arad, explained that the idea had been to 'place the names of those who died that day next to each other in a meaningful way, marking the names of family and friends together, as they had lived and died'. This was described as three groupings of 'meaningful adjacencies' that took account of where victims were when the attacks came, who they worked for and their personal relationships.[31] The attempt to bring a formulaic pattern to randomness, to invest order where there had been chaos was a form of narrative ordering of which fiction itself is another manifestation.

---

[30]Ibid., p. 118.
[31]Official 9/11 Memorial website, http://www.911memorial.org/names-arrangement [accessed 29 March 2013].

FIGURE 5.1 *Parapet of the 9/11 Memorial. Photograph by Jin Lee, 9/11 Memorial.*

What was so striking about thousands of people seeking the one name amongst the many was the urge to place their hands on the name once found. President Barack Obama did the same when it was his turn to stand in front of the names, as though by holding his hands on the written embodiment of the person it was possible to summon something back. A girl laid her face on a name. A man kissed the letters of another. Children and adults up and down the bronze rows placed sheets of paper over the names they had sought and took impressions by scoring soft pencils back and forth over the inscribed letters. The idea of 'the names' is fundamental to *The Submission*. The novel opens and closes in the same way. It begins with Claire asking, 'The names... What about the names?' and closes with 'The names... Where are they?'. The metonymical force of 'the names' is twofold. By using the term as a synecdoche, Waldman transformed those who died into more than just individuals, but rather an aggrieved mass chorus acting in concert. The concomitant effect of this is to make their role in the novel less of an absence and more of an organic presence. The names denote both individuals who once existed and a mass still acting as a protesting horde:

Names, in some ways, are the key to everything in this novel – not just the names of the dead, which is ultimately how they are remembered, but also the names of the living – specifically that of Mohammad Khan, whose name is the real problem. It was a huge shift in memorializing to start listing all of the dead (i.e. ordinary people) and has now become central to any memorial project: the name is the way we sanctify the individual, allow him or her to stand apart from collective death. It's how we say that each life matters. Which is why Claire considers the absence of her husband's name, and Asma the potential absence of her husband's, so wounding – it's an erasure.[32]

Waldman's choice of names is effective. The meaning of Alyssa is 'truth', but Spier is an archaic word, denoting 'spy'. Alyssa Spier is both a spy and a spy-er, which in combination places an ironic underscore beneath any notion of truth. There is, in addition, the unavoidable association with and memory of A. Spier's homophonic twin, A. Speer (homophonic in conventional English/American pronunciation, that is, although not German). Albert Speer, Adolf Hitler's chief architect and minister of armaments and war production, was responsible for the design of the Reich Chancellery as well as the stadium in Nuremberg where political rallies took place. The architectural connections are revealing; Alyssa Spier, as a name is a point of authority but in another sense is just a place-marker for anything that can be routed through that space. Spier is both the architect and simply the conduit at the same time.

Mohammad's name holds huge political risks for the jury, yet that perceived risk, as far as the voting panel is concerned, is dissipated by its truncation to Mo. Mo and Mohammad are the same person, but one name inspires dread for the jury, the other seems to them benign. Fred, meanwhile, is so definitively a journalist that his job title of Ed is tucked into his name like a business card. A further name that may reveal meaning is that of the aggressive, right-wing, opinionated talk show host, Sarge; Sarge evokes hints of Sarge Serge in Paul Auster's 9/11 novel *Man in the Dark*, which itself raises thoughts of *Catch 22*'s Major Major, all characters who have unearned and ultimately

---

[32]AW, interviewed by CLP, 29 February 2016.

meaningless authority. I asked Waldman how much weight she had intended the reader to place on her names:

> I was deliberate with most, including Spier and also Mohammad – not just the truncation, but Mohammad being both the most provocative name to some non-Muslims even as it's the most popular Muslim name. I didn't know about the Auster novel or character – but Sarge (which may or may not be his real name anyway) just seemed to fit the character. With Claire, I kept coming back to claire-obscure – the French translation of chiaroscuro – the way she is, in essence, trying to create herself, using both light and dark to do so.[33]

The deliberate choice of 'Claire' to connote the interplaying forces of light and dark has important connections with the work of the architect Maya Lin, who is invoked several times in *The Submission*. The novel's point of crisis is whether to allow Mohammad to proceed with his memorial design, once his identity is known. The more subtle conflict concerns the original choice itself. As the novel opens, it appears that the *Garden*, Khan's design, will be occluded by the bid known as the *Void*. A link is drawn between the *Void* and the Vietnam Veterans Memorial designed by Maya Lin. Lin's Memorial is a gash in the ground. The *Void* is a laceration in the sky:

> A towering black granite rectangle, some twelve stories high, centred in a huge oval pool, it came off in the drawings as a great gash against the sky. The names of the dead were to be carved onto its surface, which would reflect into the water below. It mimicked the Vietnam Veterans Memorial but, to Claire, missed the point. Such abstraction worked when humans could lay their hands on it, draw near enough to alter the scale. But the names on the Void couldn't be reached or even seen properly.[34]

Maya Lin was vilified when her design was chosen because her Asian identity was said to make her an inappropriate choice.

---

[33]Ibid.
[34]Waldman, *The Submission*, p. 4.

Indeed, the jury in *The Submission* makes instant reference to her when the envelope containing Mohammad's name is torn open. '"It's Maya Lin all over again. But worse."'[35] Waldman's view is that Lin's memorial has never been surpassed:

> Lin's memorial is brilliant. Partly I was trying to capture how she and that particular memorial have come to shadow, or maybe overshadow, all subsequent memorials – everyone is trying to capture the same mix of minimalism and meaning (and I'm always astounded by how every time I see an image of her memorial [...] I discover a new level of meaning). And it's elusive – no one has matched her.[36]

Lin's role as member of the 9/11 Memorial Design Competition jury placed her in an intriguing position. During the 2004 competition process, she said that she hoped her experience would help, but in some ways her position as an unmatched memorial designer who nevertheless was so tested at the time reminded everyone how difficult the final choice would be.

Twenty years after the competition to design the Vietnam Veterans Memorial was announced, Lin completed an essay about her experience. The two-decade interlude mirrors the twenty-year gap that elapses in *The Submission* between the announcement of Khan's victory and his decision to talk about the traumatic process on camera. It is surely no accident. In defining her artistic endeavour, Lin spoke of precisely the drive to commemorate 'the names' that Waldman's characters yearn to see. The sight of the names carved into a memorial wall at Yale left 'a lasting impression' on Lin, as scored into her psyche as any carved names in stone:

> The power of a name was very much with me at the time, partly because of the Memorial Rotunda at Yale. In Woolsey Hall, the walls are inscribed with the names of all the Yale alumni who have been killed in wars. I had never been able to resist touching the names cut into these marble walls, and no matter how busy or crowded the place is, a sense of quiet, a reverence, always surrounds those names. Throughout my freshman and

---

[35] Ibid., p. 17.
[36] AW, interviewed by CLP, 29 February 2016.

sophomore years, the stonecutters were carving in by hand the names of those killed in the Vietnam War, and I think it left a lasting impression on me.[37]

That lasting impression was inscribed in Lin's imagination as a narrative, which she then rendered as a form of literary text. For her, the memorial becomes a book, a book the memorial:

> The memorial is analogous to a book in many ways. Note that on the right-hand panels the pages are set ragged right and on the left they are set ragged left, creating a spine at the apex as in a book. Another issue was scale; the text type is the smallest that we had come across, less than half an inch, which is unheard of in monument type sizing. What it does is create a very intimate reading in a very public space, the difference in intimacy between reading a billboard and reading a book.[38]

It is legitimate to argue that *The Submission* is, itself, a form of memorial. It is a work that attempts to act as a memorializing meditation on the attacks, in a way that earlier works cannot. With its ten-year distance, it looks forward while works such as *Falling Man*, *Extremely Loud and Incredibly Close* and even the more oblique *The Lay of the Land* inevitably remain immersed in the trauma of the event. The guiding principle of Waldman's character Molly, the student who interviews Mo to mark the twentieth anniversary of the failed bid to build the *Garden*, is that 'the process of creating a memorial was itself part of the memorial'.[39] That distance is important to Waldman, who believes that we are suffering from a compulsion to mourn, rather than to move on:

> I believe we've become afflicted, a little, by a memorial-industrial complex, in which we pour enormous amounts of money and efforts into memorials while often ignoring the questions that hover around their edges. I think the real 9/11 memorial is very

---

[37]Maya Lin, 'Making the Memorial', *New York Review of Books*, 2 November 2000, http://www.nybooks.com/articles/2000/11/02/making-the-memorial/ [accessed 22 February 2016].
[38]Ibid.
[39]Waldman, *The Submission*, p. 286.

powerful in its design, and yet it also seems, in scale, somehow disproportionate – suggesting, somehow that we can't move on from that moment, when in fact of course we already have. It's hard to separate, now, what happened on September 11 with everything that happened as a result in the decade after – in my mind, at least, they've woven together as a single piece of history. But the memorial treats that day in isolation, puts a frame around it. With the novel, I wanted to break that frame. Also, we put a lot of focus on remembering certain events. I'm interested in what we choose to forget. Where, for example, is the discussion of a memorial for all of the people – our soldiers, the civilians of other countries – who've died in the wars that 9/11 spawned?[40]

The designs for the real 9/11 memorial were mired in argument and controversy right from the start, although the final incarnation in lower Manhattan is deeply affecting and very powerful. It has a symphonic quality in which its disparate elements of memorial, names, water, oak trees and architecture all play their part (Figure 5.2). On my last visit, the importance of this exquisite orchestration was inadvertently underscored. The waterfalls pouring into one of the pools had been temporarily switched off and without the redeeming force of its magnificent sheets of moving water, the vanished tower's huge footprint, thirty-feet deep and lined in black, was bleak, even intimidating. The sublime nature of the experiment had been stripped of its redemptive significance. Amy Waldman's view that the memorial suggests we have not moved on is another way of expressing Philip Nobel's sense that it is not 'leaning toward some future understanding; it was a summary of what was known'.[41] To impose a literary judgement on the memorial, it is not proleptic but is trapped in the past and present tenses, a quality built into the design's name: 'Reflecting Absence'. Yet, the inevitable difficulty with a memorial that fixates on the now, and not the after, is the one Maya Lin faced when it was suggested that her memorial was not, somehow, connected to its past enough. As she put it, some critics viewed it as 'a minimalist statement which they interpreted as being nonreferential and disconnected from experience'.[42]

---

[40]AW, interviewed by CLP, 29 February 2016.
[41]Philip Nobel, *Sixteen Acres: Architecture and the Outrageous Struggle for the Future of Ground Zero* (New York: Metropolitan Books, 2005), p. 252.
[42]Lin, 'Making the Memorial'.

FIGURE 5.2 *Aerial shot of the 9/11 Memorial. Photograph by Jin Lee, 9/11 Memorial.*

There was the additional difficulty for Lin that the stone she had chosen for her memorial was black, which she had to defend against those with a 'cultural prejudice against the color black'. Lin also found that she would not be allowed to source the black granite from either Canada or Sweden, despite the beauty of their stone, because draft evaders had fled to both countries and veterans would not tolerate the association. As regards the colour, a four-star general, 'who happened to be black', had to testify before a committee hearing to defend Lin's decision before the design could proceed. Lin's choice of colour was no whim:

> I always saw the wall as pure surface, an interface between light and dark, where I cut the earth and polished its open edge. The wall dematerializes as a form and allows the names to become the object, a pure and reflective surface that would allow visitors the chance to see themselves with the names. I do not think I thought of the color black as a color, more as the idea of a dark mirror into a shadowed mirrored image of the space, a space we

cannot enter and from which the names separate us, an interface between the world of the living and the world of the dead.[43]

Lin's vision of a wall that is an 'interface between light and dark' and 'an interface between the world of the living and the world of the dead' is the same vision that Waldman invoked when explaining her choice of Claire's name. Both as a character and as a name, Claire is, as Waldman confirmed, the embodiment of light and dark, the interface between the world of the living and the dead, a space we cannot enter. By adopting this reading of the text, Claire is both an anamnesis of Lin's memorial and the embodiment of its interfacial liminality and a metaphorical memorial herself. Of the four drawings provided by Khan as part of his bid, it is no accident that 'Claire's favourite was the chiaroscuro of winter'.[44] Claire is consistently presented by Waldman as a character who stands apart, separated both by her demeanour and by her inescapable position as the widow for whom life has stopped. She describes herself as being dislocated, as having 'one leg in New York and one in America'[45]and, with even more resonance, we learn that she was swimming underwater as the planes struck. 'She would think often about having been submerged in water while her husband was consumed by fire. What did this say? It was like a myth, a dark poem whose meaning just eluded her.'[46] The committee process of choosing a fictional 9/11 memorial is the way Claire attempts to reintegrate herself, to escape the 'dark poem'. Mohammad Khan's garden is ordered, peaceful, calm, organic and structured. Its classic *chahar bagh* quadrants, planted with columns of steel trees made from metal salvaged from the destroyed buildings, are divided by pathways and by two perpendicular canals.

As Waldman was completing her novel in which a disputed memorial is finally denied its place in New York, a bitter row broke out about the creation of an Islamic cultural centre to be built near Ground Zero. Waldman was journalistic in her analysis of why the row endorsed her decision to construct *The Submission* in the

---

[43]Ibid.
[44]Waldman, *The Submission*, p. 4.
[45]Ibid., p. 200.
[46]Ibid., p. 32.

way that she did: 'I took it both as confirmation of my instincts in conceiving the novel in the first place, but also a more acute sense of how the mechanics of something like this would actually play out – the spectre of violence, for example; the unexpected chain reactions.'[47] The 'unexpected chain reactions', the 'spectre of violence' were certainly familiar to Maya Lin. When she was fighting politicians, journalists and war veterans over the design, the lettering, the stone and the concept, yet another front opened up: it was suggested that a monumental statue of infantrymen and a second statue to represent women who died in Vietnam should be placed at the apex of Lin's wall. The apex of her memorial is its most important part, the place where the two pages of her book meet. The prosaic statues would have dwarfed her structure, converting her walls 'to a backdrop and violating that private contemplative space'. Maya Lin fought that battle as hard as she did the others and finally the statues were placed to one side. 'Ironically', she said, 'the compromise memorializes the conflict in the building of the piece'.[48]

Khan's conflict is memorialized too, when his garden is finally built, but on another continent. He is commissioned to recreate it in Mumbai, by 'some rich Muslim'. Khan invites Molly and her cameraman William, who is Claire Burwell's son, into the new incarnation of the *Garden*. William films the landscaping, unable to reveal to Khan his true identity, and takes the images home for his terminally ill mother to watch. The garden appears to be a transplanted replica, with its cherry trees, almond, pear, apricot and walnut trees; its rows of cypresses and steel trees, 'glinting and upside down, with roots like a distraught woman's tangled hair in place of branches and leaves'. The pavilion is there, and its canals, 'contemplative spaces' and marble columns: 'Claire closed her eyes and heard the water rippling. Khan's footsteps crunching, birds singing, chattering, telling their stories, maybe hers. Cal felt closer than he had in twenty years. Seeing the Garden alive was a gift and rebuke.'[49] But when the camera pulls out and pans along the inside walls of the *Garden*, Claire sees that where the names should be,

---

[47]AW, interviewed by CLP, 29 February 2016.
[48]Lin, 'Making the Memorial'.
[49]Waldman, *The Submission*, p. 297.

there are extracts from the Quran in flowing calligraphy. Claire's instinct is that it is a taunt, a betrayal. And yet, as an endorsement of Molly's idea that 'the process of creating a memorial was itself part of the memorial',[50] Khan leaves a parting statement on film: 'Use your imagination'. Her imagination fails her, but William urges her to look at the final frames again. In close-up, she sees 'a few small rocks stacked in a corner of the garden'. William has built his own memorial to his father in the garden, a tiny replica of the memorial cairns of pebbles that he had built as a child believing that they would help his dead father find his way home. 'In Khan's garden, her son had laid his hand. With a pile of stones, he had written a name.' It is not made clear if Claire is convinced by this gesture. It is possible, perhaps even likely, that she is not.

Claire believes that her attempts to memorialize are still being edged to the sidelines by a political process that values vindication above validation. As David Simpson observed, 'Mourning and melancholia have both been made secondary to the initiation of new states of emergency. For a national culture as committed as is that of the United States to a high level of ethical self-justification and even self-righteousness, this compression produces a definite tension in the convention of national self-presentation.'[51] The conflation of memorialization with retaliation is a now familiar response to national trauma, seen recently in the reaction to the Paris massacres in November 2015. Politicians were mourning the dead, while vigorously extending the state of emergency and the restrictions that came with it. Waldman allows some of her characters to escape the entrapments of endless memorialization, but Claire remains caught up. Her son's cairn of pebbles represents a burial mound for his father, and an embodiment of him too, with his name and identity writ large. But for Claire, it is a memorialization of 'the conflict in the building of the piece', too, just as the statues of the women and the infantrymen are at the Vietnam Veterans Memorial in Washington, D.C. Above all, the cairn of pebbles is an attempt by Waldman to crystallize her sense of what a memorial is for. As she said, 'it's not just memorializing the dead – it's also memorializing

---

[50]Ibid., p. 286.
[51]David Simpson, *9/11: The Culture of Commemoration* (Chicago: University of Chicago Press, 2006), p. 4.

what was changed in America by the way they died. I think the two go hand in hand – grieving for people, grieving for other things that were lost or sacrificed as a result of their death – and the novel is an attempt, perhaps, to conjoin them in a way an actual memorial can't.'[52] Waldman is not explicit about the things that 'were lost or sacrificed' but it would be fair to assume that liberal values, inclusivity and tolerance could be listed amongst them. In the concluding section of this chapter, I will assess the degree to which Waldman's novel not only attempts to conjoin the death of so many with the death of so much, but also whether it is able to push the narrative forward, out of retrospective memorialization and out of the confines of the American homeland.

Part three: Text as memorial

The drive to create a memorial garden in *The Submission* is as explicitly political as it is emotional. The chairman of the jury is firm in his view that the longer the space remains empty, the more it 'became a symbol of defeat, of surrender, something for 'them', whoever they were, to mock. A memorial only to America's diminished greatness, its new vulnerability to attack.'[53] But he also concedes that there are those who think it is too soon to create a memorial because 'the country hasn't yet won or lost the war'.[54] These fictional, triumphalist political impulses resonate so powerfully because they replicate historical reality. The mission to memorialize 9/11 led to an almost fetishistic quest for numerological significance, a numbers cult that was inevitably an intellectual cul-de-sac but which appeared to offer a kind of bolstering solace nevertheless. There was the collection of 9/11 short fictions called *110 Stories* in mimesis of the WTC's 110 storeys; the decision to make the newly constructed One World Trade Center 1776 feet high, as a numerical embodiment of the 1776 US Declaration of Independence; and the announcement that, with the hasty addition

---

[52]AW, interviewed by CLP, 29 February 2016.
[53]Waldman, *The Submission*, p. 8.
[54]Ibid., p. 8.

of a new steel column on top, the still unfinished building was now the tallest building in NYC one day before the first anniversary of the operation to kill Osama bin Laden.[55] Ensuring that the building was 'tall enough' with one day left to go gave the president enough time to fly to Afghanistan to bolster US troops stationed there with a fortifying message. However, since his address was at 4 am in Kabul, but prime time in the United States, it was clear who his real audience was.[56] It was announced that the rooftop parapet of the building would be placed at precisely 1,368 feet, the same height as the original World Trade Center.

In even more neurotic mode, connections were made on the day of the attacks between the date and the US emergency telephone code of 911.[57] On the internet, complex games were played with typefaces to try to bring meaning where there seemed to be none:

> typing NYC into a Microsoft Word Document, highlighting it, and then changing the font to Wingdings creates: ♋✿◊. At the same time, the widely circulated claims that Q33NY – which becomes ✿✈ ▤▤♋ by the same process – was the flight number of one of the crashed planes was false.[58]

Inevitably, the numbers game was disappointing. No genuine solace could be found by fiddling around with Wingdings, the title *110 Stories* seemed facile, and the new One World Trade Center's final finished form looked oddly dumpy. The wrangling over designs for the building had produced a very different structure than the one originally envisaged, one that could only retain its symbolic height of 1776 feet by having the distance made up with the addition of a prosaic 408-feet spire and antenna. The building's symbolic height

---

[55]'One World Trade Center becomes New York's tallest building', BBC News, 1 May 2012, http://www.bbc.co.uk/news/world-us-canada-17898138 [accessed 19 February 2016].

[56]'Barack Obama pledges to "finish the job" in Afghanistan', BBC News, 2 May 2012, http://www.bbc.co.uk/news/world-us-canada-17917750 [accessed 19 February 2016].

[57]Marc Redfield, *The Rhetoric of Terror: Reflections on 9/11 and the War on Terror* (New York: Fordham University Press, 2009), pp. 16–17.

[58]Stuart Allan, 'Reweaving the Internet: Online News of September 11', in *Journalism after September 11*, eds Barbie Zelizer and Stuart Allan (London: Routledge, 2002), pp. 119–140, 133.

was virtually the only element that finally remained of Daniel Libeskind's competition-winning design, an outcome that stands in wry counterpoint to Mohammad Khan's fictional experience. Libeskind had envisaged a building that referenced the soaring form of the Statue of Liberty holding her torch aloft in her right arm. She herself had been inspired by Eugène Delacroix's painting of the French Revolution, *Liberty Leading the People*, in which a powerful female embodiment of freedom leads the people forward to victory over the bodies of the slain. Libeskind's building became known as Freedom Tower, but the name was eventually buried along with the original designs. His offset spire soaring from the top of the building like Liberty's arm was nudged back to the middle, and now looks more like a television aerial. The twisted form of the building, emulating Liberty's powerful musculature and defiant pose, was quietly untwisted again; it needed to fit onto a new 200-feet-high concrete platform to guard the building from future attack. To look at it now is to see an office building, standing on a cardboard box. As Elizabeth Greenspan put it: 'The facts themselves spoke almost too poetically. A building called Freedom Tower had been fortified. To make it safer, designers had erased its references to the Statue of Liberty.'[59]

The publication of *The Submission* only a few days before the tenth anniversary of the 9/11 attacks was inevitably deliberate. To the extent that it was a political choice to publish precisely then, it could be argued that the decision fell within the boundary of numerological fetishism too. However, *The Submission* attempted to say what people had not dared think yet: that possibly after ten years, far from being unable to move on, according to Waldman 'of course we already have'. So, for example, Khan, who refuses to attend the retrospective of his career at the Museum of New Architecture in New York, is tacitly chastised in the text for looking backwards:

The country had moved on, self-corrected, as it always did, that feverish time mostly forgotten. Only Mo was stuck in the past. He wanted acknowledgement of the wrong done to him, awaited

---

[59]Elizabeth Greenspan, *Battle for Ground Zero* (New York: Palgrave Macmillan, 2013), p. 104.

credit for his refusal to agree that the attack justified America's suspicion of its Muslims any more than it justified the state's overreaching.[60]

Later, when Mo is interviewed by Molly and filmed by Claire's son for their documentary, he is admonished once again for failing to make that proleptic self-correction: 'America had offered his immigrant parents the freedom to reinvent themselves. Mo had found himself reinvented by others, so distorted he couldn't recognize himself. His imagination was made suspect. And so he had traced his parents' journey in reverse: back to India.'[61] This, however, is problematic. Far from embracing Rothberg's idea that the 9/11 novelist should seek a 'centrifugal literature of extraterritoriality' in which they provide 'cognitive maps that imagine how US citizenship looks and feels beyond the boundaries of the nation-state, both for Americans and for others',[62] The Submission envisages a territory in which Mo and the liminal figure of Abdul, the son of the murdered 9/11 widow Asma, no longer have a place. The centrifuge has spun them out. Indeed, Abdul's adult persona could have inhabited the pages of The Reluctant Fundamentalist. Abdul, who has never returned to the United States, speaks mournfully on camera of his sense of divided self:

Abdul had applied to and been accepted at colleges in the United States, but under pressure from his relatives decided to stay in Bangladesh. America tempted him and scared him. Both of his parents had died there. This was reason to go, reason not to. Mo remembered how his own decision not to go home had curled him in bed. How many nights had Abdul spent in the same position?

'I sometimes feel each place is the wrong place', the young man on the screen said softly.[63]

---

[60]Waldman, The Submission, p. 287.
[61]Ibid., p. 293.
[62]Michael Rothberg, 'A Failure of the Imagination: Diagnosing the Post-9/11 Novel: A Response to Richard Gray', American Literary History, vol. 21, no. 1 (Spring 2009), pp. 152–158, 158.
[63]Ibid., p. 291.

Mohsin Hamid's character speaks of that torn identity too, when a divided character moves from one territory to another, in his case from America back to Pakistan: 'I recall the Americanness of my own gaze when I returned to Lahore that winter when war was in the offing. [...] I was looking about me with the eyes of a foreigner, and not just any foreigner, but that particular type of entitled and unsympathetic American who so annoyed me when I encountered him in the classrooms and workplaces of your country's elite.'[64] Hamid defines his own identity as divided, just as Waldman's Abdul does. I asked Waldman if she had envisaged such overlaps between Abdul, Mo and Mohsin Hamid. Interestingly, she distanced her character from Hamid's protagonist, because Mo 'is an American': 'For me the essence of Mo – his character and his plight – is that he is an American, which Hamid's character was not. It is Mo's own country – his own identity – that he has become estranged from. Hamid's character begins as a foreigner in America; Mo, on some level, is made one.'[65]

The distinction in Waldman's mind between being and becoming an American is one that may be provocative to Mohsin Hamid, the 'divided man' so exasperated at never being asked if he is the American listener in his novel. Perhaps it may provoke a certain bewilderment in him too, given the fact that Kamila Shamsie defined Hamid as 'more American than me' in her interview. There is another distinction: the differentiation between the backward step, which is regressive, and progressive forward motion. At the start of the novel, when Khan first sees the destroyed Twin Towers on the day of the attacks, his thoughts are of absence, of something missing, or something having been lost:

> He had been indifferent to the buildings when they stood, preferring more fluid forms to their stark brutality, their self-conscious monumentalism. But he had never felt violent toward them, as he sometimes had toward that awful Verizon building on Pearl Street. Now he wanted to fix their image, their worth, their place. They were living rebukes to nostalgia, these Goliaths that

[64]Mohsin Hamid, *The Reluctant Fundamentalist* (London: Hamish Hamilton, 2007), p. 124.
[65]AW, interviewed by CLP, 29 February 2016.

had crushed small businesses, vibrant streetscapes, generational continuities, and other romantic notions beneath their giant feet. Yet it was nostalgia he felt for them. A skyline was a collaboration, if an inadvertent one, between generations, seeming no less natural than a mountain range that had shuddered up from the earth. This new gap in space reversed time.[66]

However, the collaboration, it would seem, is a temporal one, across generations, rather than a territorial one across national borders. In some respects, then, this is the old, revanchist way of thinking. Although *The Submission* is not yet ready to fling itself outside national borders, Kamila Shamsie, so resolute in her view that American exceptionalism should not be reinforced in fictional responses to 9/11, wrote a favourable review of *The Submission*. Her response to the novel's conclusion is revealing, in part because of what she described as her own 'disturbing' decision to leave her character Raza incarcerated in Guantanamo at the end of *Burnt Shadows*. Shamsie seemed to take heart from *The Submission*:

> Waldman's imagined America of the future has "self-corrected" away from its mood of paranoia, the suspicion between its Muslim and non-Muslim citizens a thing of the past. From another writer this might sound like unwarranted optimism, but Waldman has been so sure-footed until now that it would be churlish not to hope that she is right about this, too.[67]

Is there a trace of longing here, from an author whose own pessimistic conclusion to her novel turned out to be so prescient? Despite Shamsie's father's suggestion that President Obama's announcement about the closure of Guantanamo 'changes the end of your novel, doesn't it', Shamsie's own scepticism about its closure turned out to be correct.

While Waldman's thesis was applauded with tentative optimism by Shamsie, Waldman herself appears less sure. In December 2011,

---

[66]Waldman, *The Submission*, p. 29.
[67]Kamila Shamsie, 'The Submission by Amy Waldman – A Review', *Guardian*, 24 August 2011, http://www.guardian.co.uk/books/2011/aug/24/the-submission-amy-waldman-review [accessed 20 May 2013].

she published a short story, 'Trotter's Road'. It imagines and indeed inhabits the extraterritorial far more fully than *The Submission* does. In this story, an Afghani man, desperate to raise enough money to be allowed to marry a local man's daughter, is employed by the American military to act as translator. The US forces have appointed him to translate Pashto, without seeming to understand or even care that Dari is in fact his first language. He fills the gaps in his knowledge of the language with his own inventions, telling each side what they want to hear. Colonel Trotter yearns to hear that the warlord who controls the section of land on which he is determined to build a road will halt all attacks. The warlord desires money to raise a militia. Aziz tells each side they will get what they desire. His deceit has been an incremental one, each lie easier to tell than the last: 'War had long ago foreshortened his horizons. To take the road kilometre by kilometre – to solve this problem today, even if it created new problems tomorrow – was all he knew how to do.'[68] We are back in the present tense again, trudging 'kilometre by kilometre', trying to solve problems today that will produce more difficulties later.

In some ways, Waldman's later short story seems to step back from her sense that we have 'moved on', as she put it, from 9/11. It is difficult to argue otherwise, given the continuing tensions in international relations, political discord on so many fronts, the refugee crisis provoked by war and invasion, and the ongoing terrorist attacks that have killed and injured so many thousands since 9/11. In my Coda, I look at one particular consequence of 9/11 which turned out to score itself on my mind in a peculiarly personal way: the publication of Michel Houellebecq's *Soumission* (Submission) and the murder of twelve people working at the satirical magazine *Charlie Hebdo*.

---

[68] Amy Waldman, 'Trotter's Road', *Financial Times*, 30 December 2011, http://www. ft.com/cms/s/2/407737e0-27f3-11e1-a4c4-00144feabdc0.html#axzz1wq3gUt4V [accessed 19 February 2016].

Coda

A catastrophe, shameless in its scope and unique in its contemporaneous distribution to a global audience, produced new territory for novelists on which literary forebears did not encroach. Their only predecessors were themselves, in their earlier incarnations as journalists, essayists and commentators. It is legitimate, therefore, to suggest that post-9/11 novelists might have been liberated from Harold Bloom's 'anxiety of influence'. However, it seemed that they invented a whole new set of anxieties for themselves, based on their own perception of having been inadequate to the event already. It was a sense captured by Art Spiegelman, the artist whose home was in Canal Street, a few blocks from the WTC, and whose daughter's school at Ground Zero was turned into a triage centre on the day of the attacks. He noted in his work *In the Shadow of No Towers* that the most abiding vision of 9/11 for him was one that he could not draw:

> The pivotal image from my 9/11 morning – one that didn't get photographed or videotaped into public memory but still remains burned onto the inside of my eyelids several years later – was the image of the looming north tower's glowing bones just before it vaporized. I repeatedly tried to paint this with humiliating results.[1]

The poet and former Archbishop of Canterbury Rowan Williams articulated a related difficulty, that any attempt to represent the attacks, in words rather than pictures in his case, would inevitably be impermanent. His view that any response to 9/11 could only be mutable and faltering was why he chose the title *Writing in the Dust* for his short essay about the day:

> [W]riting in the dust is writing something that won't last, something exposed to dissolution. [...] This isn't a theology or

[1] Art Spiegelman, *In the Shadow of No Towers* (New York: Pantheon Books, 2004), n.p.

a programme for action, but one person's attempt to find words for the grief and shock and loss of one moment. In the nature of things, these words won't last, and I need to acknowledge and accept that, and hope only that they may help to take forward someone else's mourning.[2]

This palimpsestic approach was a variation on Richard Ford's familiar conundrum: not where were the words, but which words would do for the time being until better ones might be found? Yet, even when a temporary form of words was settled upon, Rowan Williams remained unconvinced that writers were entitled to use them:

It can sound as though you're gratefully borrowing someone else's terrible experience to make another pious point. And after all, not everyone dies with words of love. There will have been cursing and hysteria and frantic, deluded efforts to be safe at all costs when people knew what was going on in those planes. And would anyone want their private words of love butchered to make a sermon?[3]

It is a powerfully made point by someone who survived the attacks and who witnessed the effect on himself and on those around him of trying to outrun the collapsing North Tower.

Ultimately, it is Rowan Williams's view that it is the 'shamelessness' of the catastrophe that transmuted it into something hard to render as fictionally resonant. Perhaps perversely, he says that it is failure that the novelist should be aiming for in the end:

It is quite designedly, as far as one can tell, an atrocity for the mass communication age. It was meant to be vulgarized, it was meant to be an event on television screens all around the world. It was a show, which is one of the terrifying things about it. And it does have that effect then of potentially paralyzing the describer who says 'Am I then just colluding in another round

[2]Rowan Williams, *Writing in the Dust: Reflections on 11th September and Its Aftermath* (London: Hodder & Stoughton, 2002), pp. 79–80.
[3]Ibid., pp. 5–6.

of the show business side of 9/11?' The horror of the *Shoah* is something that you peel away the coverings from bit by bit and you think you've got to the worst, and then there's more – that sense of horrified discovery that begins with the troops going into Belsen and slowly enlarges as Auschwitz, Dachau and Birkenau come in. Whereas this is shameless. And I suspect that this is another challenge for the novelist. [...] But if I were exploring that area I think what I might look for is the exemplary failure – the novel that somehow registers the scale of the disturbance, like something on a pressure graph, so that there is enough of a jolt. In our lifetimes this has probably been one of the major imaginative disruptions. And whether or not it's on the same level as the *Shoah* – well, on one level it's obviously not. It's not about six million people being butchered and killed in cold blood. But it is for our generation probably the biggest jolt. [...] Faced with the blatant the novelist may well say that what I have to do is to be oblique. Faced with the oblique the novelist may well have the duty to be blatant. And 9/11 is blatant.[4]

This goes to the heart of the writer's difficulties. It shares in its analysis some of the anxieties raised more than thirty years ago by the poet Geoffrey Hill, who wrote with singular force about the Holocaust. He attracted near-reverence from people who declared that he wrote about the concentration camps with rare power, but it was admiration that he despised: 'the burden which the writer's conscience must bear is that the horror might become that hideously outrageous thing, a cliché. This is the nightmare, the really blasphemous thing: that those camps could become a mere "subject".'[5] The idea of tragedy as 'subject' is indeed a repulsive one and resurrects the approach to 9/11 pursued by artist Gerhard Richter, which was that the only way to contain the tragedy was to remove paint rather than add it, thereby refusing to agitate or excite the viewer. It was what Rowan Williams was referring to when he told me how much he recoiled from what he called 'trauma pornography':

---

[4]Rowan Williams, interviewed by Charlie Lee-Potter, April 2013.
[5]Geoffrey Hill, interviewed by Blake Morrison, 'Under Judgement', New Statesman (London: The Statesman & Nation Publishing Company, 16 January 1980), Ninety-ninth Volume, January-June 1980, pp. 213–214.

It does get the adrenalin flowing in some ways. I'm very wary of that. Even your own text can work that way sometimes. I don't want to get excited by it. Let's be very blunt about this. If something like that happens in the world that we're in, it makes you interesting. 'Ooh! You were *there*?' And I have to be very aware of that and I have to be very suspicious of it. [...] And there have been times when I have very deliberately backed off saying anything about it because I don't want to say 'Hey, look at me! I'm interesting. I was *there*!'[6]

It is a frank admission by a man who has resolved to back away from any such attention. He would appear to share some of the reservations voiced by Geoffrey Hill that it is language itself, as well as the rapt spectator, which can be at fault. In an earlier incarnation of Zadie Smith's warning that the towers 'were covered in literary language when they fell', Hill pointed to the dangerous allure of piling up words around a tragedy, in order to excite a reader captivated by the event's innate outrageousness:

There is an indecency in language, which has nothing to do with the superficial indecencies of the pornographic or the scatological and which is most cogently expressed in that brief entry from Coleridge's notebook: 'Poetry – excites us to artificial feelings – makes us callous to real ones'. One's fear is that through the exercise of this art of such passionate finesse one might in the end be serving callousness.[7]

Rowan Williams's notion of the 'exemplary failure' seems to resonate here as a possible powerful escape route from the path of such polished callousness. It is worth noting that despite Rowan Williams's tolerance, compassion and intellectual power, he is still marked by his experiences, a fact that would underline the idea of 'exemplary failure' being preferable to any form of perfected prose. I asked him if he still feels wounded by his experiences on 9/11. He appears to be, but that is not the term he chooses, finally:

---

[6]RW, interviewed by CLP, April 2013.
[7]Geoffrey Hill, interviewed by Morrison, 'Under Judgement', pp. 213–214.

The word I would use is scarred rather than wounded. I know that when my memory goes back to that day, it flinches and there's still a near impossibility to get close to what was going on. But I was very protected. I didn't see the worst. But I suppose just that sense of being nearer death than I have ever been and the sheer intensity of it all. And that's there. It's just there. And I know that. And I know also what I feel when I see images on television – planes going... – I can't, I just can't. It's a trigger for me ....[8]

Even for those who did not experience the day directly, the trauma continues to resonate. There are frequent reminders of 9/11's disruptive power whenever and wherever subsequent and related attacks, massacres and wars occur. 9/11 has had a long trajectory: the wars in Afghanistan and Iraq, the 7/7 bombings in London, the Boston Marathon bombings, the murder of Drummer Lee Rigby,[9] beheadings and torture in Syria, suicide bomb attacks in Afghanistan, Nigeria, Pakistan and Iraq, the mass murders in Paris and the *Charlie Hebdo* massacre.

* * *

On the morning of 7 January 2015, I flew from the United Kingdom to France. My teenage son had been seriously injured and was in intensive care in a French hospital. As my plane touched down in France, two masked men armed with Kalashnikov assault rifles were entering the offices of the French satirical magazine *Charlie Hebdo*. Affiliated to so-called Islamic State and claiming to avenge the Prophet Muhammad, Cherif and Said Kouachi murdered twelve people and injured eleven more. By the time I reached the intensive care unit where my son was being cared for, the anguished cry *Je Suis Charlie* was in full flight across France. Hospital nurses, doctors and patients bore scraps of paper and pieces of card safety-pinned to their chests, with the now-notorious words handwritten in biro or pencil. The nurse who took me to the intensive care unit was wearing a full sheet of computer paper across the front of her uniform, marked in blue ink.

<hr>

[8]RW, interviewed by CLP, April 2013.
[9]Lee Rigby was murdered near Woolwich Barracks in south east London in May 2013.

The phrase *Je Suis Charlie* expresses commonality, solidarity and resistance, redolent of President John F Kennedy's '*Ich bin ein Berliner*' of 1963, and '*Ce soir, nous sommes tous Américains*' uttered by the *France 2* television network on the evening of 9/11. 'Charlie' is both very un-French and is also my own name. Clearly, *Je Suis Charlie* had nothing to do with me, but finding myself so unexpectedly in a French hospital and with my son dangerously ill, I could not help but be affected by the sight of my name in endless visual echo wherever I looked. The effect was weirdly palindromic: I found myself radiating empathy to everyone so oddly labelled 'Charlie', while absorbing a tiny modicum of their solidarity for myself. The nurse with the computer paper on her uniform asked for my name. When I answered, she thanked me for my support.

In the peculiarly charged environment provoked by the *Charlie Hebdo* massacre, familiar laws of reticence and reserve between strangers evaporated. For the next two weeks, I spent eleven hours a day in the hospital listening to anguished conversations between patients, visitors and medical staff. They asked themselves repeatedly whether such attacks might happen again. (It was a question that received its own shocking reply eleven months later when 130 people were murdered by Islamist suicide bombers and gunmen in Paris.) A German patient, frustrated that he could not understand what was being said, asked me to translate the French into English. He then requested that I translate his views back into French so that his opinion would count for something too.

For days, a television high on the wall of my son's ward played endless loops of fuzzy video footage showing *Charlie Hebdo*'s offices, the Kouachi brothers in the road, the two of them driving off in their car, the manhunt for them. On the day the brothers were finally killed, there was a dispute between two nurses on the ward. One demanded of the other that she remove *Je Suis Charlie* from her uniform because she was not entitled to political views. The other asked furiously, 'Where's your loyalty?'

One week after the massacre, I left my hotel early to buy a copy of the new issue of *Charlie Hebdo*. It was a thirty-minute walk to the hospital and I stopped at every newsagent, food-store and garage. Each shop window bore the same notice: '*plus de Charlie*' – *Charlie Hebdo* sold out. The same note was stuck to the cash register in the hospital shop. The magazine's print run had gone from 60,000 on the day of the murders to 8 million.

In a shocking confluence of life and literature, the 7 January cover had displayed an image of the French novelist Michel Houellebecq, to mark that day's publication of his new novel *Soumission* (Submission). To describe Houellebecq as provocative is to impose demands on the term that it can barely support. In 2001, he gave an interview in which he described Islam as 'the most stupid religion' and a fatwa was issued. He went into hiding, and two days later, the 9/11 attacks took place. In 2001, he had published *Platform*, a novel about a sex tourism travel business in Bangkok that concludes with an Islamist terrorist attack. The principal character's name is Michel, as it often is in Houellebecq's novels. (The distinction Houellebecq makes is that his 'main characters are never self-portraits, but they are always projections'.[10]) *Platform*'s Michel expresses the view that 'Every time I heard that a Palestinian terrorist, or a Palestinian child or a pregnant Palestinian woman, had been gunned down in the Gaza Strip, I felt a quiver of enthusiasm at the thought of one less Muslim'.[11] When Houellebecq was asked how he dared write in such inflammatory terms, his response was: '"[I]t's easy. I just pretend that I'm already dead"'.[12] Again, this is something that he had already done: in his novel *The Map and the Territory*, Houellebecq describes his own fictional murder. Just as Don DeLillo earned the status of someone who wrote about events yet to happen, for years Houellebecq has been writing about events that his readers dread might happen and which sometimes do. His grotesque and highly graphic description in *Platform* of an Islamist machine gun assault on tourists sitting outside a café in Bangkok is almost intolerable to read post the 2015 massacres in Sousse, Paris and elsewhere. On the evening of 13 November, everyone was reminded how fragile the defiant cry of *Je Suis Charlie* was. I spoke to an old friend in Paris that night who said that the battle cry already seemed out of date: '*Nous sommes tous Charlie* was a slogan adopted to show solidarity with a targeted group. Now the group being targeted is all of us. Slogans are superfluous.'[13]

---

[10]Sylvain Bourmeau, 'At Work', Interview with Michel Houellebecq *the Paris Review*, 2 January 2015.

[11]Michel Houellebecq, *Platform* [2001] (London: Vintage, 2003), p. 349.

[12]'Michel Houellebecq, The Art of Fiction No. 206'. MH interviewed by Susannah Hunnewell, *the Paris Review*, Fall 2010, No. 194.

[13]Adrianne Ryder-Cook Joseph in conversation with Charlie Lee-Potter, 13 November 2015.

In Houellebecq's *Soumission*, François, a lethargic, alcoholic, apathetic, self-obsessed, ready-meal eating, sexually dysfunctional academic, has started to worry that '*après moi le déluge*' may be an outdated luxury: 'What if the deluge came before I died?'[14] Like his literary hero Joris-Karl Huysmans, he attempts to find religious redemption by visiting the Black Virgin of Rocamadour. Houellebecq has admitted that when he started writing the novel, he assumed there would be what he calls a 'Catholic embrace' at the end. 'It wasn't meant to be called *Soumission* – the first title was *La Conversion* (The Conversion). And in my original project, the narrator converted, too, but to Catholicism.'[15] However, he found it impossible to follow through with the idea and concludes the novel, instead, with François looking forward to the moment when he will convert to Islam, thereby earning himself the right to have three wives and a large salary. But in what I can only term a *post*-proleptic ending, Houellebecq changes the temporal drive. The past tense of the rest of the novel shifts, and Francois looks ahead to his religious conversion and to the moment when he can pick his new wives:

> Each of these girls, no matter how pretty, would be happy and proud if I chose her, and would feel honoured to share my bed. They would be worthy of love; and I, for my part, would come to love them.
>
> [...] I'd be given another chance; and it would be the chance at a second life, with very little connection to the old one.
>
> I would have nothing to mourn.[16]

But this is written in conditional tense, as though Houellebecq is hedging his potential bets. It is not the counterfactual conditional tense of Jonathan Safran Foer's Oskar in *Extremely Loud and Incredibly Close*, mournfully longing for a different conclusion to his father's life. There is a striking counterpoint between Oskar's final words: 'We would have been safe', and Francois's closing thought: 'I would have nothing to mourn.'

---

[14]Michel Houellebecq, *Soumission*, trans. Lorin Stein (London: William Heinemann, 2015), p. 58.

[15]Bourmeau, 'At Work'

[16] Houellebecq, *Soumission*, trans. Lorin Stein, pp. 249–250.

Many have assumed that Houellebecq is definitive in his assertion that François converts to Islam. I disagree and would suggest, instead, that Houellebecq chooses the conditional tense because he wishes to imbricate the possibility of an alternative ending into his fiction, thereby maintaining the novel's essential mutability. We know that he has considered the possibility of the novel having a different conclusion, first in his assertion that he had hoped to give it a Catholic overlay, and also in his admission that if he had written the novel after the *Charlie Hebdo* attacks and the murder of his friend, rather than before, the text would have been different. His interview for *the Paris Review* was published five days before the massacre in Paris. At that point, his response to the question 'In writing this book did you feel you were a Cassandra, a prophet of doom?' had been: "'You can't really describe this book as a pessimistic prediction. At the end of the day, things don't go all that badly, really. [...] Politically, one might even welcome this development – it's not really a catastrophe."'[17] But asked later that year if he would have rewritten the book if it had not been completed before the massacre, he was unequivocal:

> Yes, I think the book would have been more violent. The civil war which was threatening to explode in a part of the book might actually have exploded. The fact that the immense majority of Muslims actually disapprove of these attacks is not a reassuring thing because it's in fact the triumph of the minority. [...] Unfortunately, often the violent minority triumphs over the majority.[18]

It would seem that *Soumission* is Houellebecq's optimistic version of events, rather than the version he judged to be best suited to the new reality.

One of those murdered in *Charlie Hebdo*'s offices was Houellebecq's friend Bernard Maurice. That day Houellebecq was forced into hiding again and given police protection. In a reverse echo of the dictum *Je Suis Charlie*, the French Prime Minister Manuel Valls announced, '*La France, ce n'est pas La Soumission, ce n'est pas Michel Houellebecq.*' President François Hollande said the same.

---

[17]Bourmeau, 'At Work'.

[18]Michel Houellebecq, interviewed on *Front Row*, BBC Radio 4, 4 September 2015.

It seemed clear that neither man had read the new novel. This time it was not Islamophobic in tone, but was a bleak, dystopic thesis on the failure and lassitude of France's intellectuals and political institutions, the entropy of the State and the weakness of its journalists. To that extent, it shares the target of its attacks with Waldman in her own novel of the same name, *The Submission*. (Others have chosen the title too: *Submission* is the name of a film about violence against women in Islamic societies, written by Ayaan Hirsi Ali and directed by Theo van Gogh. Both of them received death threats after its release, and van Gogh was stabbed and shot dead in Amsterdam in 2004.) Like Waldman, Houellebecq deploys a proleptic timeframe to imagine a French state in the near future now governed by an Islamic party. However, rather than looking to the future to signal that 'the country had moved on, self-corrected, as it always did, that feverish time mostly forgotten',[19] Houellebecq's motivations appear more sinister. While insisting that the novel is not Islamophobic, he said that he set the novel in 2022 to speed up history, but only in the direction in which it was inexorably going. The apparently liberating sense of forward motion devised by Waldman to escape from the entrapments and neuroses of the present has been subverted by Houellebecq and dragged back into the present. In his hands, the future simply becomes an extreme manifestation of the dystopic present. To that extent, his approach could be seen as a retrograde step in the ongoing attempts to render 9/11 and its consequences in artistic form.

The prolepsis of Waldman's *The Submission*, while being a familiar literary convention, articulates a fundamental aspect of fiction's hesitant response to 9/11: the novelist's exploration of temporal anxieties. How could the writer look to the future, without addressing the present? And how could the present be redefined artistically when it was so unbearable to examine? Writers have been writhing and struggling to avoid 9/11, as much as they have been striving to address it. Ford was perhaps the most circumspect of them all in his response to 9/11, taking a wide arc around it. However, Auster, DeLillo, Foer and McEwan all struggled too; they may have addressed the catastrophe more directly than Ford did, but they were no less challenged, even repelled by it. Shamsie and Aslam

---

[19]Amy Waldman, *The Submission* (London: William Heinemann, 2011), p. 287.

were less fastidious and anxious in their responses, but they too
wrestled with the idea of 'what next?' Waldman, writing ten years
after 9/11, was in some ways liberated from the event itself. What
could be more substantially 'next' than a proleptic approach, with
the submission of the title becoming not just a concrete noun but an
abstract one? Waldman's submission to and accommodation with
the catastrophe was attainable in part because she benefited from
the very thing that Foer, Auster et al. were most tested by: time. She
struggled, however, to escape the confines of the homeland shunned
so deliberately by Shamsie and Aslam, while Michel Houellebecq
appears to be doing his best to speed up the doomed race to drag
things back to the petrified core.

My findings would suggest that future novelists may enjoy greater
freedoms to define 9/11 than the early experimenters. The conundrum
for the literary first responders was not just their own panic, but the
automaticity of audiences' revulsion. As I have tried to demonstrate,
there was a sense that things could not be said and, in the visual
arts, things could not be shown. The self-censorship admitted to by
TV anchor Dan Rather permeated the work of artists who seemed
anxious and overwrought about what they could write. Certainly,
further insights into the processes of defining such a globally 'known'
event are likely in the work of future novelists. There is no sense at
present that journalism will be able to provide any more assistance
than it has done hitherto; indeed, it seems likely that the work of
journalists – 'embedded' as it is in the immediacy of the moment –
will continue to be a false friend to novelists, both when they attempt
to engage in journalism themselves and when they seek its guidance
in constructing novelistic responses to global crises and conundrums.

However, as the day slips from close-up to mid-view, it has
become somehow more manageable, more definable. It looms a
little less large than it did, and for this reason, it appears to be
more containable within and by art. Incidentally, it was not just art
that struggled to contain 9/11. As soon as it became clear that the
Twin Towers had been deliberately targeted and that other flights
had been hijacked too, BBC Television's news correspondent Fergus
Walsh was told to start preparing a live studio report, giving an
overview of what had happened and where:

> I needed to bring a sense of narrative to what was essentially the
> most improbable of all improbable narratives. In the newsroom,

when we witnessed live the second plane hitting the South Tower, we realized we were watching the biggest news story ever to play out in real time.[20] As part of our extensive coverage, we decided to do what became known as a 'Big Screen'. It was the first time we'd done one on the *News at Six* and it became a trend. I would stand in the studio, the presenter would throw to me and some maps behind me would animate. I would then try to bring sense to what seemed impossible – not how it was done or why it was done but *what* was done. But the graphics department was working on information that was changing all the time and once the map was made, it was very difficult to change it. At that stage, we couldn't imagine we'd need a map not only with Boston, Washington DC and New York on it, but with Pennsylvania too. When I came to do the live studio piece, the Pennsylvania crash site was too far west for the maps and I just had to point in that direction. We couldn't make any sense of it at all, and our graphics showed that. But when I went into the mundane details of flight numbers and airports and take-off times, in a sense it made it more real. It anchored it in the imagination, when we were still thinking it was impossible. What we were looking at was beyond terrible, but some of the simple facts can take you from images on the screen into the realm of the real. We weren't doing it for that reason, either consciously or unconsciously, – but retrospectively that's what we did.[21]

The idea of entering the 'realm of the real' is a potent one for novelists. To co-opt Frank Bascombe's phrase, 9/11 has assumed a more 'human scale'[22] than it had at first, but the 'realm of the real' is still, even now, a way off.

The old stricture that I touched on earlier in this work, Virginia Woolf's counsel that the close-up would present novelists with a 'painful jolt in the perspective', turned out to be prescient in its

---

[20]There are only three known recordings of the first plane hitting the North Tower: one was shot by a Czech tourist making a video to send to his family, another was captured by documentary makers shooting a film about a novice fireman and the third was a sequence of CCTV still frames.

[21]BBC News correspondent Fergus Walsh interviewed by Charlie Lee-Potter, 8 November 2015.

[22]Richard Ford, *The Lay of the Land* (London: Bloomsbury, 2006), p. 485.

definition of the difficulties of rendering 9/11 in artistic form. Not that Woolf could have imagined a novelistic responsibility to respond quite so swiftly as future novelists would be expected to do. But neither could she or those future novelists have imagined an event that would prove to be so traumatic and so testing to render in artistic form. For those who continue to maintain that 9/11 cannot or even should not be fictionalized, it is worth noting the words of the Russian poet Anna Akhmatova, whose son had been imprisoned by the Soviet secret police. Akhmatova was queuing in the snow outside the prison with others who were trying to find out what had happened to their relatives:

> I spent seventeen months in the prison lines of Leningrad. Once, someone 'recognized' me. Then a woman with bluish lips standing behind me, who, of course, had never heard me called by name before, woke up from the stupor to which everyone had succumbed and whispered in my ear (everyone spoke in whispers there):
> 'Can you describe this?'
> And I answered: 'Yes, I can.'
> Then something that looked like a smile passed over what had once been her face.[23]

There is an ambivalence to Akhmatova's words; a dutiful resolution to describe the horror, a conviction that it would be done, and yet combined with a '... but how?' That obligation clearly resonates with Rowan Williams. It is the reason, perhaps, why he has finally resolved to speak about his experience of 9/11. More than a decade and a half later he exemplifies, in a fragmentary way of course, the evolutionary path that novelists have explored. He could not speak about it, but now he has elected to do so. Kevin Marsh's invocation, cited at the outset of this work, that novelists who responded immediately in essays and non-fiction were denying themselves the one commodity that they needed, which was time, turns out to have been wise. The old idea, voiced by Audrey Niffenegger, of 'nodding

---

[23]Anna Akhmatova, 'Instead of a Preface', Leningrad, 1 April, 1957, *The Complete Poems of Anna Akhmatova*, trans. Judith Hemschemeyer, ed. Roberta Reeder (1997: Brookline, MA: Zephyr Press, 2006), p. 384.

at' 9/11 has grown tired, the 'love-spectrum' was an exhausted mode before it began, the neurotic fumbling for artistic expression has faded from view, and the swift and easy journalistic response is out of date. It is the wide sweep of history and the landscape beyond which has produced the richest and most assured ground for novelists. It would perhaps have been the surest territory for journalists, commentators and politicians too.

REFERENCES

Ahmed, Bonya. Voltaire Lecture, 2015, The British Humanist Association, 2 July 2015.

Akhmatova, Anna. 'Instead of a Preface.' Leningrad, 1 April 1957. *The Complete Poems of Anna Akhmatova*, translated by Judith Hemschemeyer, edited by Roberta Reeder, 384. 1997; Brookline, MA: Zephyr Press, 2006).

Allan, Stuart. 'Reweaving the Internet: Online News of September 11.' In *Journalism after September 11*, edited by Barbie Zelizer and Stuart Allan, 119–140. London: Routledge, 2002.

Amis, Martin. 'Intoxicating, free – the novelist life', *Daily Telegraph*, 15 October 2011.

Amis, Martin. *The Second Plane*. London: Jonathan Cape, 2008.

Amis, Martin. *Time's Arrow*. 1991; London: Vintage, 2003.

Arad, Michael and Peter Walker. Extract from memorial design statement for 'Reflecting Absence', 9/11 Memorial website, http://www.911memorial.org/design-competition [accessed 23 May 2016].

Arendt, Hannah. *Crises of the Republic*. Kindle edition. New York: Harcourt Brace & Co., 1969.

Armstrong,Tim. *The Logic of Slavery*. Cambridge: Cambridge University Press, 2012.

Aslam, Nadeem. *The Blind Man's Garden*. London: Faber & Faber, 2013.

Aslam, Nadeem. *The Wasted Vigil*. London: Faber & Faber, 2008.

Aslam, Nadeem, interviewed on *The Strand*, BBC World Service, 6 February 2013.

Aslam, Nadeem, interviewed on *Nightwaves*, BBC Radio 3, 6 February 2013.

Auster, Paul. *The Brooklyn Follies*. 2005; London: Faber & Faber, 2006.

Auster, Paul. 'Ghosts.' In *The New York Trilogy*, 1985; London: Faber & Faber, 1987.

Auster, Paul. Interviewed by George Miller, 'Paul Auster: *Man in the Dark*', Faber Books SoundCloud, November 2008, https://soundcloud.com/faberbooks/paul-auster-man-in-the-dark [accessed 24 May 2016].

Auster, Paul. *Leviathan*. London: Faber & Faber, 1992.

Auster, Paul. *Man in the Dark*. London: Faber & Faber, 2008.

Auster, Paul. *The New York Trilogy*. 1985; London: Faber & Faber, 1987.

Auster, Paul. 'Random Notes – September 11, 2001, 4.00 p.m.' In *110 Stories: New York Writes After September 11*, edited by Ulrich Baer, 34–36. New York: New York University Press, 2002.

Auster, Paul. *The Red Notebook*. London: Faber & Faber, 1995.

Auster, Paul. *Sunset Park*. London: Faber & Faber, 2010.

Auster, Paul. *Winter Journal*. London: Faber & Faber, 2012.

Auster, Paul, interviewed by George Miller. Accessed 24 May 2016. https://soundcloud.com/faberbooks/paul-auster-man-in-the-dark.

Auster, Paul, interviewed by Andrew Van Der Vlies, 'The Tyrannies and Epiphanies of Chance', *Oxonian Review*, 15 June 2004. Accessed 7 May 2013. http://www.oxonianreview.org/wp/the-tyrannies-and-epiphanies-of-chance/

Auster, Paul, interviewed by Helena de Bertodano, *Telegraph*, 16 November 2010.

Auster, Paul, interviewed by David Daley, Salon, 19 August 2012. Accessed 26 February 2013. http://www.salon.com/2012/08/19/paul_auster_i_think_of_the_right_wing_republicans_as_jihadists/.

Baudrillard, Jean. *The Intelligence of Evil or the Lucidity Pact*, translated by Chris Turner. Oxford: Berg, 2005.

Baudrillard, Jean. *Simulacra and Simulation*, translated by Sheila Faria Glaser. Ann Arbor: University of Michigan Press, 1994.

Baudrillard, Jean. *The Spirit of Terrorism*, translated by Chris Turner London: Verso, 2012.

BBC. 'Artists write "Homeland is racist" on set', BBC News, 15 October, 2015. Accessed 4 February 2016. http://www.bbc.co.uk/news/world-us-canada-34536434.

BBC. 'Barack Obama Pledges to "finish the job" in Afghanistan', BBC News, 2 May 2012. Accessed 19 February 2016. http://www.bbc.co.uk/news/world-us-canada-17917750.

BBC. 'One World Trade Center Becomes New York's Tallest Building', BBC News, 1 May 2012. Accessed 19 February 2016. http://www.bbc.co.uk/news/world-us-canada-17898138.

BBC News. 26 February 1993. Accessed 4 May 2008. http://news.bbc.co.uk/onthisday/hi/dates/stories/february/26/newsid_2516000/2516469.stm.

BBC World Service Poll, carried out in October 2007. Accessed 25 March 2013. http://news.bbc.co.uk/1/hi/7134918.stm.

Beigbeder, Frédéric. *Windows on the World*. English edition, translated by Frank Wynne. London: Harper Perennial, 2005.

Beigbeder, Frédéric. *Windows on the World*. French edition. Paris: Éditions Grasset & Fasquelle, 2003.

Bellow, Saul. *Dangling Man*. 1944; London: Penguin, 2007.

Belsey, Catherine. *Critical Practice*. 1980; London: Routledge, 2002.

Binelli, Mark. 'Bruce Springsteen's American Gospel', *Rolling Stone*, 22 August 2002. Accessed 17 January 2016. http://www.rollingstone.com/music/news/bruce-springsteens-american-gospel-20020822.

Binelli, Mark. 'Intensity of a Plot', *Guernica*, 17 July 2007. Accessed 15 May 2013. http://www.guernicamag.com/interviews/intensity_of_a_plot/.

Bird, S. Elizabeth. 'Taking It Personally: Supermarket Tabloids after September 11.' In *Journalism after 9/11*, edited by Barbie Zelizer and Stuart Allan, 151. London: Routledge, 2002.

Blumenberg, Hans. *Shipwreck with Spectator: Paradigm of a Metaphor for Existence*. Cambridge: MIT Press, 1997.

Bourmeau, Sylvain. 'At Work', Interview with Michel Houellebecq, *Paris Review*, 2 January 2015.

Bradbury, Malcolm. *The Modern American Novel*. 1983; Oxford: Oxford University Press, 1992.

Bush, George W. *Address to a Joint Session of Congress and the American People*, 20 September 2001. Accessed 16 March 2013. http://georgewbush-whitehouse.archives.gov/news/releases/2001/09/20010920-8.html.

Bush, George W. Archives, 'Press Gaggle with Scott McClellan Aboard Air Force One En Route Andrews Air Force Base, MD', 31 August 2005. Accessed 30 March 2013. *The White House Archives*, http://georgewbush-whitehouse.archives.gov/news/releases/2005/08/20050831-2.html.

Campbell, Alastair. *The Burden of Power: Countdown to Iraq, The Alastair Campbell Diaries*. 2012; London: Arrow Books, 2013.

Campbell, James. 'The Mighty Quinn', *Guardian*, 12 November 2005. Accessed 6 May 2013. http://www.guardian.co.uk/books/2005/nov/12/fiction.shopping.

Cauchon, Dennis and Martha Moore. 'Desperation Forced a Horrific Decision', *USA Today*, 2 September 2002. Accessed 21 February 2016. http://usatoday30.usatoday.com/news/sept11/2002-09-02-jumper_x.htm.

Chaudhuri, Amit. 'Qatrina and the Books.' *London Review of Books* 31 (16) (27 August 2009). http://www.lrb.co.uk/v31/n16/amit-chaudhuri/qatrina-and-the-books [accessed 22 February 2016].

Cochrane, Kira. 'Barbara Kingsolver: From Witch Hunt to Winner', *Guardian*, 10 June 2010. Accessed 8 September 2014. http://www.theguardian.com/books/2010/jun/10/barbara-kingsolver-orange-prize.

Combat Paper Project. Accessed 15 March 2013. http://www. combatpaper.org/index.html.

Connerton, Paul. *How Societies Remember*. Cambridge: Cambridge University Press, 1989.

Conversations with Don DeLillo, edited by Thomas DePietro. Jackson, MS: University Press of Mississippi, 2005.

Cowart, Courtney. *An American Awakening: From Ground Zero to Katrina: The People We Are Free to Be*. New York: Seabury Books, 2008.

Crownshaw, Richard. 'Introduction.' In *The Future of Memory*, edited by Richard Crownshaw, Jane Kilby and Antony Rowland, 4. New York: Berghahn Books, 2010.

Cuomo, Mario, quoted by the BBC 26 February 1993. Accessed 4 May 2008. http://news.bbc.co.uk/onthisday/hi/dates/stories/february/26/ newsid_2516000/2516469.stm.

Curran, James, interviewed on *Making News: The Endless Cycle*, BBC Radio 4, 9 April 2013.

De Man, Paul. 'Literary History and Literary Modernity.' *Daedalus* 99 (2) *Theory in Humanistic Studies* (Spring 1970): 384–404.

DeLillo, Don. 'Assassination Aura.' In *Introduction to Libra*, v. 1988; London: Penguin, 2005.

DeLillo, Don. 'Baader-Meinhof.' In *The Angel Esmerelda*: Nine Stories, 105–118. 1 April 2002; London: Picador, 2011.

DeLillo, Don. *Cosmopolis*. 2003; London: Scribner, 2004.

DeLillo, Don. *Falling Man*. London: Picador, 2007.

DeLillo, Don. 'In the Ruins of the Future', *Guardian*, 22 December 2001. Accessed 22 January 2016. http://www.theguardian.com/books/2001/ dec/22/fiction.dondelillo.

DeLillo, Don. *Mao II*. 1991; London: Vintage, 1992.

DeLillo, Don. *Players*. 1977; London: Vintage, 1991.

DeLillo, Don. *Underworld*. 1997; London: Picador, 1998.

DeLillo, Don, interviewed by Mark Binelli, 'Intensity of a Plot', *Guernica*, 17 July 2007. Accessed 15 May 2013. http://www.guernicamag.com/ interviews/intensity_of_a_plot/.

Dickens, Charles. *A Tale of Two Cities*. 1859; London: Penguin Classics, 2003.

Doran, John. 'Time Becomes a Loop: William Basinski Interviewed', *The Quietus*, 15 November 2012. Accessed 4 January 2016. http:// thequietus.com/articles/10680-william-basinski-disintegration-loops- interview.

Eaglestone, Robert. *The Holocaust and the Postmodern*. Oxford: Oxford University Press, 2004.

Eaglestone, Robert. Keynote address at Institute of English Studies conference *After the War*, 6 May 2009.

Evans, Stephen. 'Ground Zero.' In *The Day that Shook the World: Understanding September 11th*, edited by Jenny Baxter and Malcolm Downing, 23. London: BBC Worldwide, 2001.

Faludi, Susan. *The Terror Dream*. 2007; London: Atlantic Books, 2008.

Fassin, Didier and Richard Rechtman. *The Empire of Trauma: An Inquiry into the Condition of Victimhood*, translated by Rachel Gomme. Princeton: Princeton University Press, 2009.

Finnegan, Lisa. *No Questions Asked: News Coverage since 9/11*. Westport, CT: Praeger, 2007.

Fisk, Robert. *Pity the Nation: Lebanon at War*. 3rd edition. Oxford: Oxford University Press, 2001.

Foer, Jonathan Safran. *Extremely Loud and Incredibly Close*. London: Hamish Hamilton, 2005.

Ford, Richard. 'The Attack Took More than the Victims' Lives. It Took Their Deaths', *New York Times*, 23 September 2001. Accessed 30 March 2013. http://www.nytimes.com/2001/09/23/magazine/23WWLN.html.

Ford, Richard. 'Elegy for My City', *Observer*, 4 September 2005. Accessed 13 March 2013. http://www.guardian.co.uk/books/2005/sep/04/hurricanekatrina.features.

Ford, Richard. *Exclusive Extract from the Lay of The Land: Special Edition for Richard Ford's UK Tour*, December 2004, produced by OSCAR (South East Literature Promoters Network), courtesy of Random House Publishers.

Ford, Richard. *Independence Day*. 1995; London: Bloomsbury, 2006.

Ford, Richard. *The Lay of the Land*. London: Bloomsbury, 2006.

Ford, Richard. *Let Me Be Frank with You*. London: Bloomsbury, 2014.

Ford, Richard. *The Sportswriter*. 1986; London: Collins Harvill, 2006.

Ford, Richard, interviewed by Chas Bowie, *Portland Mercury*, 19 October 2006. Accessed 16 May 2013. http://www.portlandmercury.com/portland/richard-ford-interview/Content?oid=73912.

Ford, Richard, interviewed by Phil Hogan, 'To Be Frank', *Observer*, 24 September 2006. Accessed 25 March 2013. http://www.guardian.co.uk/books/2006/sep/24/fiction.features.

Ford, Richard, interviewed by Ramona Koval, *The Book Show*, Radio National, 4 June 2007. Accessed 25 March 2013. http://www.abc.net.au/radionational/programs/bookshow/richard-fords-the-lay-of-the-land/3242570#transcript.

Ford, Richard, interviewed by Ramona Koval, Sydney Writers' Festival: 4 June 2007. Accessed 4 May 2008. http://www.abc.net.au/rn/bookshow/stories/2007/1941373.htm.

Franzen, Jonathan. 'Tuesday, and After', *New Yorker*, 24 September 2001.

Freud, Sigmund. 'A Note upon the "Mystic Writing Pad"', *General Psychological Theory, Chapter XIII*, 1925. Accessed 20 May 2013. http://home.uchicago.edu/~awinter/mystic.pdf.

Freud, Sigmund. *The Uncanny*, translated by David McLintock. 1919; London: Penguin, 2003.

Giuliani, Rudy, interviewed by Steve Forbes: 'Remembering 9/11: The Rudy Giuliani interview', *Forbes*, 9 September 2011. Accessed 18 January 2016. http://www.forbes.com/sites/steveforbes/2011/09/09/remembering-911-the-rudy-giuliani-interview/#2715e4857a0b6e050 4a45897.

Goldsmith, Kenneth. *Seven American Deaths and Disasters*. New York: powerHouse Books, 2013.

Gray, Richard. *After the Fall: American Literature since 9/11*. Malden, MA: John Wiley & Sons, 2011.

Greenspan, Elizabeth. *Battle for Ground Zero*. New York: Palgrave Macmillan, 2013.

Gunaratna, Rohan. *Inside Al Qaeda: Global Network of Terror*. New York: Columbia University Press, 2002, p. 4, ProQuest ebrary. Web. 15 December 2015.

Hamid, Mohsin. 'A Beheading', *Granta 112: Pakistan*, Autumn 2010.

Hamid, Mohsin. 'Discontent and Its Civilizations.' In *Discontent and Its Civilizations*, 123. 2010; London: Hamish Hamilton, 2014.

Hamid, Mohsin. *The Reluctant Fundamentalist*. London: Hamish Hamilton, 2007.

Hamid, Mohsin. 'Silencing Pakistan', *Express Tribune with the International Herald Tribune*, 4 June 2011. Accessed 21 February 2013. http://tribune.com.pk/story/181760/silencing-pakistan/.

Hamid, Mohsin, interviewed by Hamish Hamilton for Hamid's official website, February 2007. Accessed 22 May 2013. http://www.mohsinhamid.com/interviewhh2007.html.

Hamid, Mohsin, interviewed by Anna H. R. Khan, *Stanford Daily*, 23 April 2007.

Hamid, Mohsin, interviewed by Harcourt for Hamid's official website, March 2007.

Hamid, Mohsin, interviewed on BBC Radio 4's Book Club, 4 September 2011. Accessed 25 March 2013. http://www.bbc.co.uk/programmes/b0144ybj.

Hamid, Mohsin, interviewed by John Mullan for Guardian Book Club: '*The Reluctant Fundamentalist* by Mohsin Hamid', 21 May 2011. Accessed 26 February 2016. http://www.theguardian.com/books/2011/may/21/book-club-reluctant-fundamentalist-hamid.

Harris, Robert R. 'A Talk with Don DeLillo', *New York Times Books*, 10 October 1982. Accessed 25 March 2013. http://www.nytimes.com/books/97/03/16/lifetimes/del-v-talk1982.html.

Hill, Geoffrey, interviewed by Blake Morrison, 'Under Judgement', *New Statesman*. London: The Statesman & Nation Publishing Company, 16 January 1980, Ninety-ninth Volume, January-June 1980.

Hitchens, Christopher. 'Believe Me, It's Torture.' In *Arguably*, 448–454. London: Atlantic Books, 2012.

Hoskins, Andrew and Ben O'Loughlin. *War and Media: The Emergence of Diffused War*. Cambridge: Polity Press, 2010.

Houellebecq, Michel. *Platform*, translated by Frank Wynne. 2001; London: Vintage, 2003.

Houellebecq, Michel. *Submission*, translated by Lorin Stein. London: William Heinemann, 2015.

Houellebecq, Michel. Interviewed on *Front Row*, BBC Radio 4, 4 September 2015.

Huffington, Arianna. 'The Flyover Presidency of George W. Bush', *Huffington Post*, 31 August 2005. Accessed 28 May 2013. http://www.huffingtonpost.com/arianna-huffington/the-flyover-presidency-of_b_6566.html.

Hunnewell, Susannah. 'Michel Houellebecq, The Art of Fiction No. 206', *Paris Review*, Fall 2010. No. 194.

James, David. 'A Renaissance for the Crystalline Novel?' *Contemporary Literature* 53 (4) (Winter 2012): 845–874.

Jenkins, Roy. *Churchill*. London: Macmillan, 2001.

Junod, Tom. 'The Falling Man', *Esquire*, 8 September 2009. Accessed 24 March, 2013. http://www.esquire.com/features/ESQ0903-SEP_FALLINGMAN.

Kakutani, Michiko. 'A Man, a Woman and a Day of Terror', *New York Times*, 9 May 2007. Accessed 25 February 2016. http://www.nytimes.com/2007/05/09/books/09kaku.html.

Karim, Karim H. 'Making Sense of the "Islamic Peril".' In *Journalism after September 11*, 102. London: Routledge, 2002.

Keane, Fergal. 'The Mind of the Terrorist.' In *The Day that Shook the World*, edited by Jenny Baxter and Malcolm Downing, 56. London: BBC Worldwide, 2001.

Kennedy, Charles, speaking in the House of Commons, 14 September 2001, *Hansard*, 14 September 2001. Accessed 29 February 2016. http://www.publications.parliament.uk/pa/cm200102/cmhansrd/vo010914/debtext/10914-02.htm#10914-02_spnew1.

Kermode, Frank. *The Sense of an Ending*. 1967; Oxford: Oxford University Press, 2000.

King, John. 'Administration Defends Bush Flight to Carrier', *CNN International*, 8 May 2003. Accessed 4 May 2008. http://edition.cnn.com/2003/ALLPOLITICS/05/07/bush.lincoln/.

Kingsolver, Barbara. 'And Our Flag Was Still There.' In *Small Wonder*, 238. London: Faber & Faber, 2002.

Kirn, Walter. 'Extremely Loud and Incredibly Close: Everything is Included', *New York Times*, 3 April 2005. Accessed 25 March 2013. http://www.nytimes.com/2005/04/03/books/review/0403cover-kirn.html?pagewanted=all&_r=0.

Laqueur, Thomas. 'We Are All Victims Now.' *London Review of Books* 32 (13) (8 July 2010): 19–23.

Lethem, Jonathan. 'To My Italian Friends.' In *The Ecstasy of Influence*, 222, 227. 2012; London: Jonathan Cape, 2013.

Lin, Maya. 'Making the Memorial', *New York Review of Books*, 2 November 2000. Accessed 22 February 2016. http://www.nybooks.com/articles/2000/11/02/making-the-memorial/.

Litt, Toby. 'The Trembling Air', *Guardian*, 26 May 2007. Accessed 26 March 2013. http://www.guardian.co.uk/books/2007/may/26/fiction.dondelillo.

Mallarmé, Stephane. *A Tomb for Anatole*, translated by Paul Auster. San Francisco: North Point Press,1983.

Man on Wire, film dir. by James Marsh, Wall to Wall production in association with Red Box Films, 2008.

Mars-Jones, Adam. 'As His World Came Tumbling Down', *Observer*, 13 May 2007. Accessed 15 May 2013. http://www.guardian.co.uk/books/2007/may/13/fiction.dondelillo.

Marsh, Kevin. 'Afghanistan, Truth and the Unexamined War.' In *Afghanistan, War and the Media: Deadlines and Frontlines*, edited by Richard Lance Keeble and John Mair, 81. Bury St Edmunds: Arima Publishing, 2010.

Martin, Father James. Interviewed on 'Fresh Air', National Public Radio, 12 August 2002.

Mary Boone Gallery, Notes from the Mary Boone Gallery, New York. Accessed 25 March 2013. http://www.maryboonegallery.com/exhibitions/2008-2009/Eric-Fischl/Eric-Fischl-2008.pdf.

McCann, Colum, interviewed by Bret Anthony Johnston, National Book Award Winner Fiction Interview, National Book Foundation, 2009. Accessed 1 February 2016. http://www.nationalbook.org/nba2009_f_mccann_interv.html#.Vq9cBhiLQ0Q.

McChesney, Robert W. 'September 11 and the Structural Limitations of US Journalism.' In *Journalism after September 11*, edited by Barbie Zelizer and Stuart Allan, 91–100. London: Routledge, 2002.

McEwan, Ian. 'A Message from Paris', Edge.org, 14 November 2015. https://www.edge.org/conversation/ian_mcewan-a-message-from-paris [accessed 23 May 2016].

McEwan, Ian. 'Only Love and Then Oblivion', *Guardian*, 15 September 2001. Accessed 1 March 2013. http://www.guardian.co.uk/world/2001/sep/15/september11.politicsphilosophyandsociety2.

McEwan, Ian. *Saturday*. London: Jonathan Cape, 2005.

McGrath, Charles. 'A New Jersey State of Mind', *New York Times*, 24 October 2006. Accessed 4 May 2008. http://www.nytimes.com/2006/10/25/books/25ford.html?fta=y.

McInerney, Jay. 'The Uses of Invention', *Guardian*, 17 September 2005. Accessed 22 January 2016. http://www.theguardian.com/books/2005/sep/17/fiction.vsnaipaul.

Metres, Philip. *Abu Ghraib Arias*. Denver/Rosslyn: Flying Guillotine Press, 2011.

Middleton, Peter and Tim Woods. *Literatures of Memory: History, Time and Space in Postwar Writing*. Manchester: Manchester University Press, 2000.

Morandi, Giorgio, cited by Museo Morandi, Bologna. Accessed 24 March 2013. http://www.museomorandi.it/index_net.htm.

Morley, Catherine. 'How Do We Write about This? The Domestic and the Global in the Post-9/11 Novel.' *Journal of American Studies* 45 (4) (November 2011): 717–731.

Morrison, Blake. 'Future Tense', *Guardian*, 17 May 2003. Accessed 25 March 2013. http://www.guardian.co.uk/books/2003/may/17/fiction.dondelillo.

Murdoch, Iris. 'Against Dryness: A Polemical Sketch.' In *The Novel Today: Contemporary Writers on Modern Fiction*, edited by Malcolm Bradbury, 23–31. London: Fontana, 1990.

Murray, Don. 'Behaving in the Face of Tragedy.' In Forward *Crisis Journalism: A Handbook for Media Response*, ii. American Press Institute, 2001.

Niffenegger, Audrey, interviewed by Veronica Bond, December 2003. Accessed 14 March 2013. http://www.bookslut.com/features/2003_12_001158.php.

9/11 Memorial website. Accessed 29 March 2013. http://www.911memorial.org/names-arrangement.

Nobel, Philip. *Sixteen Acres: Architecture and the Outrageous Struggle for the Future of Ground Zero*. New York: Metropolitan Books, 2005.

Noonan, Peggy. 'The Right Man', *Wall Street Journal*, 30 January 2003. Accessed 18 March 2013. http://online.wsj.com/article/SB1043895876926710064.html.

O'Hagan, Andrew. 'Racing Against Reality', *New York Review of Books*, 28 June 2007. Accessed 26 January 2016. http://www.nybooks.com/articles/2007/06/28/racing-against-reality/.

O'Leary, Stephen. 'Rumors of Grace and Terror', *Online Journalism Review*, University of Southern California, 2 April 2004. Accessed 4 May 2008. http://www.ojr.org/ojr/ethics/1017782038.php.

O'Neill, Joseph. *Netherland*. London: Fourth Estate, 2008.

Paulson, Ken. 'A Patriotic Press Is a Vigilant One.' In *Crisis Journalism, A Handbook for Media Response*, 46–47. Sunrise Valley, Reston, VA: American Press Institute October 2001.

Phillips, Kevin. *The Politics of Rich and Poor: Wealth and the American Electorate in the Reagan Aftermath*. New York: Random House, 1990.

Pozorski, Aimee. *Falling After 9/11: Crisis in American Art and Literature*. New York: Bloomsbury, 2014.

Rakoff, David. 'Post-9/11 Modernism', *New York Times Magazine*, 27 October 2002. Accessed 25 March 2013. http://www.nytimes.com/2002/10/27/magazine/27QUESTIONS.html.

Rather, Dan, interviewed by Madeleine Holt, BBC *Newsnight*, 6 June 2002. Accessed 15 March 2013. http://news.bbc.co.uk/1/hi/programmes/newsnight/archive/2029634.stm.

Rawnsley, Andrew. *The End of the Party: The Rise and Fall of New Labour*. London: Penguin, 2010.

Redfield, Marc. *The Rhetoric of Terror: Reflections on 9/11 and the War on Terror*. New York: Fordham University Press, 2009.

Richter, Gerhard. In conversation with Nicholas Serota. Extract taken from recording for the Tate Channel and reprinted in *Tate Guide*, December 2011–January 2012.

Rosen, Jay. 'September 11 in the Mind of American Journalism.' In *Journalism after September 11*, edited by Barbie Zelizer and Stuart Allan, 27. London: Routledge, 2002.

Rothberg, Michael. 'A Failure of the Imagination: Diagnosing the Post-9/11 Novel: A Response to Richard Gray.' *American Literary History* 21 (1) (Spring 2009): 152–158.

Santner, Eric. 'History Beyond the Pleasure Principle: Some Thoughts on the Representation of Trauma.' In *Probing the Limits of Representation: Nazism and the 'Final Solution'*, edited by Saul Friedlander, 143–154. Cambridge, MA: Harvard University Press, 1992.

Self, Will, interviewed on *Making News: The Endless Cycle*, BBC Radio 4, 9 April 2013.

Shamsie, Kamila. *Burnt Shadows*. London: Bloomsbury, 2009.

Shamsie, Kamila. 'Our Dead, Your Dead', *Guardian*, 6 September 2011. Accessed 12 February 2016. http://www.theguardian.com/books/2011/sep/06/9-11-stories-kamila-shamsie.

Shamsie, Kamila. 'The Submission by Amy Waldman – a Review', *Guardian*, 24 August 2011. Accessed 20 May 2013. http://www.guardian.co.uk/books/2011/aug/24/the-submission-amy-waldman-review.

Shenk, Joshua Wolf. 'Living to Tell the Tale', *Mother Jones*, May/June 2005. Accessed 9 November 2015. http://www.motherjones.com/media/2005/05/jonathan-safran-foer.

Simpson, David. *9/11: The Culture of Commemoration*. Chicago: The University of Chicago Press, 2006.

Smith, Zadie, talks with Ian McEwan, *The Believer*, August 2005. Accessed 6 January 2016. http://www.believermag.com/issues/200508/?read=interview_mcewan.

Smith, Zadie. 'Two Paths for the Novel', *New York Review of Books*, 20 November 2008. Accessed 18 March 2013. http://www.nybooks.com/articles/archives/2008/nov/20/two-paths-for-the-novel/?pagination=false.

Solomon, Norman. 'Foreword.' In *No Questions Asked: News Coverage since 9/11*, edited by Lisa Finnegan, xiii. Westport, CT: Praeger, 2007.

Sontag, Susan. *Regarding the Pain of Others*. London: Penguin, 2003.

Sontag, Susan. 'Tuesday, and After', *The New Yorker*, 24 September 2001.

Spiegelman, Art. *In the Shadow of No Towers*. New York: Pantheon Books, 2004.

Storr, Robert. *September: A History Painting by Gerhard Richter*. London: Tate Publishing, 2010.

Stubblefield, Thomas. *9/11 and the Visual Culture of Disaster*. Bloomington: Indiana University Press, 2014.

Suskind, Ron. 'Faith, Certainty and the Presidency of George W. Bush', *New York Times Magazine*, 17 October 2004. Accessed 21 February 2016. http://www.nytimes.com/2004/10/17/magazine/17BUSH.html.

Townsend, Frances Fragos. Quoted by Spencer S. Hsu, *Washington Post*, 14 February 2006. Accessed 4 May 2008. http://www.washingtonpost.com/wp-dyn/content/article/2006/02/13/AR2006021300679.html.

Versluys, Kristiaan. *Out of the Blue: September 11 and the Novel*. New York: Columbia University Press, 2009.

Vollard, Ambroise. *Cézanne*. New York: Dover, 1984.

Vonnegut, Kurt. *Slaughterhouse Five*. 1969; London: Vintage, 2000.

'Waiting for a Leader', Editorial, *New York Times*, 1 September 2005. Accessed 30 March 2013. http://www.nytimes.com/2005/09/01/opinion/01thu1.html.

Waldman, Amy. *The Submission*. London: *William Heinemann*, 2011.

Waldman, Amy. 'Trotter's Road', *Financial Times*, 30 December 2011. Accessed 19 February 2016. http://www.ft.com/cms/s/2/407737e0-27f3-11e1-a4c4-00144feabdc0.html#axzz1wq3gUt4V.

Wilder, Thornton. *The Bridge of San Luis Rey*. 1927; London: Penguin, 2006.

Williams, Rowan. *Writing in the Dust: Reflections on 11th September and Its Aftermath*. London: Hodder & Stoughton, 2002.

Wood, James. 'Shallow Graves', *The New Yorker*, 30 November 2009.
Woolf, Virginia. 'Before Midnight', *Times Literary Supplement*, 1 March 1917, Issue 789.
Wright, Lawrence. *The Looming Tower*. London: Allen Lane, 2006.
Zelizer, Barbie and Stuart Allan. 'Introduction: When Trauma Shapes the News.' In *Journalism after September 11*, edited by Barbie Zelizer and Stuart Allan, 1–24. London: Routledge, 2002.
Zinn, Howard. *A People's History of the United States: 1492–present*, 3rd edition. 1980; Harlow: Pearson Education, 2003.

Works of art cited

Delacroix, Eugène. *Liberty Leading the People*, 1830, The Louvre, Paris.
Fischl, Eric. *Tumbling Woman*, bronze, 2002.
Richter, Gerhard. *18 October 1977*, 1988, Collection of the Museum of Modern Art, New York.
Richter, Gerhard. *September*, oil on canvas, 2005, Collection of the Museum of Modern Art, New York.
Stidworthy, Imogen. *The Whisper Heard*, 2003.

Music cited

Basinski, William. *The Disintegration Loops*, 2002.
Springsteen, Bruce. *Darlington County*, 1984, *Born in the USA*, Columbia Records.
Springsteen, Bruce. *The Rising*, 2002, *The Rising*, Columbia Records.

INDEX

Note: The letter 'n' following locators refers to notes.